To

a shipmate and
dear friend!

Doc Davis

Hilario

SEAL Doc

The Story of the First US Navy SEAL Team in Vietnam

✦

Lt. Cmdr. D.R. Davis, MSC, USN (Ret.)

iUniverse, Inc.
New York Bloomington

SEAL Doc
The Story of the First US Navy SEAL Team in Vietnam

iUniverse books may be ordered through booksellers or by contacting:

iUniverse
1663 Liberty Drive
Bloomington, IN 47403
www.iuniverse.com
1-800-Authors (1-800-288-4677)

ISBN: 978-1-4502-7145-5 (pbk)
ISBN: 978-1-4502-7146-2 (cloth)
ISBN: 978-1-4502-7147-9 (ebk)

Library of Congress Control Number: 2010916424

Printed in the United States of America

iUniverse rev. date: 11/11/2010

To Honor

SEAL Doc honors the men of US Navy SEAL Teams, the men and women of the Navy Hospital Corps and, in particular, the members of that Corps who serve on independent duty aboard ships, with the Marine Corps Fleet Marine Forces and with Special Operations Forces the world over.

Acknowledgement

This book would have not been possible without the priceless and tireless efforts of my loving wife who devoted hundreds of hours to editing and proofreading it while offering meaningful and valuable suggestions to add clarity and readability to the work.

Thanks for all of your help!

I Love You!

The One Called "Doc"

By

Harry D. Penny, Jr. HMC (AC), USN

Copyright 1975

I'm the one called "Doc" I shall not walk in your footsteps, but I will walk by your side. I shall not walk in your image I've earned my own title of pride. We've answered the call together, on sea and foreign land. When the cry for help was given, I've been there right at hand. Whether I am on the ocean or in the jungle wearing greens, giving aid to my fellow man, be it Sailors or Marines. So the next time you see a Corpsman and you think of calling him "squid", think of the job he's doing as those before him did. And if you ever have to go out there and your life is on the block, look at the one right next to you...I'm the one called "Doc".

Reprinted with permission of the author

INTRODUCTION

Since first authorized by order of President John F. Kennedy in 1962, the US Navy SEALs have forged an unmatched record for clandestine and covert operations within the Special Operations Branch of the US Armed Forces. To date, little has been written of the early activities and deployment of the first unit of the first SEAL Team . Though the formation of a special warfare unit, within the US Navy, had been discussed since the earlier formation of the US Army Special Forces, it took a man with the foresight of President Kennedy to bring those discussions to fruition. Probably because of his experiences during WW II, Kennedy saw the evolution of world warfare, and naval warfare in particular, changing from the big guns and big ships of prior wars to a covert insurgent-based series of conflicts. His wisdom and foresight hold significant meaning for those who have served in the Armed Forces, and have encountered unconventional warfare in virtually every conflict since the Korean War.

The conceptual design and formation planning for the Navy SEAL Teams began to take shape in late 1960 with a coordinated effort of the East and West coast Amphibious Warfare Commands. While initial training formats and content were assembled, a select group within these two commands assessed the personnel qualifications and team mix for the incremental assembly of the first units. The Amphibious Warfare commands served as the parent organization of Navy Underwater Demolition Teams (UDT) organized for underwater warfare during WW II and were the perfect choice to oversee the assembly and training of these new special purpose units. Qualifications of UDT members were extremely high in terms of covert and underwater operations. The requirements for SEAL Team members were even broader and required greater diversity, which would include operations centered on sea, air, and land missions. Classified as Secret at the outset, the word SEAL was chosen as the name for the new special operations team to describe its capability for diverse operations, i.e. **SE**a, **A**ir, **L**and- **SEAL**.

The development of naval units specializing in sea/air/land operations was something new for navy planners although specialized units, such as the Seabees, landing parties, and occasionally increments of UDT, had functioned successfully on land in prior conflicts. The decision was made at the outset that SEAL training would include parachute jump training, jungle warfare training, survival training, small arms fabrication, and theater specific language training. These requirements would be in addition to the rigorous and physically demanding training received in underwater warfare and explosives during basic underwater demolition school (BUDS) the acronym for UDT training. East and west coast units of the Naval Amphibious commands initiated training protocols for the first SEAL Teams with resources and personnel contained in their respective UDT teams. Volunteers were solicited from existing east and west coast UDT teams.

The Naval Amphibious Command at Coronado, California was the first to assemble a select group of enlisted men and commissioned officers from west coast UDT teams. These first selectees represented a broad range of rating skills. Ratings within the navy are the job specialties in which individual sailors have received special training. These personnel were then assigned supplemental training in specialties and skills not included in their previous UDT training regimen. While a portion of this first unit attended parachute jump training at Fort Bragg, North Carolina, others attended Jungle Warfare training in Panama, language training at the Naval Post-Graduate School in Monterey, California, and small weapons fabrication training. When each member had cycled through these various training assignments, the final training evolution for the unit was completion of survival training program at a place called Pickle Meadows in California.

Upon completion of their training, this select group of men comprised Increment One of SEAL Team One. They were scheduled for deployment to Vietnam in April 1962 as an advisory group designated Mobile Training Team 10-62 (MTT 10-62). At this early point in SEAL Team deployment, permanent assignments were not considered practical so units were typically sent on assignments under temporary additional duty (TAD) orders, which did not extend beyond a period of six months. The 10-62 designation indicated the end of the temporary assignment, which would end in October 1962. At this point, since the word SEAL and its meaning were classified as SECRET and did not appear on written transfer orders, hence the designation MTT 10-62 was used.

Navy Regulations (1962) mandated that each functional diving unit of Naval forces include at least one independent duty qualified Hospital Corpsman, who had completed First Class Diving School, to provide the medical support and services required by the units operational mode.

Corpsmen who served with units involved in diving operations such as fleet diving ships (salvage and rescue vessels), Explosive Ordinance Disposal units (EOD) and UDT teams were required to receive extensive special training in all phases of diving operations and diving medicine. A corpsman, who desired duty with one of the above units, had to be Second Class Hospital Corpsman (E5). Normally three to five years of active service as a corpsman were required to attain this level. Next, they must be a graduate of the navy's Independent Duty training program. This concentrated and specialized training prepared the individual corpsman to function in a comprehensive healthcare delivery mode independent of a navy physician. Finally, all corpsmen meeting the above qualifications had to be a graduate of the navy's First Class Diver training program. The program required thirty weeks to complete, it was open only to volunteers. This program trained the individual to a proficiency in all types of air based and mixed gas-breathing media diving. It provided in-depth training in underwater mechanics, underwater cutting and welding, salvage operations, hyperbaric chamber operation, explosives/demolition, and diving physiology. The program also included an extreme regimen of physical training and conditioning consistent with the demands of diving. If the corpsman was able to complete all of these phases of training and graduate, he then advanced to the specialized phase dealing with the medical aspects of diving. This training concentrated on the diagnosis and treatment of diving injuries and their associated conditions. On average, only a small percentage of the corpsmen who volunteered for this training were able to complete the entire program, due to its academic rigor and extreme physical demands.

The net result of this high rate of attrition among corpsmen admitted to the program, left many diving units in the fleet and special operations units such as SEAL and UDT short of their medical support requirements. As a result, the limited number of qualified diving corpsmen carried multiple assignments in multiple diving units simultaneously.

SEAL training, operations, and equipment described herein pertain to the first unit of SEAL deployed to Vietnam in 1962. They do not represent SEAL training and equipment as it exists today.

Chapter One

April 1962

The Military Air Transport Service (MATS) flight had left Travis Air Force Base outside San Francisco three days earlier and now was on the ground at Tan Son Nhat airport outside Saigon. Crew changes and rest stops at Hickam Air Force Base in Hawaii and the Clark Air Force Base in the Philippines were required, causing delay of the flight.

Lieutenant (junior grade) Bill Evans, USNR, gathered his gear and headed for the forward exit of the C 133. The C 133 was easily converted to cargo or passenger transport as the mission required. It had no windows. The primitive canvas and metal frame seats, in tight rows, facing aft, make an irregular seat arrangement. Bill hoped that the rest of the men in his new unit would be able to make better flight arrangements.

The "transfer immediately" wording in his orders left him little choice but to take the first available flight from San Diego, the nearest commercial airport to his home base at the Naval Amphibious Base (NAB), Coronado, California. Bill was an Ivy League graduate and the product of the Navy Reserve Officer Training Corps (NROTC) program. He completed his degree in math under the navy's scholarship program. Of slim but muscular build with dark hair and blue eyes, his first assignment after graduation from college had been at the Naval Submarine Base in New London, Connecticut. This first tour of duty was uneventful and, after a few months, Bill found himself wanting more action and activity. He volunteered for UDT training at NAB Coronado, CA.

Although physically demanding, he completed the basic phases of the program and when it was available, requested additional training that would qualify him for duty with the soon to be formed SEAL Teams. Early deployment scheduling placed him as the Commanding Officer (CO) of MTT 10-62, the first SEAL unit assigned to Vietnam.

The ramp leading from the aircraft door was wet from a heavy rain and, as Bill stepped out of the plane, the press of heat, humidity, and stench in the air hit him like a brick wall. *This climate will take some getting use to*, he thought, as he walked to the terminal for check-in and transportation to Military Advisory Command Vietnam (MACV) headquarters in Saigon. A disinterested US Air Force airman, after stamping his orders, directed him to a blue bus in front of the terminal. Bill took a seat directly behind the US Air Force driver as he threw his gear under the seat. A heavy metal grid covered all the windows in the bus making it resemble a bus for transporting prisoners; it made him uncomfortable. He leaned forward and asked the driver the purpose of the window coverings.

"Bombs," was his response. "The locals throw grenades and home-made bombs into busses on a regular basis. Last week, a kid on a bike rode up alongside a cab and threw a loaf of bread into it; the bread had a hot grenade inside. The two army personnel in the cab are in the morgue. The driver bailed out before the kid threw the bread…knew it was coming."

In a few minutes the last passenger boarded the bus. On the way out of the terminal area, Bill noticed several commercial aircraft and a few military transports. Considering the hour, 1500, the airport was relatively quiet. Passing through a chain link gate, the bus emerged onto what appeared to be a city street jammed with cycle cabs, small automobile taxis, and pedestrians. A throng of activity the likes of which Bill had not experienced. The street the bus traveled was narrow and the driver was constantly blowing the horn to avoid running down bicycles and foot traffic. Small sidewalk front shops crowded one another like chickens lined up at a feeding trough…people were everywhere. The heat in the bus was oppressive, in spite of the pounding rain, there wasn't a breath of fresh air. It appeared to Bill that everyone was in a hurry to get somewhere but the rain did not seem to play a part in the haste. Hundreds of young women moved along the sidewalk dressed in long white sarong type attire with blue and green shirtwaists on top. They were the only group who carried umbrellas and most carried an armful of books.

Near the center of Saigon, the bus passed the presidential palace that showed severe structural damage to the wing furthest from the street. Bill had read in a newspaper in Hawaii that a renegade South Vietnamese Air Force pilot, with strong ties to the North Vietnamese cause, had dropped a bomb on the palace the preceding week in an attempt to assassinate the president. The president wasn't home that day!

As the bus entered the heart of Saigon, Bill was surprised to see the array of large modern buildings, a sharp contrast to the structures in the less urban portion of the city. After several turns, the bus approached a large walled enclosure covering several blocks. Atop the wall were rings of barbed wire and a steel entry gate guarded by an armed U.S. Marine. On the wall next to the gate was a primitive painted sign identifying the enclosure as Military Advisory Command and in block letters below that sign appeared the abbreviation "MACV". The marine waved the bus through the gate, the bus proceeded to the center of the compound, stopping by a central flagpole.

The driver turned to Bill telling him the Navy section was to the right at the first corridor. The interior of the compound looked like the inside of a fort. The only thing missing was a cannon. At a door marked Navy Personnel Office, Bill saw a large counter with a Chief Petty Officer seated behind it.

The chief got to his feet as he entered and asked, "checking in, Sir?"

Bill responded by laying his bundle of paperwork on the counter.

"Lieutenant Evans, yes, Sir, we've been expecting you. Go down the hall three doors, to check in with the commanding officer's office, in the mean time I'll get your paper work in order and assign you billeting in a nearby hotel. Come back here after you check in with him."

Bill followed the chief's directions and found the office of the commanding officer of the Navy section. A navy Wave, the CO's secretary, informed him that the CO was in a meeting and would meet with him at 0900 the following morning. Bill returned to the personnel office as requested. The chief gave him directions to a nearby hotel and the MACV Armory for a weapon issue.

The only weapons available were old Smith and Wesson revolvers in caliber.38 Special, not the weapon of choice. He received six rounds of ammunition in addition to the revolver. The Sergeant at the armory told him to keep track of each round fired so he could account for its use when he turned in the weapon.

"That's a ridiculous rule, Sergeant. If I shoot someone, I'm going to run back to my quarters and record their name, rank, and service number in my diary along with how many of your stupid .38s it took to do the job?"

"I don't make the rules, Lieutenant. You might want to take it up with the Commanding Officer of MACV. However, the General is in Washington at the moment but I'm sure he would be glad to hear from you when he returns."

Bill picked up the weapon and cartridges and headed for the door saying under his breath, "horse shit system."

After checking in at the hotel front desk, it was time for a long nap. It had been over twenty hours since he had slept.

Bill awoke to another day of monsoon rains and after a small breakfast of eggs and rice cakes headed for the MACV compound. He arrived at the office of the commanding officer a little early and found the CO, Captain Joe Witt, at his desk with a cup of coffee. Captain Witt invited Bill to help himself to coffee and take a seat. After informal introductions, Captain Witt asked Bill what he knew of his assignment. Bill related the details of the briefing he had received at Coronado and asked what the Captain could add. Captain Witt told him that the location of his training group would be DaNang, about 300 miles to the north. He went on to tell him that at present there were about twenty-five air force personnel in the DaNang area and one Army Special Forces team of about twelve men. They were working for a group in Okinawa. He explained that he did not know the identity of the Okinawa group. Captain Witt expanded on his knowledge of Bill's primary mission, which was to train a group of volunteers from the Vietnamese Junk Force in counterinsurgency tactics, demolition, and jungle warfare. He also told him he was aware that Bill's unit was the first contingent of a new navy Special Warfare Unit. He understood the secret classification of the term SEAL, its meaning, and its mission. Captain Witt told Bill he should use the Naval Intelligence Officer there at MACV as his primary point of contact for future interaction and assistance. Bill assumed that meant there would be no further contact with the CO.

"I have scheduled a meeting for you tomorrow at 1300 with Commander Rudd, the Head of Navy Intelligence here at MACV. He will be able to fill in the details on what questions you may have about your operation. I realize you also have a command reporting responsibility to Coronado, please info me on those communications. I think that about covers it for now, good luck with your assignment. If you need anything beyond routine please let me know."

Bill got to his feet and thanked the Captain who responded that the officers' mess in the compound had a good menu for lunch. As Bill left the office he decided to take a walk around the compound to familiarize himself. He might end up spending time here. His first stop was at the Chief Master at Arms office where he thought he could get a briefing on the compound. As he entered, a First Class Gunners Mate (GM1) wearing a sidearm got up from behind the desk and came forward. Bill introduced himself and asked about background information on the compound.

The GM1, whose nametag read "Donald", told Bill the compound was built as a French garrison position back in the early fifties when they occupied the country. This explained the fortified nature of the base and the high wall with barbed wire. After chatting for a few minutes, he thanked Donald and left the office.

Bill found Commander Rudd in his office the next afternoon and introduced himself. The Commander was a red-faced man in his early forties with a medium and somewhat overweight build based on what had most likely once been a very muscular body.

"I don't have a lot to tell you about your operation, Mr. Evans, except that you will be playing it by ear. The men you will be training have been selected from the Junk Force rank and file and probably aren't much. It will be your initial task to screen out those that have potential for this training and get rid of the rest, send them back to their units."

"I was told we would have a Corpsman on our team. We'll need one to conduct the physical evaluations. What kind of support can I count on in terms of training materials, weapons, billeting?" Bill questioned with concern.

"Most, if not all, will have to come from your ingenuity. We have no funds or support for your operations." The Commander added that he had been in contact with the group that supported the Army Special Forces team near DaNang and asked if they could help with logistic support, they had responded positively.

"The army team up there is supported by direct air from Okinawa so some support could come by that avenue if you coordinate with the army team CO."

Bill asked about the identity of the Okinawa group.

Commander Rudd hesitated for a moment. "They call themselves Combined Studies. They are the same group that operates Air America and you know the driving force behind that operation, right?"

Bill nodded his head. He knew it was the CIA.

"Your operations in DaNang will have to be strictly covert, the government in power doesn't want to acknowledge our presence that far in-country, it tends to color our mission as advisory. You and your team will have to surrender all forms of identification that could reveal your identity as US military personnel or as US citizens. We don't anticipate any great difficulty. However, if a situation should develop, we officially don't know you…understand?"

"I do, but I don't like it." Bill was barely able to conceal his resentment.

"Your contact person with the Vietnamese Junk Force is a guy by the name of Vinh. He is a pompous asshole who came down from the North after the French got their ass kicked out of the country in the fifties. Through political ties, he managed to gain a commission in the South Vietnamese navy at the rank of Commander and ended up as the senior coordinator between the Junk Force and us. I don't trust the son of a bitch and I would advise you not to! His allegiance is questionable. He is planning a raid at Hai Phong, the major port in North Vietnam. I would like you to go along as an observer. Let me know how he handles himself but stay out of it."

After questioning the coordination of his role in this operation, Bill learned that notification would be by message to the air force unit in DaNang as to when and where. He sensed the meeting was nearing its end and rose to leave.

Commander Rudd took hold of his arm saying, "teach those guys up there how to beat the Viet Cong (VC) at their own game, Bill, that's the only way we'll ever win this thing."

When Bill returned to his hotel, he found a familiar face waiting for him in the lobby. Chief Volkert, the best demolition expert in UDT and now SEAL Team One, saluted Bill and shook his hand.

"When did you get in, Chief?"

The Chief responded with a list of delays and frustrations, which surrounded his trip to Saigon. The plane had made five stops between Hickam Air Force Base in Hawaii and Saigon. The Chief then asked about their assignment, its location and duration. Bill filled him in on the details over a beer in the hotel lounge. He also informed him that they could catch a flight to DaNang the next day and asked the Chief to meet him at the airport the following morning at 0700.

As they waited in the terminal the next morning, the two men discussed the training plan that they would launch in the following weeks and outlined the material and logistic needs as best they could. They had arrived with nothing in the way of supplies for such a training mission, not the least of which was weapons.

The Chief asked, "what about a Corpsman, Skipper?"

"They are in short supply, Chief. The requirements for them far outstrip the number who volunteer for the training and, of those who do volunteer, a very small percentage make it through. I sent a message to Coronado when I arrived stating an urgent need for one. I hesitate pushing the training too far until we have some medical support. I'm told the nearest military M.D., to Da Nang, is over a hundred miles."

The morning dragged on, Bill checked frequently with the flight operations desk on departing DaNang flights. The time of the next departure was unclear. They would page him when they had more information.

Finally, at 1100 they were approached by an Air Force Captain in a greasy flight suit. "You guys looking for a ride to DaNang?"

The Chief responded with a vehement, "hell yes…Sir." Chief Volkert was over six feet tall with a slender but muscular build, blond hair, and a deeply tanned complexion.

The pilot looked at him for a moment and prepared to respond, thought better of the idea, and told them that the plane was in front of the terminal to the left and would leave in about ten minutes. As they exited the terminal, they noticed that the rain had stopped but steam rose from the concrete apron in front of the terminal and the humidity was severe. Bill could feel the sweat running down his back. He noticed the Chief's shirt was wet through to the waist. As they walked across the apron, they both looked at the plane that would carry them north.

"Wow, we are going first class today, Skipper."

Bill looked at him with a smile. The plane they were looking at was old, bedraggled, and probably not in the best condition. They boarded through the forward hatch and moved aft into the cavernous fuselage. The plane was an old Fairchild C-119, which had seen better days. The seats were made of steel frames covered with canvas, temporarily bolted to the floor of the aircraft and aligned along the outer bulkhead facing inward.

After several aborted attempts, the pilot managed to get the engines running accompanied by many backfires and clouds of white smoke. The plane taxied to the end of the runway and applied full take off power. It sat motionless for what seemed like several seconds and with a jolt started down the runway. The vibration and noise within the plane were deafening but finally it began to rise making a sharp left bank and headed north.

The Chief leaned close to Bill shouting over the roar of the engines, "I am not happy about giving up my I.D. to those people in Saigon and the weaponry they issued me is sad to say the least."

Bill acknowledged the statement with a sorry look of displeasure and a shrug of the shoulders, the noise level in the aircraft was too intense to carry on a conversation.

The weather over DaNang was sunny with scattered clouds at about 3000 feet and the runway appeared dry. After landing, the plane taxied over the steel matting to a position in front of the makeshift terminal building. They loaded up their gear and deplaned into stifling heat and humidity.

As they walked toward the terminal, an Army Captain in fatigues and jungle boots extended his hand and introduced himself as Captain Marz, Commanding Officer of Unit 762 Special Forces.

He went on to tell them that he had received word of their arrival with instructions to give them a hand in getting set up.

"You're welcome to bunk in with us until you find a better place to hang out. I doubt your troops will want to spend the next six months in a tent. We are located out of town a ways and I understand you'll be conducting training at the old French Naval Base near town. You might want to consider renting a house near the base. I have a contact that can help you with that."

Bill was relieved at this news as he had been wondering where he could quarter his team. After a rough ride over badly rutted dirt roads, the Captain's Jeep entered an area of heavy tree growth that was contained within a high combination wood and rock fence. Scattered among the trees were tents of various sizes with exterior ropes and poles. The Special Forces' compound contained a large mess tent, a canvas roofed motor pool, and a tent with a red cross on the front signifying a medical aid station. Locations of multiple tents for berthing and administration appeared functional.

Bill questioned the Captain about the compound, including the rock and wood wall. The Captain explained he believed the rock was the remains of an old Buddhist monastery. His troops added the wood to enhance the security of the compound. Bill further questioned him about the purpose of his team. Marz responded by explaining they functioned as a special training unit for a select group of men from Army of the Republic of Vietnam (ARVN) to teach Ranger tactics. He added that they were about half way through the training schedule and should complete the cycle in early July, another unit from Fort Bragg would then replace them.

At this point Captain Marz directed Chief Volkert to one of the tents on the outer edge of the compound, telling him that he needed to talk with Master Sergeant White about providing logistics support for the new navy unit.

The following day was spent working out logistic support details and renting a two story furnished house in Da Nang. Captain Marz accompanied Bill to act as his guide around Da Nang and as part of the tour, took him out to the old French Naval Base, now a Vietnamese Junk Force base, where Bill would conduct most of his training. The old base consisted mostly of Quonset type buildings, a long stretch of open beach, and assorted old blockhouses. There was little sign of activity, no fences and no security was visible. A few men wondered about the area, mostly clad in black pajama type clothing. It did not look like any naval base Bill had ever seen.

After a brief look around, Marz stopped in front of a small frame building. "You need to meet the senior Junk Force officer present, his name is Vinh, somehow he holds the rank of Commander."

As they entered the building, a small slightly built man rose from behind an old wood desk and extended his hand. "Nice to see you again, Captain Marz, and I assume you are Lieutenant Evans?"

Bill responded affirmatively taking a seat next to the desk. He noticed that Vinh's English was almost perfect, with only a slight French accent.

After a brief introduction of his role with the Junk Force, Vinh looked at Bill, "you and I have a few things to discuss, Lieutenant."

Captain Marz took the hint and left the building with a look at Bill and a nod to indicate he would wait outside.

Vinh took a seat behind the desk and began to explain his upcoming mission. The plan was to place contact mines on ships in Hai Phong harbor, the major shipping port in North Vietnam. Operating from a motorized junk, disguised as a fishing vessel, self-contained underwater breathing apparatus (SCUBA) equipped swimmers were to attach the mines. Junks normally used sail power but these junks had been equipped with diesel engines to increase their speed and versatility. He went on to say, he was surprised when Commander Rudd had suggested that Bill accompany him on this mission. He welcomed the idea as long as Bill understood his role as an observer. It was a Junk Force mission; he was not to interfere. He went on, in an attempt to impress Bill with his qualifications, telling him about the extensive training in SCUBA and explosives he had received in Taiwan. The training had lasted four months.

It was all Bill could do to keep from laughing. Bill's training had taken more than a year.

The junk was to depart from Da Nang with six Junk Force divers trained by Vinh and three Junk Force sailors to serve as crew. They would pose as fishermen working their way 350 miles up the coast to Hai Phong. They would move little during the daylight, making maximum speed at night, in order to reach offshore of Hai Phong harbor by the third night. Vinh expected little trouble since intelligence indicated that the North Vietnamese had light security in the harbor and no costal patrols. Posing as fishermen was just an added precaution.

Vinh told Bill he expected him to remain below decks during daylight, appropriate clothing would be available aboard the junk. The junk would leave for the north in three days and return immediately to Da Nang, once the operation was complete.

Bill wondered about the planning for this mission. It sounded slipshod and off-the-cuff to him. He questioned Vinh regarding the type of ships he hoped to sink and their country of origin.

"Intelligence indicates there are always Chinese and Russian ships in Hai Phong. Those countries represent the major suppliers of war materials to the North Vietnamese Army and the VC. The charges we will use are designed to disable a ship by cracking hull plates and welds or to disable a propeller but are not intended to actually sink a ship in the short term. I selected this type of charge because they are easily transported underwater. I got them from my supplier at no charge. I can't divulge the identity of that supplier."

This raised even more questions for Bill but he decided this was not the time to pursue the matter.

The junk departed Da Nang just after dark and put to sea with all aboard seemingly in a jovial mood. One of the Junk Force SCUBA divers, named

Kaye, spoke good English and immediately began to converse with Bill. He explained that he had attended college in Japan, where English was required as a core course. He left college, after two years, to return home and fight for his country against the VC. He expressed his conviction that the war was necessary to prevent the overthrow of his government and the spread of Communism into South Vietnam.

He questioned Bill's presence on the mission but Bill could only respond in platitudes and half-truths.

Using sail power during daylight hours, to enhance their image as a fishing junk, the trip north progressed smoothly. At night, they ran on diesel power to increase their speed. There were no signs of North Vietnamese gunboats or any presence of costal security.

Late in the evening of the third day, the junk arrived off Do Son beach at the entrance to Hai Phong where it slowed to maintain a steady position for swimmer insertion. As the divers assembled their gear and donned wet suits, Bill noticed that Vinh was unpacking a box of explosives. They were small rectangular units in a waterproof plastic covering. On the end of the rectangle was a small timing device that resembled the face of a watch. Bill had never seen this type of device. The markings on the devices were in a language that resembled Chinese characters. The timing face used Roman numerals.

As the men donned their SCUBA gear, fins, and facemasks, Vinh had the men file past him, handing each of them two explosive devices. He directed them to stand by the gunwale and prepare to enter the water.

Two large ships, that appeared to be freighters, were clearly visible in the mouth of the harbor, illuminated by onboard lighting and scattered lights on the pier. Bill estimated the distance to the ships to be 600-700 yards. Not a long underwater swim in calm water but a difficult one with tidal currents and the tide was running. The junk had to maintain steady power to hold its position against the outgoing tide. Bill estimated the tide to be running at between two and three knots, a difficult swim, submerged, for an experienced swimmer.

As the men stood by the rail ready to enter the water, Vinh went to each of them telling them to set the timers on the explosives at fifteen minutes and instructing them to arm their charges!

Dumbfounded, Bill reacted in a low and menacing voice. "No, that's not a good idea, Commander."

Vinh glared at him, "I told you at the outset this was a Vietnamese operation, remain quiet, Lieutenant, you have no authority over my men. Your advice is not needed or wanted."

Bill shook his head and turned away, sick with the thought of what might befall these men.

The men quietly entered the water, submerged, and began their swim toward the ships in the distance. Vinh was the last to enter the water. Bill noticed that Vinh did not arm his explosive.

The night had become pitch black as a thick layer of clouds covered the moon. Bubbles from the swimmers were not visible once they were thirty feet from the junk. Minutes dragged by. Bill could appreciate the struggle the young men must be going through to swim against an active tide. Suddenly, there was a series of low thumps that sounded like someone striking a hollow log with a baseball bat. Bill knew immediately what the sounds represented and felt sick and angry. The explosives had detonated long before the men reached the ships.

The three man crew of the junk looked at Bill for direction. He indicated to them in sign language and broken Vietnamese to remain in the area as long as possible in order to pick up swimmers who might make it back to the junk. The only reaction in the harbor had been the appearance of several more lights and a series of spotlights sweeping the water around the ships. There was no sign of any swimmers.

After thirty minutes had passed, Bill decided they could not continue to risk discovery. He directed the crew to put about and head south for Da Nang.

Chapter Two

The return to Da Nang was uneventful, except for some rough weather just south of Dong Hoi. Bill was unable to pay much attention to the weather or the crew of the junk during the trip. The remorse and anger he felt after the experience at Hai Phong was overwhelming. He had actually stood by and watched seven men commit a death act with full knowledge that the technique used could prove disastrous. He was having difficulty dealing with his own guilt, but from that guilt, came a strong personal commitment. He would never again let an operation go forward that had a high probability of failure. He knew that he must talk to Commander Rudd in Saigon to fill him in on the questionable operation he had just witnessed.

In Da Nang, he found that Chief Volkert had taken charge, as is typical of Navy Chief Petty Officers and the reason they form the backbone of the Navy. In Bill's absence, the Chief completed setting up the house they had rented, including hiring a housekeeper and laundress. He had given the largest of five bedrooms to Bill, reserved a second for himself, and structured the other rooms to accommodate the remainder of the team.

The house was large, having five bedrooms and a bath with a large dining area on the main floor and a large open space with a kitchen and sleeping alcove on the ground floor. The monthly rent, including salaries paid to the housekeeper and laundress, would be about fifty dollars per month for each team member. A much better set-up than a tent.

"I need to make a quick trip to Saigon," Bill said.

Chief Volkert knew immediately that something was not right with his CO. "I assume, from the look on your face, the trip up north didn't go well." It was obvious that Bill was under a great deal of stress as he explained what had occurred in Hai Phong.

Chief Volkert took the news in his usual quiet manner. "The rest of the team is in Saigon, they arrived over the last two days. I sent a message for them to sit tight until we could arrange their trip up. Maybe you could herd them up when you go down. When do you plan to leave?"

Bill thought for a minute. "First thing tomorrow, there's a flight at 0630."

"Sergeant White loaned me one of his vehicles while you were gone, it needs to be back as soon as we can come up with one of our own, and I am working on that with him."

Bill arrived at MACV headquarters and found Commander Rudd in his office with a young Lieutenant he had not met.

"Come in, Bill, I would like you to meet Tom Beck, he is my assistant and will be your contact here when I am involved in other things."

Bill shook hands with Beck, poured himself a cup of coffee, and sat down across the desk from Rudd.

"How was the trip? I haven't heard anything from Vinh and was beginning to wonder."

"It was a goddamn mess, Commander. Vinh put his men in the water for a 700-yard swim against a significant outgoing tide, with all the charges armed except his. I tried to stop him, but he reminded me that I had no authority. The charges started detonating before they could reach either of the two ships that were in range. None of the men returned to the junk. I hung around for a half hour or so but couldn't risk further exposure."

"Christ. I knew he was a devious son of a bitch but I did not think he would pull anything that stupid. On second thought, was it stupid? Yes, from an operations standpoint, but... How was the security along the route and at Hai Phong?"

"We saw nothing on the way up and no apparent security on the water in the harbor, except for normal lighting. I was pissed beyond belief at the time but I remember being a little surprised that there wasn't more reaction in the harbor after the little charges went off, although you could barely hear them."

"Do you get the impression they might have known you were coming?"

"Yes, that is possible but how could it be?"

Lieutenant Beck entered the conversation, "we have suspected Vinh to be a VC agent for some time. He was very precise about your arrival time in Hai Phong wasn't he?"

"Yes, almost to the hour."

"What do you make of that, Commander?"

"I suspect that Vinh has more than confirmed our suspicions but, even if he is alive, we would have one hell of a time convincing the Vietnamese high command that he is VC. In the meantime, let it go. I can tell how upset you are but you had damn well better move on. Whether they acknowledge it in Washington or not, this is a war and people are being killed. I need to cut this short. I have an appointment in a few minutes. I would like you to spend some time with Tom and work out a communications mode so you can talk with each other on a regular basis. See you in a couple of weeks."

A few minutes later in Beck's office, Bill opened the conversation by asking about Tom's background.

"NROTC. Finished a degree in electrical engineering at Purdue and came directly on active duty. Had a chance to go into submarines but couldn't pass the pressure test. Did a couple of tours of duty stateside and wormed my way into intelligence, don't let that term fool you, Rudd is the real brains in this outfit."

"What can you tell me about him?"

"First off, he is the original maverick. Academy class of 1942, on the first UDT team formed in the latter part of WW II. From there he went to flight school at Pensacola and within three years was executive officer of a squadron. Here was where his career went sour. He likes his booze and during the wetting down party celebrating his selection to the rank of Commander, he got a snoot full. He found himself outside the Officer's Club at Naval Air Station North Island having to take a leek. There was no hidden space available so he thought he could avoid discovery by climbing up a short palm tree across the street. He was about half way up the tree when the urge hit him. Like most of us, he preferred to pee at a target. Now it happens, the Admiral had parked his new Cadillac convertible under that very palm tree. The bright shiny center hub of that big steering wheel was just too good a target to miss. Now a real problem arose. Soon after he had finished but before he could descend the tree, the Admiral and his wife decided to leave the party early and came out of the club to drive home. His wife decided to drive their new car for the first time and crawled into the driver's seat where a very wet steering wheel and a soaking wet leather seat confronted her. It had not rained in San Diego for weeks so her immediate reaction was to look up at the sky and try to determine where the water had come from. Low and behold, there was the newly selected Commander Rudd clinging to the palm tree above her new Cadillac. You can almost guess the rest. As a result, Rudd was not promoted and was quickly assigned to duty in Adak, Alaska. He later managed to qualify for submarine duty and ultimately ended up with command of a fast attack submarine. From duty in the boats, he made the logical transition to intelligence. That pretty well sums up the career of Commander Rudd. He never married but has had plenty of girl friends; his current girl and his "roomie" is the disbursing officer for MACV and a real knockout." (Many in the navy refer to submarines as boats)

"Wow, what a career. I don't think I'll try to match it. I didn't realize he had been UDT, we do have something in common."

"Not to change the subject, Bill, but some of your men are here waiting to go to Da Nang when you head back. I have open seats for all of you on tomorrow's flight at 1000, if that doesn't work for you, let me know and I can change it. Your men are at the Exeter hotel about four blocks north. I knew you were on your way down from Da Nang so I told them to hang around until you contacted them."

"Do you know if one of the men is a Corpsman?" Bill asked with a note of eagerness in his voice.

"I'm afraid not. We haven't gotten any word on when a medic may join your team," Tom regretfully answered.

At the Exeter, Bill found his team lounging in the hotel lobby. Each had a beer. They were all dressed in civilian clothes. Bill had met each individual team member at Coronado, at various times during preparation for deployment. All eight appeared to be glad to see their skipper and greeted him warmly. This marked the beginning of the SEAL brotherhood!

"What's with the civies? You guys think you are in the movies or something?"

After looking around the area to determine that there was no one close enough to overhear, Les Barter, one of the new team members with a super solid, almost square build, spoke up, "the CO at Coronado told us this was to be a cloak and dagger operation. He thought we should present as low a profile as possible. We finessed him into authorizing civies for the trip."

"You guys are a real prize. I can see this is going to be a marvelous tour. We head out for a place called Da Nang at 1000 tomorrow. Da Nang is about 350 miles north and about a one and a half hour flight on a C 119. I rented a house up there for us."

Aye, aye, Skipper, the team answered in unison.

Les added, "sure beats a tent," before he went on to say, "we had decided to have a look around the area once you showed up. Do you want to join us?"

Bill indicated he had some other things that needed doing.

Les looked around the group to see how many were still interested in a little exploration.

Boatswain Mate, First Class Vail nodded his head.

Bill felt the need to expand on the details of their assignment before they left for Da Nang. He gathered the group in a quiet corner of the lobby to avoid being overheard. Then in a subdued voice he explained, "as you were told in Coronado, our primary task is to train a group of Vietnamese sailors who are members of the Junk Force. The training will center on counterinsurgency, jungle warfare, demolition, and water insertion tactics. We will have to screen these men well before we start training them since we have no idea of their qualifications or previous training. We really need a Corpsman for the physical screening. I'm hoping he shows up soon. As you have also been told, the primary insurgents in South Vietnam are called Viet Cong (VC) and there is no way to identify them, unless they try to hurt you. Chief Volkert and I have worked out a training outline that we can review once we get onsite."

BM1 (Boats) Vail asked, "if these VC are so unrecognizable shouldn't we have something that can detect things we can't? In some operations with east coast UDT, we took a dog along for its ability to detect bad guys."

"Not a bad idea, Boats. Kick it around among yourselves, its O.K. with me."

Les jumped to his feet. "We can go doggie shopping, Boats."

At the front desk of the hotel, the dog shopping detail composed of Barter and Vail inquired about the best place to buy a dog, a puppy preferably.

The desk clerk replied, "butcher shop. Good one right down street."

The two men looked at each other with a puzzled look and headed out the door and down the street.

They came to a shop with carcasses of various dead animals hanging in the window. Inside the shop were several caged dogs, cats, and monkeys with prices in Vietnamese currency marked on tags. The men looked in the cages. Partway down a row, they saw a German Shepherd puppy.

"This is the one, she's a great breed and looks in good condition," Boats Vail said, as he stuck his finger in the cage, the dog responded by licking it.

Les pointed to the cage as he looked at the clerk. "How much for this one?"

"Very fine choice," replied the clerk. "Do you want her dressed or just skinned?"

"What she's wearing is just fine," said Vail. "What's the price?"

The clerk looked at the cage for a moment. "Three thousand Peastries (Ps)."

Les had already learned that the official exchange rate was about 120 Ps to the dollar but the black market rate on the street ran closer to 500.

"We will pay six American dollars."

"No, no," screamed the clerk, "I must have twenty dollar."

"O.K., Vail, let's hit the next shop, I am sure we can find another dog just as good down the street."

The two men started for the door but the clerk stepped in front of them. "You have dog for ten dollar."

There was no response from the men.

"O.K. O.K. Your special price be five dollar."

"We'll take her if you throw in a leash," Les said smiling at Vail.

Later, with the pup on a cord leash, they headed back to the hotel with their purchase and laughed at the price they ended up paying. They guessed that the clerk must have become confused and gotten his numbers mixed up.

CHAPTER THREE

May 1962

THE SUBMARINE ESCAPE TRAINING TANK at Pearl Harbor is unique as one of only two like structures in the navy. The other escape training tank is located at the Naval Submarine Base, New London, Connecticut. These escape training tanks are 120 feet high, twenty feet in diameter, steel structures, designed to hold 225, 000 gallons of water that is heated to a temperature of between eighty-eight and ninety-two degrees. The heated water is essential since staff instructors averaged seven to ten hours per workday in the water. A lesser temperature would bring about severe fatigue and hypothermia, a dangerous reduction in body temperature that can cause unconsciousness and cardiac arrest.

The function of the escape training tank at Pearl Harbor is to train the crews of all Pacific fleet submarines in buoyant assent techniques. This training, hopefully, enables submarine crews to escape from a sunken submarine, in the event of a pressure hull rupture or other emergency. However, the submarine escape tank staff and the submarine crews are aware that, under many circumstances, escape would be impossible. This can be attributed to the extreme operating depths of contemporary submarines.

The staff of each escape tank is composed of first class divers drawn from the fleet, after they have gained a high level of experience and expertise in the various aspects of advanced underwater techniques. Typical staffing of each tank includes twelve to fifteen first class divers, a diving medical technician, a master diver, and a diving officer, who functions as the officer in charge.

A tour of duty at one of these tanks is a rewarding, unique, and demanding experience, since all submarine crews in the fleet must re-qualify in buoyant accent each calendar year. This training must be integrated into their operating schedules. Submarine deployments last months and are frequent so the ascent training must often be sandwiched in on weekends and holidays.

In addition to their training duties, all staff divers assigned to Subase escape training tank carry out diving operations on in-port submarines that include hull inspections, propeller replacement, and other underwater repair projects. The diving medical technician functions as a first class diver and participates in all diving functions and training, along with other divers on the staff. This person is also responsible for detecting emergent medical conditions resulting from the buoyant assent training of submarine crews, operation of the re-compression chambers used in the treatment of many diving injuries, and conducting pressure and oxygen tolerance tests. These tests are a required part of the physical examination for personnel applying for submarine and diving training. Escape training tank staff divers often work fifty to seventy hours per week and value their free time. Consequently, the tank staff obviously resented the Saturday personnel inspections that put them behind schedule.

"Another personnel inspection, seems like we just had one."

"They come around once a month, Doc, but I agree it does seem like the last one was a week ago." Chief Mausey responded to Doc David's complaint.

Doc expanded on his first comment by adding, "the first damn weekend in a month that we haven't had extra training scheduled or a diving job on a boat and we have personnel inspection. Oh well, as they say, it all goes on twenty." (All time served, regardless of the assignment contributes to the twenty years required for retirement from the navy, a common navy saying usually said in jest)

Chris David,(Doc) Hospital Corpsman First Class, First Class Diver, Diving Medical Technician, had been on the staff of the Subase escape training tank for slightly more than a year and had previously completed a tour of independent duty on a Submarine Rescue vessel home ported in Pearl Harbor. He managed to arrange a no cost transfer from that ship, to the escape training tank, in order to complete work on the undergraduate degree he had started seven years before at Purdue University.

"How's school going, Doc?"

"Good, I have about one semester left and I get a Bachelor of Science degree. Sure has taken me long enough. I hope this will open the door for a commission later on. It's hard to go to school while on sea duty, I did quite a bit with correspondence courses through the United States Armed Forces Institute but you can just take that so far, until you get to the more advanced courses."

The two men joined the rest of the tank staff in formation in front of the first level of the tank. Then, in formation, they marched to the nearby softball field, the site of monthly personnel inspections. At the field, they broke off into two ranks and waited for the Officer in Charge and the inspecting officer.

After a few minutes, the tank master diver, who also functioned as the assistant division officer and senior enlisted coordinator, broke ranks from his position at the front left of the first column and walked up to Doc David.

"Hey, Doc, I hate to ruin your inspection but I got a phone call from the personnel office just before we came over here. They have a set of Temporary Additional Duty orders for you that are immediate, you better go over there now, you're excused from inspection."

"Are you kidding, Chief?"

"Nope, straight scoop, Doc."

David broke ranks and headed for personnel at a trot. On the first level of the personnel office, the receptionist looked up from her typewriter, recognized David and pointed at the Chief behind a double set of swinging doors. David smiled at her and nodded his head.

In the personnel office proper, a Chief Personnelman sat behind a grey metal desk, leaning back in his chair.

"HM1, David?"

"Yes, Chief."

"Got a set of TAD orders for you to Vietnam, you will be attached to a Unit called MTT 10-62, the length of this assignment is 180 days and you need to get out there ASAP. You also need to go to the Federal building in Honolulu first thing Monday and fill out a passport application. The Bureau of Naval Personnel sent them a copy of your message orders to set the passport thing in motion. You need to ask for the State Department representative, they will take it from there. Any questions?"

David sat down in a chair beside the desk and looked at the Chief. "Only about fifty or so, Chief, but let's start with a very basic one. Where the hell is Vietnam?"

"It's in Southeast Asia, Doc. It used to be called French Indochina. There is something going on over there but I don't know what, maybe a new war."

"I know where it is now but why do I need a passport? I have been all over Asia, Japan, China, the Philippines, but I never had to have a passport."

"Part of it may be that the organization called Southeast Asia Treaty Organization (SEATO), is involved in this thing, whatever is going on over there. I do know that Vietnam is not a member of that organization and never signed on to any of its rules or agreed to participate in joint defense efforts of the other members. Maybe that's the reason a passport is required? Does that clear it up for you, Doc?"

"It's a step in the right direction, Chief."

"I have copies and the original of your orders coming from upstairs, they should be ready for you in about thirty minutes. You can come back and pick them up or wait."

"I'll come back, Chief. Should I thank you now or in six months?"

"Get the hell out of here, Doc. You tank people are all a bunch of smart asses."

Later that afternoon, Doc picked up his orders and read them carefully. In summary, the orders stated that he should be transferred immediately, he was authorized to use commercial air to travel to Vietnam, a passport and secret clearance were required, and he should take seven sets of dress white uniforms and two pairs of dungarees. He had no idea of the extent or type of duty he was being assigned and did not question the white uniforms; later this would become laughable.

When he arrived at the Federal Building the following Monday morning, the State Department representative was waiting for him. After completing several forms and having his picture taken, he was told that he could return on Wednesday to pick up his passport. The middle-aged clerk commented that this must be some special deal, since they had never before seen a passport issued in less than six to eight weeks.

Doc discovered there was very limited commercial air service to Saigon from Hawaii and, consequently, opted for military air transport as the quickest way to get to Vietnam. He was able to book onto a MATS flight that would depart from Hickam Air Force base on Wednesday evening. It was a multi-stop flight. The flight would go first to Wake Island, next to Guam, then Clark Air Force Base in the Philippines, and eventually Saigon. Scheduled overnight stops were in Guam and Clark. A long, slow flight but it was the best he could do.

When Doc finally heard the screech of the tires on the runway in Saigon, he was glad that the old plane had made it in one piece. The bus ride from Tan Son Nhat airport was hot and dirty. Having previously spent several months in Asia, the crush of people was not particularly interesting to him. The climate seemed very similar to what he had experienced in the Philippines and other South East Asia locations.

When the bus stopped at the MACV compound, he grabbed his sea bag and headed for the Navy Personnel office. A sweaty Chief Petty Officer rose from behind the counter and took a copy of the orders that Doc laid on the counter.

"Ah, another MTT 10-62 guy. How many more of you are coming?"

"I can't answer that, Chief. I don't know what the unit is. I heard some scuttlebutt on the plane that it is a newly formed navy unit call SEAL?"

The Chief came half way across the counter and took hold of Doc's wrist. "Don't ever use that word in public again, it is classified Secret...get it, David?"

"I do, Chief, but don't overreact."

"I am sorry, Doc, it's just that I get these damn directives and I have to enforce them, even through I don't know anything about them. There is just too much going on and I don't get the word. O.K., that said, give me your dog tags, I.D. card, passport, drivers license, and anything else that identifies you as an American."

"What the hell is this about, Chief?"

"It's more of those rules I was just telling you about. Anyone checking in who is assigned to MTT 10-62 must surrender all of their personal identification. For your information, we got word earlier today that your CO will be coming down day after tomorrow to take you back up country with him. In the meantime, I will assign you billeting in a hotel down the street. Be back here tomorrow for an in country briefing and to be issued a weapon. After that just hang loose until your CO shows up."

"Where is up country?"

"Your unit is operating in the Da Nang area about 350 miles north, you get there by flying. Here's your hotel assignment, down two blocks, then right three blocks. See you in the morning, about 0900."

The hotel was what might be described as clean but crummy. Doc's room did have a nice little balcony that overlooked the street. After a shower and a change into dungarees and a T-shirt, Doc got a soda out of a machine in the hall and sat on the balcony. The sun was going down and the heat had abated slightly, it was almost pleasant on the balcony. The usual rush of people seemed to be less than normal and those who were present appeared to be in a hurry to get off the street.

Doc was taking a sip from the soda when he saw a man run out the front entrance of another hotel about five doors up and across the street. There was a huge explosion as a fireball burst from the doorway the running man had just exited. Doc could feel the heat and concussion from the blast, it knocked him backward in his chair. The entire front of the hotel across the street disappeared, as giant flames leaped up the front of the brick and frame building. In just a couple of minutes sirens seemed to be converging from every direction. Within a few minutes, a military ambulance and a small fire truck arrived. The Saigon police cordoned off the entire block and a dozen armed U.S. Marines were onsite within minutes.

Doc had left the door to his room open to help with air circulation. He looked away from the street for a moment and saw a large, fat man standing in his doorway.

"Them fuckers did it again. That's the third US billeting hotel they've hit in the last two weeks," the man said with a vigorous shake of his head.

Doc frowned at the man."Who's them?"

"VC, who else? I've been in this stinking town for seven months now and all it does is get worse. Soon we'll have armed guards in every lobby and a curfew for US personnel. This place sucks."

"I'm HM1 David, passing through."

"Passing through to where?"

"Up north, attached to a MTT, I think." He was hesitant to say more.

"I'm Sharlot, I'm stationed at the dental clinic at MACV and so far this month we have pulled two dogs' teeth and done one filling on a Marine PFC…a challenging assignment."

"So the VCs are trying to kill US military personnel, right?"

"Yeah, and anyone else who gets in the way. It makes you feel like you're not wanted, doesn't it? Well, I have to get a move on. Got a date with a hot mama on the other side of town and she won't wait."

Doc spent the remainder of the evening watching the rescue activities down the street. He considered going down to offer help but thought better of it, when he remembered he had no form of identification. There were many Vietnamese and military police onsite, not a good environment for someone without a way to verify his identity. Sleep escaped him for the remainder of the night and left him wondering if there would be another bomb.

The next morning, at MACV headquarters, he was accosted by questions from the staff in Navy Personnel about the bomb and the reaction in the area. The Chief told him that he thought four army men had been killed and three more were in the hospital. Evidently, this type of attack was becoming all too common and an effective means for dealing with it was still in the planning process. The Chief directed Doc to a room, on the other side of the compound, to attend the orientation class for personnel assigned outside the Saigon area.

He entered the room that had about thirty school desks, finding almost all of them occupied by air force men.

An Army Major, Doc assumed was the instructor, entered the room and walked to the front. Someone called out attention and the entire group came to their feet.

The major then introduced himself as Major Doug and launched into a monologue of dos and don'ts while in country, most of which were common sense to Doc. The lecture lasted about thirty minutes and, in conclusion, the Major asked for questions.

An airman raised his hand, when acknowledged asked, "how do I tell who, is VC and who isn't?"

The Major hesitated and smiled. "Well I can tell you from my own experience, if you see someone pointing a weapon at you, chances are he is VC. Other than that, I know of no way! The problem we are dealing with is a mixture of loyalties among the people. Some are committed to the Saigon government, some feel loyalty to the VC. Some are VC at night and loyal to Saigon in the daytime. Most couldn't care less who runs the government. The VC raid villages in the countryside and attempt to gain the villagers' support, if that doesn't come willingly, then they get it at gunpoint. Eventually, if the support isn't available, they return, kill everyone in the village and burn it to the ground."

This gave Doc some understanding of what he would be dealing with during his deployment up north.

Later, he made the trip to the MACV armory and was issued the venerable .38 Special revolver and six rounds of ammunition. He received the same instructions as Bill and others in his team had received when they were issued weapons. This was the first time Doc was issued a weapon in his career, because of the restrictions under the Geneva Convention, which prohibited the arming of medical personnel. He guessed, when it came to men in SEAL, that didn't apply? Doc was no stranger to firearms. He had grown up target shooting and hunting. He was an accomplished rifle shot by his early teens.

Next, he went to the Navy Personnel section where he was told his team CO would be in at 1000 tomorrow and he should be there ready to move out.

After another sleepless night, he returned to the personnel office where the Chief told him, "your CO is in the Naval Intelligence office down the hall, David. He asked that I have you go down there when you came in." The Chief returned to reading his Playboy magazine.

A navy Wave in the Intelligence Office directed David to Commander Rudd's office where Lieutenant Beck opened the door after David knocked.

"HM1 David, we've been waiting for you, come in. Would you like some coffee?"

"Yes, Sir, that sounds good."

Lieutenant Evans got up and held out his hand, "I'm Mr. Evans, welcome, Doc, sure glad you finally made it. We need medical support before we can do much more up North."

During the next hour, Evans, Beck, and Rudd briefed David on the mission of MTT 10-62, the problems associated with lack of support available and the challenges that David was likely to face. The absence of M.D. back up was a major concern, but David was quick to tell them that he was accustomed to working independent of a physician and, in fact, much of his training had focused on that type of duty.

"Are you a First Class Diver?"

"Yes, Sir," David responded to his new CO.

"I take it, from your earlier response, that you have had tours of duty with various diving groups. Have you ever been with a UDT unit?"

"Yes, I've been TAD to UDT 11 a few times in the last year. I just returned from a three week tour with them. They were doing some work off the island of Kauai."

Commander Rudd then asked, "are you jump qualified?"

"No, Sir, never had the opportunity to go through that training."

Lieutenant Evans looked at Rudd with a smile. "Well we can solve that problem when we get up to Da Nang. We'll give you a good run of on-the-job training. All team members are jump qualified so we have many instructors to teach you the basics. You need to have that capability, Doc, in case we need to make an air insertion. The first thing I would like you to do, when we get up there, is a medical screening of the trainees to insure they're capable of withstanding the rigorous training we will put them through. I sure don't want to kill any of them but you know, from personal experience, that it can be tough. We won't lay it on as heavily in the beginning but we have a level we must attain, if we hope to make them effective."

"I'll start on that as soon I can, Mr. Evans. What about the team members, are there any health problems that you know of?"

"None, but you're welcome to check them over if you like."

The discussion continued for another half hour with an open exchange about the trainees and personal qualifications of the other team members.

In parting, Doc and Lieutenant Evans said goodbye to Commander Rudd and Lieutenant Beck, left MACV headquarters, and headed for the airport. The ride was hot and crowded through the streets of Saigon and there was little exchange between the two.

At the airport, Lieutenant Evans headed through the terminal and onto the apron in front. He pointed to an older, twin tailed aircraft. "That's our ride, Doc. Not much for looks but it will get us there."

They entered the plane through the left forward hatch and Doc was amazed at the open space inside. This plane was known as the "Flying Boxcar". It sure was named right. In addition to the canvas seats, there were several crates of materials in the cargo bay marked "Explosives-Handle With Care." Doc wandered what would happen if they made a rough landing. The crew chief had mentioned that the crates were bound for a US Army detachment in Nha Trang. Oh well, he had handled and worked with plenty of explosives in the past and he was still here. An Air Force Captain, dressed in a green flight suit, entered the plane through the same hatch and walked back into the cargo bay. He looked at the two passengers and without any expression said, "if we lose power on takeoff, we'll crash." With that, he turned and headed for the cockpit where the copilot had already began the coughing, smoking ordeal of starting the cranky engines.

Chapter Four

The C 119 taxied to take off position and began an engine run-up. It sounded as though the engines had reached take off power but the plane still wasn't moving. Then, suddenly, it lurched forward and began a laborious take off run. Doc began to wonder if the damn thing was ever going to lift off when he had the sensation of a modest climb. The climb out continued at a very slight angle and then a gentle bank to the right as the climb resumed on a northerly heading. Doc thought the weight of those crates must be near maximum payload for the old Fairchild. Eventually, the plane reached a cruising altitude and leveled off. Doc began to settle back in the hard, uncomfortable seat as he thought about what awaited him in Da Nang.

He leaned close to Lieutenant Evans to speak over the deafening noise, when the speaker of the onboard communications system blurted out. "This is the pilot. We have just lost generator power in the port engine. We will try to maintain partial power until we return to Saigon for an emergency landing...buckle up!"

Lieutenant Evans looked at David, rolled his eyes and threw up his hands, hollering to be heard. "Not a routine flight, Doc, but you'll get used to it after a while flying these antique birds."

The power in the port engine remained sufficient to make the airport and, under bad conditions, the pilot did a great job of pulling off a smooth landing.

After stopping in the taxiway, the pilot came aft to tell them that there would be another flight headed their way in about an hour. It was destined for Nha Trang but would divert to Da Nang en route.

The hour passed quickly. It wasn't long after boarding the second C 119 that the engines were started and the plane began to taxi to the runway. Take off was uneventful and the aircraft assumed an angle of climb more to Doc's liking, the crates of explosives in the other plane must have made the difference.

The small portholes in the plane's fuselage gave Doc a restricted view of the ground below. He saw nothing but jungle laced with small brown streams and rolling hills in all directions.

The approach to Da Nang was bumpy with severe turbulence. The windsock alongside the runway indicated nasty crosswinds. The plane had just touched down when there appeared to be an explosion under the right side. The plane lunged down to that side and began a sideways slide that continued into a spin. The force inside the aircraft was a brutal circular spinning effect that slammed Lieutenant Evans and Doc back in their seats one minute, then threw them forward the next.

As the spinning decreased in frequency, the plane began to slow its slide along the side of the runway. Smoke, welling up in the cabin, smelled like burning rubber. As soon as the motion of the plane had slowed enough to move, Doc and Lieutenant Evans unbuckled and raced for the forward hatch. The pilot had already flung the hatch door open and quickly pushed them to the ground outside, shouting, "run, this son-of-a-bitch may blow."

As they ran, Doc fought with the weight of his sea bag, taking a moment to look back over his shoulder, he saw that most of the plane was engulfed in flames that shot a hundred feet in the air. Fire trucks were on their way down the runway. At about 100 yards from the plane, the pilot, crew chief, and co-pilot caught up with them and stopped to look at their plane. The trucks stopped at a safe distance sensing that there was a good chance the plane would explode. The flames were so intense that, in minutes, the plane had disintegrated into a pile of aluminum and steel.

All had escaped from the plane with no injuries except for the pilot, who had some minor burns on his arms.

Doc offered to look at the burns to see what might be needed to treat them but the pilot declined, saying that he would have them checked out later. Doc then looked at his CO, "Bill, that's quite a ride you got us on, next time let's take the train."

Lieutenant Evans looked away and said under his breath, "goddamn air force junk."

As they resumed their walk to the terminal, Doc saw a man running toward them, waving both hands in the air.

"Someone is trying to get our attention, Skipper."

"Yes, that's Chief Volkert, he's our team Chief. He came to pick us up. I'll bet he's been waiting for hours."

"Hey, Skipper, you really know how to make an entrance, that was a spectacular landing but a little hard on the plane. Are you alright? You must be the Doc. Welcome aboard."

As they moved toward the makeshift terminal, Doc noticed it was not much of an airport, a few little buildings and hangers.

Chief Volkert led the way toward a Jeep parked near the terminal building. "Are you sure you're both okay? That was one hell of a fire! I didn't know when you would get in, I got one arrival time but then they changed it and I didn't know if you would be in today. I took a chance and came back out about five minutes before your ill-fated landing. In the future, Skipper, let me schedule your flights, I think the odds are against you."

"I know it was an introduction to Da Nang I won't forget. Damn, you guys live dangerously up here." Doc smiled as he threw his sea bag into the Jeep.

The drive through the edge of Da Nang exposed Doc to the area he would be living in for the next few months. In all, it was not unlike many other Asian settlements with many small shops and closely grouped buildings. It was more like a group of small villages, in that each community seemed to have its own shopping area.

The Jeep pulled into an alley next to a large two-story house and angled into a parking area immediately behind it. An eight-foot high steel fence, with two strands of barbed wire topping it, surrounded the rear of the house.

"This is home, Doc. You'll meet our newest team member just inside the back door, she's friendly." The Chief smiled at Evans as he led the way through the iron gate to the back door.

Inside, a half grown German Shepherd puppy greeted them with a happy bark, her tail wagging in welcome.

"This is Junk, Doc. We got her a few weeks ago in Saigon, thought it would be a good idea to have a pooch around after dark. We named her Junk because we're training Junk Force people. Not the most original name but it works for us."

Doc patted the dog on the head and she responded with a whine.

"You can leave your gear down here, Doc. This will be where you bunk until we can arrange for you upstairs." The Chief pointed to a metal double deck bunk in the corner of a ground level basement room.

Doc nodded and threw his sea bag on the lower bunk. There was a small metal locker in the far corner and a small alcove in the opposite corner that looked like a kitchen. Up a long set of wide stairs, Doc entered a huge room dominated by a ten foot long wooden table surrounded by straight back chairs. Around the table sat several men drinking what appeared to be beer. One of the men got to his feet and approached Doc.

"I'm Les Barter, welcome aboard. Your name is David, right?"

"That's right, Les, hot off the plane from Pearl and points in between,"

Doc looked around the table, the other men seated there looked up and either nodded or raised a hand in greeting.

No one said anything for a minute, then Chief Volkert spoke up, "Doc is going to be with us for the remainder of our tour, we need to make him feel at home…right? How about a beer, Doc?"

"I'll have one, Chief, can I buy?"

"Next time."

With that, the Chief walked through a large set of double doors, leading to a narrow balcony that stretched all the way across the front of the house and slightly overhung the narrow sidewalk below.

"Din, hey, Din."

Doc had followed the Chief partway onto the balcony and saw that there was a small storefront across the street. A small Vietnamese boy appeared in the doorway of the store and looked up at the Chief.

The Chief held up three fingers and shouted, "mochi bomeba."

The boy answered by holding up three fingers and nodding his head. In a few minutes Doc heard footsteps of someone running up the stairs and the boy from the store appeared at the head of the stairs carrying three bottles of beer. Chief Volkert reached in his pocket, pulled out a handful of paper money handing the boy a single bill. The boy smiled at him and ran back down the stairs. The Chief handed Doc a beer, one to Les, and kept the third for himself.

"Thanks, it actually feels cold." Doc looked at the bottle in his hand and read the label, "Tiger Beer."

"It's not the best beer you ever drank, Doc, but it's the best we have out here."

Most of the men had left the table and wandered off to some place else in the house without saying anything. Those who remained at the table pushed out a chair and motioned for Doc to sit down.

"I'm Jim Vail. I have to ask you, since you have your ice cream suit on, where in the hell did you park your ice cream truck? I really need a Dilly bar."

"No Dilly bars, Jim. Would you believe that they told me to bring seven sets of these things?"

"That's typical of the Washington Navy; frequently they can't hit their ass with both hands. Do you have anything else to wear? You sure won't want to be running around in those things." As Doc shook his head, Les continued, "we'll scare you up some greens until we can requisition some camouflage for you. Hey troops," Les shouted, "Doc needs some greens, and anything you got that will fit him. What size, Doc?"

"Thirty-two inch waist." Doc was sturdily built at five foot eleven and

170 pounds. His dark complexion and brown eyes were typical of his Welch/Pennsylvania Dutch heritage. The years of strenuous diving activity and physical conditioning had developed his muscles to a refined tone.

Within an hour, there was a pile of greens on the end of the big table, enough to see him through several changes.

"I've got an extra pair of jungle boots in here, Doc, if you want to try them on?"

"Thanks for the offer, Chief, I brought my navy high top work shoes, they should work for the time being. I think I'll go unpack my gear and get squared away."

Doc began sorting his gear and trying to arrange it in the small locker. He put his six extra pairs of whites in a bag he had brought with him, to avoid ruining them on the rusty shelves of the locker.

As he was finishing up, he saw Lieutenant Evans coming down the stairs.

"Doc, there are a couple of things I need to talk to you about. I wouldn't count on doing too much for the next few days, it may not have gotten to you yet, but the water contamination will hit you soon. You won't be able to get more than fifty feet from the head, just pretend you made a trip to Mexico. We all went through it when we got here, for some it lasted several days, others less. There isn't anything we can do about it, we tried the water purification tablets but the water tastes so bad we didn't figure it was worth it. We have no other source of water. Most of us stay away from drinking the water as much as possible by having soda, beer, or canned milk."

Bill was apologetic as he continued, "we don't really have regular meals yet either, I'm trying to find a cook, until we do everyone is on their own. We have canned milk, bread, peanut butter, jelly, crackers, and chips…usually. Not much of a diet but we can survive until I make better arrangements. Lastly, we use first names only. Since we are supposed to be covert or something like that, names are easily overheard and that might endanger our presence here."

"O.K., Bill. I have some questions for you. What about medical supplies, nothing fancy, but I do need some things to work with; like a stethoscope, blood pressure cuff, thermometers, a minor surgical kit. You know just basic stuff?"

"There are some things out at the Junk Force Naval Base but I don't know what. The first time you go out you can look, what you don't have we can probably bum from the army Special Forces docs. I'm having a meeting upstairs at 2000, why don't you come up and join in."

Later that evening, Doc found the entire team seated around the big table. On the table was a big bag of potato chips and several unopened sodas.

Les directed Doc to an empty chair next to him.

Bill looked at the group, "I want to go over our preliminary training plan and work up how we'll proceed from here. I want Doc to do a physical check on all of the trainees, but that will have to wait for a couple of days. When we get to that point, you can break the trainees off from whatever they are doing and send them to him in groups of say ten. Does that sound about right, Doc?"

Doc thought that was about enough to check at one time and agreed.

"You have all read the plan, let's talk about the problems you see in it."

Vail looked at the group, then at Bill. "We are supposed to give these people weapons and explosives training, with what?"

Chief Volkert answered for Bill, "I'll have a dozen M1 Carbines coming in a day or two with 5000 rounds of ammo. The explosives training is going to be limited to TNT and grenades, that's all army Special Forces can get. Sergeant White also said he would send over some pistols, 9mm semi-autos and ammo for our personal use, he knows about the issue of the old .38s.

Bill grinned, nodding his head at the Chief. "Good work, Chief, you're a cumshaw artist. Are there other comments?"

Les pushed his chair back from the table and looked at Bill. "What about vehicles, I mean how are we going to cart these guys around and get back and forth to the base? We can't all ride in that one Jeep the Chief borrowed."

"If you haven't figured it out by now, this is a shoestring operation and they told me in Saigon to use my ingenuity. Our team ingenuity is all we have. I don't think Coronado has any idea of the job we have to do, nor what we need to do it. We'll work with what we can get from army Special Forces and "liberate" the rest from whatever source we can. I've been told that our air force has a few new vehicles in a compound out at the airport that might be available to be checked out, I'll give that a try tomorrow."

Chief Volkert joined the conversation, "Sergeant White told me that vehicles given by the US to the Vietnamese army are distributed to various regions throughout the country. One of those regions happens to be Da Nang and the storage yard is about five kilometers beyond the Junk Force Naval Base. He also told me they often arrive after dark. They park them outside the compound, unguarded, until the next morning, when the Vietnamese guard force arrives. The keys are taken to a central office in Da Nang, but I don't see that as a problem. Do you, Les?"

"Not in the least, Chief. Give me about two minutes per vehicle and it's ours. If they are like most vehicles I've seen, they'll have serial numbers stenciled on the hood and other places. Can you handle that, Chuck?"

Chuck Ramsey, Damage Controlman, Third Class, looked at Les. "I'll need more than two minutes, it may take as much as ten but I can fix those numbers so no one will ever guess that they weren't painted on in San Francisco."

"Are there any other questions or comments?" No one responded as Bill turned away from the table and headed for his room. He shook his head and said to himself, "a great crew."

A few days later Doc had recovered from intestinal upset. He was anxious to get to work on screening the trainees and establishing his medical presence. Chief Volkert woke Doc at 0500 and told him the Jeep would be leaving for the base in an hour. After dressing in a suit of the greens collected for him, he went upstairs to a canned milk and cracker breakfast.

Clear skies dominated the day with heavy humidity and stale air. The trip to the Junk Force Naval Base took a route through the edge of Da Nang and then headed out into the countryside. The roads were poor, many places were full of potholes. Chief Volkert drove, while Barter and Vail rode in the back.

Barter leaned forward speaking in Doc's ear, "nice roads. The French taught the Vietnamese how to fix them. If a hole develops you fill it with dirt for a patch that works fine until the next rain, in this climate, that won't be long. The French built most of these roads and it's interesting because they built them from points where resources exist to the coast. It made it much easier to haul stuff back to France. They built very few roads that the people could use, like from village to village."

After a twenty-minute ride over the rough gravel road, the Chief made a left turn onto a narrow spur road running past a small village of rough wood huts. Small children played in the dirt in front of them while an older child watched from the shade of a hut door. The village didn't look very prosperous, the children were scantily dressed, no men or women were in sight. There was an explanation for the absence of women. On the drive to the base Doc had seen lines of women trotting along the side of the road with poles over their shoulders. On the ends of the pole hung heavy baskets or buckets, the women were used as beasts of burden. They were one of the major sources of transportation of all sorts of commodities including food, water, and even rock and gravel for building projects. Doc had seen these phenomenon elsewhere in Asia but it never ceased to amaze him. The brutal physical exertion would be exhausting except for the common practice of chewing the narcotic Beatle Nut that left a dark brown stain on teeth but provided enough of a high to continue the brutal labor.

Another half mile brought them to a group of Quonset type buildings interspersed with small frame structures.

The Chief stopped the Jeep under a large tree next to one of the Quonsets and said, "the building on the right is being used to house our trainees and as the center for portions of the training that require a makeshift classroom setting. That building across the road is empty, you can use that for a sick bay. What we have for medical supplies are in a locker up there. When you're ready to start screening the trainees let us know, we'll start sending groups to you. I'll have Lieutenant Lin come up with them to interpret for you. He is the officer leader of the trainees and speaks good English."

Doc made his way up to the building the Chief had pointed out and opened the rusty metal door. It was a one-room building with a few rusty metal chairs and a large metal cabinet. Doc opened the doors of what he thought might be the medical supply cabinet. It was almost empty. On the middle shelf, he found a partial box of tongue blades, an old glass jar filled with dirty cotton tipped applicators, a small bottle of Merthiolate, and an empty aspirin bottle. He walked over to one of the rusty metal folding chairs, sat down and gazed out the open door feeling a strong sense of frustration and anger. He realized that the screening of the trainees would have to take on a very simplistic format. Well, he thought, I can do a fundamental gross evaluation and do the blood pressure, ear, nose, and throat after I get some equipment. He wished he had known the conditions he would face in this assignment, he could have come better prepared by bringing the equipment and supplies he needed from Subase.

The first group of ten trainees arrived along with Lieutenant Lin, who extended his hand to Doc in greeting.

"Can all of these men write, Lieutenant?"

"Yes, they can, but not in English. I can interpret for you. What is it you want them to write?"

"If we can get some pencils and paper, I would like them to write down a list of injuries and illnesses they have had and any health problems they have today. You think they can do that?"

"Yes, certainly."

"Once they have that written, I will talk to them, with your help, and do a basic gross exam of their body, muscles, and bone structure."

"I'll send one for the pencils and paper."

Lin turned to a man seated nearest him saying something in Vietnamese. The man jumped to his feet, ran out the door, and across the road.

"I'm glad you're here. I feel much better having someone with medical training around for the good of my trainees."

Doc looked at him and saw a handsome, well-built Vietnamese man in his early twenties with dark hair and sun tanned brown skin. "While we're waiting for the paper, would you tell me about your background, Lieutenant?"

"I was born near here. My father had a plantation and I was educated through primary school by tutors who lived at our home. My father sent me to France for my advanced education and later I attended the French Naval Academy. I graduated from the academy two years ago and came home. I was able to do that since my mother was born in France, my father is Vietnamese. The French played a major role in our country until they were ejected in the early fifties. I learned English at the academy."

"You probably do a better job with English than I do, Lieutenant."

"I would be happy if you would use my first name, Doc. It is Lei."

The paper and pencils arrived and Lei set about telling the men what they should write. In a few minutes, several of the men were finished and Lei motioned the first over to a chair in front of Doc.

The trainee handed the paper to Lei and he read it carefully. "This man claims no major illnesses and no injuries. He states he is in good health."

Doc had the man stand in front of him and carefully examined his head, neck, shoulders, arms, legs, and feet. He had good muscle conformation and appeared to be reasonably well nourished. Then, with a tongue blade, he examined the inside of his mouth and teeth. He checked his outer ear canal as well as he could without proper tools. Next, he conducted a hand-eye coordination test, took the man's pulse in both arms, then checked range of motion in shoulders and arms, and had the man do a deep knee bend. Next, using a rough chart he had made, he checked his visual acuity in each eye. Finally, after draping an old blanket he had found across the corner of the room, he had the man enter that enclosure and drop his shorts to conduct a visual exam of his penis and rectum. He recorded a summary of this information on the trainee's questionnaire. Doc nodded to the man telling Lei, "this man looks like a good candidate, from a physical perspective."

Lei said something to the man in Vietnamese and the man left the building.

Doc followed this routine for the remainder of the day, examining sixty men. The first man examined was one of the fit, while many of the others had physical abnormalities, or a history of injury or diseases that would disqualify them from participating in the rigorous training they would undergo. In several men, he discovered symptoms of venereal diseases such as gonorrhea as well as what appeared to be syphilitic lesions. He saw some conditions he could not identify that caused him considerable concern. He told Lei that he should tell these men to seek treatment from a Vietnamese military doctor. At the end of the day, Doc had rejected twenty-five of the sixty men in this first group, fearing that subjecting them to the training would worsen their physical condition or cause permanent injury.

The next day, using the same routine, with Lei's assistance, he examined the remaining forty trainees and found only fifteen of them he could approve for the training.

The initial group of trainees had numbered 120. By the end of the second day of physical fitness training, prior to Doc's arrival, eight men were missing and twelve quit. Doc's physical screening eliminated fifty more who he considered unfit for the demands that would be placed on them. The result was that out of 120 men, fifty reasonably fit men would advance to the training program.

Chapter Five

The next evening, a quiet discussion was in progress when Doc went upstairs to assemble anything he could find for dinner, peanut butter and crackers again. In the process, he overheard vehicles mentioned. He tuned into the conversation at that point.

Chuck Ramsey, a strapping young man in his early twenties had blond hair and a weightlifter's body. With a can of soda at his lips, he looked at Les. "Are you sure you can wire a vehicle that fast?"

"Shouldn't be a big problem. I've done a lot of them, in fact I made a living for a while doing it for a "repo" outfit in L.A. We averaged ten to twenty a week and I did about half of them. You know folks don't make payments on their ride, the finance company wants their money, so, they would give us the info on the dead beat and tell us where they lived. We'd watch the place, maybe where they worked or where they lived, until we had a line on the vehicle. Then I'd take over, wire the car and drive it to our lot. Sometimes the owner wasn't too happy but we always left a copy of the paper work. They had no legal beef with us. If they wanted the car back, all they had to do was pay up what they owed, which they seldom did. It wasn't a profit sharing deal, I got 150 dollars per hit and, at a ripe age of seventeen, that wasn't bad money."

Chuck countered, "I am impressed. I didn't realize we had such a professional in our midst. Aren't you impressed, Doc?"

"Yeah." Doc noticed a bottle of pills on the table. The expression on his face was so serious he had everyone's attention. "Hey, have you guys taken your malaria pills today? You have to take them every day or you'll get messed up and I don't have the time to nurse you back to health." Doc reached across the table and picked up a bottle of pills marked Chloroquin, he washed one down with a sip of soda.

"When do we stop taking these things, Doc?" Les asked.

"You can never stop while you're in a malaria region. When you're back to the states, you'll need to take another drug called Primaquin, for seven days. The Clorquin keeps the malaria virus in your bloodstream inactive. The Primaquin will kill it once you are out of the malaria area. There's no point in killing the bug until you are no longer exposed to it."

"Mosquitoes carry the virus, don't they?" Les needed more details.

"Yes, the Anopheles. You can tell it's that kind of mosquito when they bite because they stand up on their front legs, I guess so they can get deeper penetration. The major species that we have in the states can carry diseases, but not malaria."

Suddenly, realizing he had changed the topic, Doc went back to the subject of vehicles. "You guys were talking about vehicles when I came in, what's the story, Chuck?"

"We're planning a trip to the Vietnamese vehicle storage yard tonight. The Chief got word from army Special Forces today that they have a delivery tonight and we plan to pay them a visit."

"Who's we?"

"Les, Vail, and, me, do you want to come along and play lookout, Doc?"

"Sure, I've never been involved in grand theft auto before."

"Did you see that monster truck in the backyard when you came in, Doc?"

"Yeah, Chuck. It says US Air Force all over it. It must be one that Bill got from the air force motor pool. A Ford no less and a 6x6, the bed on that thing must be twenty feet long?"

"No actually only eighteen, Doc. The nice part is the sixty-gallon fuel tanks. We can fill the other vehicles we liberate from it until we find a bigger source."

At that point, BM1 Vail entered the room. "Are you guys ready?"

Les got to his feet. "Let me get my tools, I'll be right down."

All four men piled into the Jeep, Vail drove while Doc and Les rode in back. Ramsey rode shotgun. The night was black with a heavy overcast of dark clouds. It felt like rain. The streets on the edge of Da Nang were deserted and most of the shops closed. As the Jeep rumbled along over the rough gravel road, Doc thought of late night raccoon hunting at home in Ohio and the thrill of listening to the dogs and following their progress through the woods. However, this was no coon hunt. The risks of being caught were real, oh well, life on the edge!

They passed the entrance to the Junk Force Base and in a few minutes saw a lane angling off to the right, Vail followed it and within 100 yards came to a fenced compound about seventy-five yards square. New vehicles and heavy equipment of every description, including dump trucks, road graders, bulldozers, Jeeps, and busses, resembling school busses painted gray/green, filled the fenced area. A heavy chain and padlock secured the large gate. It was a relief to see two Jeeps and four pickup type trucks, called weapons carriers, parked outside the gate. The weapons carriers had canvas covered bow tops over their beds. The Jeeps were lacking tops but appeared to have everything else.

Les grabbed his tool bag while throwing his legs over the back of the Jeep. No one said a word as he approached the nearest weapons carrier and quietly opened the door. Flashlight in hand, he checked the dashboard and ignition for possible keys. As expected, there was none. Next, he took a tool from his bag and lay down on his back on the floor in front of the driver's seat. It was dead quiet except for the snap of Les cutting wires. In another minute or two, he sat up reached across the dashboard and pulled on the choke. In a few seconds, the engine started with a cough.

Les motioned to Vail, whispering, "why don't you start back to the house in this one, we'll be right behind you in the others. It looks like it'll rain so any tracks we leave will be washed out before morning."

Vail got into the vehicle, keeping the engine RPMs to a minimum, quietly drove out the lane to the road. He avoided turning on the headlights until well down the road.

Les was already working on one of the Jeeps and in minutes had it started. He motioned to Ramsey, who followed the same pattern of departure as Vail. The second weapons carrier was soon running and Les motioned Doc to drive the Jeep they had come in, he would follow in the weapons carrier.

Back at the house, the four gathered around the table for a soda and had a good laugh while slapping each other on the back. It had almost been too easy, but they acknowledged that if it were not for the lax Vietnamese security, it would have been much different.

Les looked at the group. "The sad part, as I see it troops, is that these damn vehicles were bought with our tax dollars and yet, we can't even borrow them. Well you know the old saying goes, *What thou can't beg or borrow, thou may steal.*"

The next morning, driving a newly acquired weapons carrier, Doc and Vail arrived at the Junk Force base by 0600. Doc was interested in working out with the trainees and going along on their morning run. It had been two weeks since he had done any serious running. As they sat outside the trainee barracks, Doc noticed a group of trainees trotting down the road with baskets on their shoulders.

"What do they have in those baskets, Boats?"

"Breakfast, Doc, they go to the base pay office and draw money each day to buy their food. They bring it back here and take turns cooking or whatever needs doing. Mostly, they have vegetables and some fruit but seldom any meat or protein. There is no mess hall or cooks. They're strictly on their own to select what they eat. There's a little farmers' market about one kilometer up the road, you may have noticed it when we've come by, that's where they go to get the food. What they buy in the morning is all the food they will have for meals for that day."

"Not much of a diet, particularly considering the physical conditioning we will be putting them through. I'll talk to Bill about trying to get more protein and carbohydrates into their diet, if we don't, they won't be able to withstand the physical demands."Doc thought for a moment. "Boats, I've been meaning to ask you, why don't we buy some fresh fruit at that farmers' market?"

Boats contemplated the question. "I think we're hesitant to be seen, locally, more than necessary."

Doc nodded his understanding although he doubted they could maintain their cover for long.

After finishing their first meal of the day the trainees fell out in formation and limbered up, they knew the run would be next.

"How far are we going, Boats?"

"Ah, only about three miles, Doc, we're going easy on them as we build them up. We'll be up to about five in another week or so."

The run progressed well. As they returned to the starting point, Doc could feel tightening of the muscles in his legs and lower back. It had been too long since running that distance and he vowed to run at least three mornings a week until he was back to his usual level of four to six miles.

When the team returned to the house late that afternoon, they found a new face. An older Vietnamese man was in the basement working in the kitchen. As they approached him, he looked up from a cutting board and spoke to them in broken English, with a heavy French accent. "Good evening, gentlemen, I am the cook, just hired this morning. I cook for army Special Forces before but left because of sick child. Child better now so I come back to work. Army not need me, they hire another cook while I gone. Lieutenant Evans offer me job, now I here. Would either of you care for a cup of coffee, made a short time ago?"

"It sounds great to me," Les quickly responded.

"Me too. Haven't had a decent cup for weeks. Will you be here to cook breakfast, what is you name?" Doc asked.

"Kin Verone. I was trained in Paris in a cooking school and then had to return home to care for family, I have five children."

"Welcome, Kin, we'll sure be glad to have some regular meals for a change, peanut butter gets old after a few weeks. I assume you've met our dog, Junk. Please make sure she gets a good meal twice a day. We've been feeding her the same things that we eat, she must be sick of crackers, milk, and peanut butter by now."

Doc walked across the room to undress and get ready for a shower. As he pushed back the curtain to enter his cubicle, he noticed a weapon lying on his bunk. He picked it up and saw that it was an M2 carbine. He remembered Chief Volkert had said he had some M1 carbines coming from Sergeant White but he didn't expect any to be the M2 nor did he expect to be a recipient. He remembered the major difference between the two was that the M2 had a small lever on the right side of the action that, when moved to its forward position, converted its mode of fire from semi-automatic to full automatic. The weapon was in excellent condition, as he opened the breech to make certain that it was not loaded, the inner portions of the action shone as though they were new. He knew that millions of these carbines were used in WW II. He had read that they were designed to take the place of a handgun for those whose duties made carrying the larger standard M1 rifle unhandy. He also remembered reading that many of these carbines were returned for armory rebuild. He assumed this must be one that had been returned.

At dinner that evening, they were treated to fried eggplant, some green lettuce like vegetable, bread, butter, and fried fish, a real banquet after crackers and soda. During dinner, Bill spoke of his recent visit to Saigon and the meetings he had with Commander Rudd. He also mentioned putting in a request to Combined Studies for SCUBA gear, a boat, and outboard motor.

After dinner, Vail asked Doc if he would like to go have a look at some of the shops in Da Nang. It was dark by that time so they wouldn't attract much attention if they left their immediate neighborhood.

"Sure would. Is anyone else going?"

Les and Chief Volkert indicated they would go along for the ride.

They all jumped into the new Jeep noticing the freshly inscribed numbers on the hood. Chuck Ramsey had done his thing. They did not look too new, Doc guessed they had been subjected to some wear and tear with a sand rub.

Small shops, that protruded onto the sidewalk, lined the main streets of Da Nang. Finding a jewelry shop, Doc saw beautiful items that looked hand made. He questioned the shopkeeper who assured him they were hand made. He got the idea of ordering a class ring, since he knew it would be a short time after his return to Pearl that he would be graduating with his degree. He sketched out a couple of ideas for the design of the ring and after looking at them closely; the shopkeeper said he could make the ring and add a birthstone for the centerpiece. He told Doc to return in about five days and he would have the preliminary work done for his approval. The ring would be made of eighteen-karat gold. With the stone it would cost about twenty-five dollars. Doc thought the price to be more than reasonable, in fact a bargain.

The following day, on their way to the Junk Force base, they passed a group of ARVN Officers training Vietnamese Army trainees to use a rifle. Les was driving; he pulled to the side of the road so they could watch the training. The trainees stood facing the targets with M1 rifles to their shoulders. The men were all Vietnamese and, typically, on the small side; the rifles were much too heavy for them to properly shoulder. An M1 rifle, the standard US military rifle of WW II and Korea, weighs slightly over eleven pounds, empty. The recoil, as they fired, caused several of the men to be slammed back and three fell to the ground squarely on their butts. It really was not funny, but Les and Doc could hardly control their laughter. Obviously, the M1 was too much rifle for these small framed men.

On the base, they parked in the usual place adjacent to the trainee barracks and across from the building Doc used for sickbay. Down the road another 100 feet stood a group of low trees, which provided a large umbrella of shade from the sun. Under the trees sat a group of about twelve Vietnamese men with cloths wrapped around their heads to serve as blindfolds. A Vietnamese Army Corporal, with a weapon, stood next to the group. Doc and Les walked a little way down the road to get a better look.

"Those guys have their hands tied behind their backs, Doc."

At that moment, they noticed Lieutenant Lin walking toward them from the opposite direction.

Les held out a hand to stop him.

Lin stopped in front of them and smiled.

"Are those men some sort of prisoners?" Les demanded looking at him.

"They are believed to be VC and are being held for questioning by army intelligence. They were captured last night during a raid the army held on a village about ten kilometers from here. No one thought there were active cells of VC this close but it looks like there is proof enough now. They will probably be released after they are interrogated, which is often the case. When it's done that way, you can go back to that village in a few days and capture them again. It looks good on paper for the people in Saigon."

"Are they really VC, are they hostile?"

"Yes, Doc, they are. They don't look very dangerous but turn them loose and give them a weapon and see how their attitude changes. They might be working in a rice paddy during the day and setting up an ambush, along a trail, at night."

"Then why would they be released, if we know they are VC?" Doc was trying to understand the logic.

"It's the way things are done here. I don't agree but, as I said, it looks good on paper. Few, if any, VC that are taken prisoner are held, unless they are known to be truly hard core VC leaders."

Chapter Six

A few evenings later, the team was treated to a steak dinner with a side of eggplant. The meat was tough although the flavor was good. After dinner, a debate arose over the possible origin of the meat, through a process of elimination, they determined it must be water buffalo, no wonder it was tough. Junk emerged from the basement kitchen looking extremely satisfied, no doubt she had received a choice cut of the buffalo for dinner.

This dinner was attended by the entire team because of the menu and Bill's announcement of a team meeting to discuss the progress of the training program. It was the first time, since his arrival, Doc had seen the entire team at one time.

Lieutenant Evans took a chair in the center of the table while Chief Volkert and Vail occupied the end chairs. Les and Doc sat across from Bill Evans while the rest of the team scattered out on the remaining chairs.

Bill opened the discussion by congratulating them for their success in the 'liberation' of the three new vehicles now parked at the rear of the house. "You guys did a top notch job getting those trucks for us. I think they'll fill our needs for now. The one thing we need to think about is how we are going to keep them fueled. We can draw unlimited gas from the air force motor pool but you can just put so much in two thirty gallon truck tanks. Those weapons carriers get poor gas mileage and the sixty gallons won't feed them for long. Think about how we can transport more at one time. Next, the boat, motor, and SCUBA gear I requested from Combined Studies are at the airport, someone can pick that gear up tomorrow. Chief, are we making enough progress on physical conditioning to start some water work soon?"

"I think we are in good shape, Bill, the number of push ups, sit ups, deep knee bends, and run distances are growing daily. We should be to our target in a couple more sessions. We can start water workouts by the middle of next week."

"The water work will require the entire team; we'll start out with some preliminary swim screening and work toward a 200 yard swim then progress to our target of two miles. Our training schedule also includes a night compass swim at the completion of the swimming segment." Looking around the table, Bill asks if there were any questions or comments.

Electronic Technician, Third Class, John Smith, spoke up, "did everyone see the VC prisoners at the base last week?"

Everyone around the table acknowledged that they had. Smith continued, "I know that many of us go out to the base unarmed but I wonder if that's such a good idea? I think we need to rethink the ongoing need to carry a weapon and be prepared, with the VC operating that close to the base."

Bill joined the conversation, "I have been assured by intelligence in Saigon that there has never been an officially confirmed report of VC activity in the Da Nang area."

Les spoke up in his usual direct approach. "Bull shit, Sir. What would you call those blindfolded people with their hands tied behind them, sure not den mothers. I think those intell desk jockeys should look around and really see what's going on. I had Junk with me that day. She really reacted, the hair was standing up on her neck and the growling never stopped. She seemed to recognize that they were bad guys. I don't know how she did it. Maybe it was the blindfolds or their odor. I think we should offer her services to intell."

"O.K., O.K., Les, I think your point is well made. From a team commander's view, I can evaluate our local situation and let intelligence in Saigon know; it would appear that ARVN intelligence is not sharing with our navy folks…nothing new."

Radioman, Third Class, George Soule, looked, at Bill. "I can tell you that I don't intend to take fire, I *will* carry my weapon and at the slightest indication that our trainees or team are in danger, I *will* shoot to disable."

Bill looked at the group around the table, moving his eyes from man to man, "I'm only going to say this once. This unit is supposedly here as an advisory group, our designation as a mobile training team makes that point loud and clear. Our deployment orders indicate we are not an operational combat team, maybe there will be teams in the future that are, I suspect that will happen. However, for the record, I find it difficult to train a group of men in counterinsurgency and not have them exposed to insurgents."

Bill went on to say, "I have spoken to Captain Marz about our trainees being involved in the Special Forces training program for the Vietnamese Army troops under his control, he thought that would be possible. This would involve integrating a select group of our men into real exercises against active VC contingents in this area. We need to talk more about this to build time into our training schedule. I suggest our team be armed and stay alert for VC activity that might interfere with our training or endanger the trainees or us.

We are a team and I want all of our involvement, regardless of the task or mission, to be a team effort and a team decision. Questions?"

The team members around the table looked at one another and rolled their eyes, Bill had just undergone a complete reversal of his position on VC activity.

"Not a question but a comment. That steak had to be water buffalo."

"I don't know, Tom, but I will check it out with the cook," Bill responded, giving Tom a disgusted look.

Bill left the table, indicating to the Chief that he had a meeting with Madam Chang, the owner of the house. The Chief frowned thinking, *these meetings with Madam Chang are becoming more and more frequent, what is the attraction?* The premise for these frequent meetings was the mastery of the Mandarin dialect, Madam Chang was supposedly teaching Bill Chinese. She was also a very wealthy attractive woman in her thirties and she owned one of the largest, most palatial homes in Da Nang. The Chief doubted she was a teacher as well.

As the group broke up, some of the men headed for their rooms, others went out on the balcony to check out the activity on the street below. An unusual amount of activity at the house next door was obvious. An American missionary couple with two children occupied the house. It was normally quiet. Tonight something was going on. Tom Carey walked to the end of the balcony to investigate. From that position he could look directly into the living room of the missionaries, they were sitting in a circle on the floor. It looked like an old time revival in progress.

Barter, Chief Volkert, Smith, and Vail remained seated at the table with Doc.

"We haven't had much of an opportunity to talk to you, Doc, we're curious about your training. What can you tell us?" The Chief leaned back in his chair and looked around the group.

"What would you like to know?"

Les turned in his chair to face Doc, "We got the word that you are a first class diver. I for one don't know exactly what that means. Have you been trained in SCUBA?"

"Yes, as well as hard hat, shallow water gear, mixed gas, underwater mechanics, and welding. The first class diver program takes about nine months. As a corpsman, I had an additional three months training in diving and submarine medicine at the Experimental Diving Unit in D.C."

"Didn't you find that the big metal helmet restricted your movement?" Les asked.

"Yes, it can, but there are advantages to that equipment. If you have a heavy job to do, you know, lots of pushing, pulling, or lifting, you can't beat the helmet diving gear. You also have the advantage of an unlimited air supply for heavy or long jobs, that's a real advantage."

Les leaned forward in his chair. "What is the deepest dive you've made, Doc?"

"285 feet on air and 385 in mixed gas equipment."

"How deep have you been with SCUBA?"

"About 150, the limit in the fleet is less than that but sometimes you need to go deeper to get the job done."

Les shook his head, "I don't know how the rest of you feel but that sounds too deep for me, don't know if I want to get down that far."

"So you've had all this diving training, what about the medical stuff? As team Chief, I need to know what I can expect from you."

"I've been trained to function as the medical representative for units that don't have an M.D. I can do minor surgery, diagnose and treat diseases and injuries, and prescribe medications to treat those conditions. I recently completed a two-year tour as the medical representative on a submarine rescue vessel home ported at Pearl. I've also been TAD to UDT 11 when their corpsman got hurt. I provided medical support for their operations in Hawaii for a short period."

Soule then asked, "did you like your duty with UDT? I know a couple of guys in team 11."

"Yeah, a great bunch of guys. During one of my brief tours with them, we pulled off an operation that you may have heard about. In Pearl, there is a new type of destroyer called a destroyer leader. It's about 100 feet longer than the old type. When it arrived in Pearl, the CO knew he had a showboat and took advantage of it by telling everyone that the ship would maintain maximum security for the vessel's integrity, including topside guards. An officer from team 11 overheard his claims in the Officers' Club and thought they needed testing. He put together an operation to do that. A few nights later, he led a contingent of the team to the pier area near where the ship was moored. We placed simulated underwater explosives on the keel. To verify our feat, we had taken along a small container of white paint and painted a sign on the port side of the hull, the side most visible to other ships in the harbor, SUNK - UDT 11. The next morning, almost every ship in Pearl and everyone at Sub Base saw the sign on the ship. The shit hit the fan. Team 11 was placed on report and ordered to remove the sign and apologize to the ship's CO and crew."

Les led the group in laughing and asked the others if they had heard of the incident, two said they had.

Doc enjoyed the laughter of his team-mates and asked if they would like to hear another 'sea story'. He thought they might enjoy hearing about a submarine rescue vessel called the USS Coucal on which he had served. In answer to his question most of the men answered with an, "oh, yeah." Sailors always like to hear sea stories. Doc grinned and related one of his experiences on the Coucal.

He explained that the ship's company included up to thirty first class divers. That number was necessary to provide deep diving capability in the event the ship was called to perform a submarine rescue using its rescue chamber. The ship was also expected to perform other jobs and the least popular was towing a submarine converted from a WW II boat to an antisubmarine warfare practice target. The submarine had the WW II name of the Asonet, after conversion, it had been renamed the Tenosa. The Coucal, from time to time, was tasked with towing the Tenosa submerged. The submarine was equipped with special valves on the main deck so it could be flooded from there. The inside of the submarine had been stripped of all equipment. After flooding, the submarine was supported by huge salvage pontoons that suspended it at a depth of 150 feet. Needless to say, this load was very difficult to tow because of the underwater drag.

Doc shrugged his shoulders when he said, "the crew hated the job, but someone had to do it."

"Sorry to interrupt," Les apologized, "but I just figured out that Tenosa is Asonet spelled backwards."

"Leave it to you, Les, to figure that out, I should have explained that when I mentioned the Tenosa."

"Go on, Doc, I for one want to hear the rest of the story," the Chief urged.

Doc went on to explain that the Coucal's last tow of the Tenosa came in the winter of 1960 when the ship was ordered to pick up the Tenosa and tow her submerged in the open sea between the islands of Oahu and Kauai. The CO of the Coucal cautioned the officer, who issued the order, that it was very dangerous to tow the Tenosa in the heavy seas, that were running between the two islands, at that time. He was ordered to proceed. Once in position between the two islands, the tow became progressively more difficult, due to heavy seas and a strong wind from the north. Midway between the islands, the main tow cable parted and the Tenosa started its plunge into two thousand fathoms of water. The crew manning the sonar equipment heard her breaking up at about 500 feet.

Doc concluded his story by saying, "the USS Coucal can go down in Naval History as the only submarine rescue vessel to have sunk a submarine.

The story raised a round of questions for Doc that he enjoyed answering.

When the questioning played out the Chief spoke up, "we now have some SCUBA gear, Doc, how about a little dive tomorrow?"

"Nothing I would like better, Chief. What are we diving on?"

"Lieutenant Lin told me that there is an old Japanese troop barge in the Da Nang harbor about 500 yards out from the harbor area. It's a carryover from WW II, the Japanese moved much of their supplies and troops with barges because of their shallow draft and the load they could carry. I thought we might give that old barge a shot and see what we can come up with."

"What's the depth, Chief?"

"Judging from the charts we have, it looks about 130 feet."

"O.K. Sounds like a good way to spend a Sunday. At that depth we should have a ten minute bottom time to avoid decompression, I hope the chart is accurate."

Late the next morning, Chief Volkert, Les, Vail, and Doc launched the newly acquired boat on a small sandy stretch of beach adjacent to the main harbor in Da Nang. The boat, provided by Combined Studies, was a UDT beach assault craft made of fiberglass coated foam with a hard fiberglass bottom and wood transom. A forty horsepower outboard powered the boat.

"Lin told me that the best way to locate the wreck was to triangulate from that end pier on the left and that power pole on the far beach. That should get us close, we should be able to find it, looks like there's decent visibility."

"I think you're right about the visibility, Chief, but we'll know better once we get in the water."

After setting up the dual 2250-p.s.i. tanks, Doc and Volkert assembled the rest of their gear, checked the air supply, and entered the water. The water temperature was very comfortable probably in the eighty-degree range. A quick look at the depths below them indicated a visibility range of about seventy feet. With hand signals indicating they were ready to dive, the two men started a rapid decent. As they reached the sixty-foot level, indicated by their depth gauges, they leveled off to make a visual survey of the bottom beneath them. A faint outline of a hull was visible, in the silty bottom, at a forty-five degree angle from their position. With a nod, they continued their decent. As they approached the hull, they began to see huge schools of fish congregated around and above it. A little deeper, at ninety feet, they could clearly see the outlines of a flat decked barge with very faint markings that appeared to be in an Japanese script. They looked at each other and gave a thumbs up, Lin's information had been correct. It was obvious why the barge was on the bottom, a huge hole was present in the port bow section caused by an explosion. Spikes of jagged metal were pointing out from the hull; the explosion had come from inside the barge. Above the hole they could see several holes which had probably been caused by a large caliber gun, possibly a .50 caliber or even larger. The bullet holes had set off a huge explosion of something being carried inside the barge. At their present depth, the schools of fish began to swarm around them. In hundreds of dives all over the Pacific, Doc had never seen such a concentration of fish in one small area.

A check of dive time on Volkert's watch showed that they had almost used up their bottom time. He gave Doc the signal to head for the surface.

As they broke the surface, the boat changed position to pick them up. They had covered a distance of more than 100 yards from the boat. They turned their backs to the boat while Les and Vail pulled their tanks into the boat and gave them each a hand over the gunwale.

"Good dive, Doc, did you ever see so damn many fish?" Chief Volkert was more excited about finding the fish than the barge.

"Not in one place. I don't know what kind they are but they all seem to be about the same size."

Les began pulling the anchor and looked at the divers. "Well, what's the word, is there a wreck down there, Chief?"

"Yeah, just like Lin said, looks like a Japanese barge that was carrying explosives of some kind. It has a hole in the bow as big as pickup. Bullet holes in the hull near the site of the explosion look to have set the thing off, it blew outward."

"What's next, Chief?" Vail wanted to know.

"Well, I thought we should go fishing. We could get enough for several good meals. Fresh fish for supper sounds good to me. I need to run back to the house to get my fishing tackle. You guys can hang out on the beach while I'm gone."

As the Chief drove away, Les looked at Vail. "Did you ever see the Chief with any fishing tackle?"

"No. I've never heard him talk about fishing, I've known him for a couple years. How big is that barge, Doc?"

"The beam would measure close to forty feet and the length should hit about 100. It looked like there was some sort of a pilothouse toward the stern but the silt has covered most of it. If it wasn't so deep we could find out more but it's not worth the risk to re-dive to that depth without backup tanks. The bottom time is just too short to really do much looking around."

"Is it actually at 130 feet?"

"It's probably closer to 110 feet where it lays now; it looked considerably deeper beyond the hull toward the mouth of the harbor."

The Chief drove into a small parking area near where they had launched the boat and grabbed two olive green bags from the back of the weapons carrier.

"That's funny looking fishing gear, Chief." Vail looked at Les and Doc with a twinkle in his eye.

"Yeah, this is the only kind I know that can catch hundreds with one cast, the good old satchel charge."

"If you get the depth right, we should get enough for a lot of meals. What's in the other bag?" Doc asked with a smile.

"I thought you guys would like a beer. Help yourself, Doc, before they get warm."

Each man withdrew a beer from the bag and popped the caps off, on a nearby post edge, before boarding the boat and heading out to the wreck location. As they got nearer, the Chief was measuring the fuse and estimating the sinking speed of the charge pack.

"I think about ninety seconds should do it, troops. We'll pull over the area where Doc and I surfaced and then pull off a hundred yards or so. We can use features on the shore to position the boat."

The Chief ignited the fuse after setting the cap in the charge and lowered it into the water. The boat quickly withdrew to a safe distance, while they waited for the explosion.

The time seemed to pass slowly, but in the estimated ninety seconds, a deep thump resounded in the water around them. A gush of foam and bubbles erupted on the surface above where the charge had been dropped, fanning out in an ever-widening circle. Reaction among the fishermen on the shore was quick. Soon, many boats began to make their way toward the explosion site. In a couple more minutes the first wave of fish began to reach the surface, stunned or dead, they did not move.

"Let's go gather them up men, before the fishermen arrive," the Chief said in a voice revealing more excitement than his usual calm approach. "Hand me that burlap bag, Vail. You can use the other one, Doc. We can leave most of them for the locals, fifty or so should be enough for our needs."

As they headed back toward shore, a small fleet of Vietnamese fishing boats descended on the location and they could hear the gleeful shouts of the fishermen as they scooped fish from the water. A few of the fishermen waved at them shouting a happy greeting.

The cook prepared the fish that night and served them with a side dish of eggplant.

A satisfying day!

Chapter Seven

June 1962

Doc was gathering and sorting his clothes for washday when he heard a noise in the space next to his cubicle. He stuck his head around the partition and saw Les just getting up from the floor.

"What's up, Les?"

"Doing my daily PT routine, Doc. I can't miss a day or I start to loose it and that's unacceptable. I usually get in on the runs with the trainees but that doesn't keep my muscles in the condition they need to be." As he said this, he dropped to the concrete floor on his back on top of a layer of blankets he had placed there. In a prone position, he began doing sit-ups. He wore tan swim shorts and he was sweating heavily. The heat in the basement area was oppressive, although still cooler than outside. His well-developed upper body, arm, and leg muscles were impressive. He looked like a miniature Charles Atlas.

"How often do you push yourself like this, Les?"

"Everyday, unless I can't fit it in. I am not as tall as many men I might encounter in a hostile environment, therefore, what I lack in height I must make up in personal strength. When it comes to hand-to-hand combat, I do not want to be the looser because I didn't keep myself in top shape. That's pretty much the mind set behind SEAL and how we see ourselves. In any situation, we must prevail and that success is based on our physical and mental readiness. There is a saying that most of us live by, probably not original but useful, "*the difficult we do immediately, the impossible takes a little longer.*"

Doc was amazed that Les could talk while doing sit-ups and not ever sound winded.

Les continued with his workout, after fifty set-ups, he turned on his stomach and began doing two-handed push-ups. At the count of fifty, he retracted his left hand against his chest and did fifty with his right arm then, without missing a count, switched to his left arm and did fifty more.

"That's enough for today. I did work up a little sweat for a change, and tomorrow is another day."

Around the table for breakfast, the team was talking about the training schedule for the day. The trainees had progressed to a level of conditioning that made them ready to start the water-training phase of the program. The initial stages of this training were to be conducted on the beach adjacent to the Junk Force base.

Bill entered the room and sat down across from Doc. "Doc, there's not much involvement for you in the initial stages of the water work but we have several who are complaining of sore muscles, it's not surprising. Is there anything you can do for them?"

"I have no medication of any kind, I'm not sure there is anything available that would help much anyway. Soon after I got here, I sent a batch of requisitions to Saigon for some medical supplies. I got them all back stamped in big red letters, 'CAN NOT IDENTIFY YOUR UNIT'. What do I try next? I've hit the Special Forces people for some of the basics but there is a limit to what they can spare."

"Can you get what you need in Saigon? I can set up a flight for you if you think you can."

"I think so, it's worth a try, Skipper."

Everyone at the table lost interest in medical supplies, the conversation shifted to other topics.

"I think I have a way to get more gas for the vehicles," the Chief said, addressing Bill.

"What's that, Chief?"

"When I was picking up the boat and the other gear at the airport, I did a little checking on the air force fuel dump. As you know, its US gasoline but we give it to the Vietnamese and they maintain the security of it. For air force vehicles like our big Ford, it is on a take as you need basis with no accounting that I can determine. I spoke to one of our air force sergeants, he said it's a lousy system but that's how the officials in Saigon want it done. The Vietnamese monitor the supply levels in the dump, when it gets to a certain point, they notify him and he has more flown in. Based on that info, we should be able to put a couple of fifty-gallon drums in the Ford, go out, and fill them up. The air force man I spoke to said the Vietnamese back off on the security in the evening. There is only one guard at the gate. He can't leave his post to check on what we are doing so we should be able to pull it off."

"Let's try it. Can you come up with the drums?"

"I have drums coming, all I have to do is pick them up."

As the team readied to head for the base, Doc grabbed a facemask and fins from the gear locker in the rear of the house. If he were needed, he would be there, in the process he would get in some water time. As he headed for the back door, Boats Vail met him at the base of the stairway.

"Are you going to take a weapon with you, Doc?"

"No. I took the carbine with me a couple of times but it keeps getting in the way, not real handy."

"Hang loose for a minute, Doc, I can fix that problem."

In a minute, Vail was back down the stairs carrying a pistol in his hand."I know you have that .38 revolver they issued in Saigon but I have something better you can have and you can have more than six rounds of ammunition too."

He handed Doc a semi-automatic pistol that Doc recognized as a WW II German P 38, the standard sidearm of the German Army during that war.

"It's loaded, Doc, there are several thousand rounds of 9mm in the gear locker. There is also a holster and cartridge belt in there that will fit it. They were mine but I replaced them with a Browning 9mm a couple weeks ago. Here are two extra magazines for it; the belt has a pouch that will hold them."

"Thanks, Boats. How do you and the rest of the team come up with this stuff?"

"It all comes from Combined Studies, Doc. I know you haven't been briefed on them, I'll do that the next time we have a chance."

They headed out the door toward the vehicle where the rest of the team was waiting. On the way out, Doc retrieved the holster and belt from the gear locker so that he could have his new sidearm available.

They arrived at the base and found the trainees lined up and ready to begin the day.

Lieutenant Lin walked up to the Chief and pointed at the ranks. "We have four men missing, a trainee told me they went to the Vietnamese Army hospital to be treated for sore muscles. They know better than to take off without my approval, there will be disciplinary action waiting for them when they return. I wonder if we should ask Doc to go to the hospital and check."

The Chief motioned to Doc who trotted up a few yards from his position on the beach. "Four men took off for the ARVN hospital before muster, would you go check on them?"

"Why did they go, Chief?"

"They were complaining of muscle pain."

"So who doesn't have muscle pain? Can I take the Jeep?"

"Sure, Doc, have a ball."

Doc walked to the far side of the building where the Jeep was parked, got in, and started the engine. He had driven past the ARVN hospital once before and when he got on the right road he remembered the directions. The ARVN hospital was a sprawling complex of several old white stucco buildings on the north side of town with dirt roads leading through the complex. He pulled up in front of a building with a sign depicting a stick figure of a man bent over in pain and holding his abdomen. Doc figured that it might be a sign indicating a trauma center. He had no other indication of where to look for the men; this was as good a place as any. There was a long glassed in veranda running the length of the building parallel to the road. Doc parked the Jeep. He noticed a large opening without doors in the center of the veranda and decided that must be the entry, since he saw no other means of getting into the building. Entering the building, the odor of disinfectant was heavy, irritating his nostrils. In the hallway, he saw a Vietnamese woman in a white uniform setting at a desk. Walking up to the desk, he asked if she spoke English.

Looking at him she replied, "yes, also French and Mandarin. May I help you?"

"I'm the medic responsible for the care of a group of Junk Force men we are training. I was told they came here to be treated for muscle pain."

"They were here. They've seen the doctor and were sent back to their training site."

"What did he do for them?"

"I don't know. Would you care to talk to him?"

"Yes, I would."

She got up from behind the desk and motioned Doc to follow her. They moved down the veranda a few steps and she turned into a short hall that led to a room at the end. In the room, which appeared to be some sort of a treatment room, was a Vietnamese man in a white coat. The nurse introduced Doc, adding that the doctor spoke English, and then left the room.

"What can I do for you, Sir?"

"You examined some of my trainees this morning. I would like to know who gave you the authority to do that. Those men are my responsibility. I can't monitor their health or physical condition if they come to you for treatment," Doc stated indignantly.

"I am very sorry, I had no idea what unit they were from. They didn't volunteer that information."

"I'll instruct them not to bother you again, but if they should, send them back to me and tell them not to return unless I refer them. May I ask about your training?"

"I completed two years at the School of Medicine in Saigon and entered the army. This is my first experience in treating people in the military."

"Did you prescribe anything for their pain?"

"I can't recall. I've seen so many people this morning."

"How do you remember my group?"

"I assume they were your men, they came in a group, all complaining of muscle pain."

Doc turned and headed down the hallway, saying over his shoulder,

"Thanks DOCTOR"

Back in the Jeep, Doc headed for the base, mad as hell. About a mile from the base he saw four men walking along the side of the road, he recognized them and pulled to the side in their path. Doc could not figure out how he had missed them on his way to the hospital, they must have taken a route that did not follow the roads. They all stopped and stood still behind the Jeep. Doc got out and walked up to them questioning why they had gone to the hospital and not to him for their pain.

"We go Bac Si to get medicine," one of the trainees responded belligerently.

"I'm your Bac Si, don't go to the hospital again. Did they give you any medicine?"

Each of them reached into their pockets and withdrew something, from the look on each face it was as if he held a crown jewel. Doc walked over to the first man to see what he held in his hand. A glass vial. They each held a glass vial. Doc took one of the vials to read the fine print, 'Injectable Strychnine'. It was apparent none of them had ever seen a glass vial before because they treated it with such reverence.

"When were you to take this?"

"They say not to take. When muscles hurt again, come back and bring medicine."

"Give me the vials, now!" They reluctantly handed them to him. *My God, I wonder what they would have done then, give them an injection*, Doc thought as he got back into the Jeep and headed back to the hospital. As he pulled away, he instructed the four trainees to return to the base immediately and report to Lieutenant Lin. He reentered the ARVN hospital compound, stopping at the first building that looked like an administration building. He had not noticed it on his earlier visit. He entered the building and was greeted by a young Vietnamese soldier sitting on a chair in the hallway.

Doc glared at him, "Commanding Officer?"

The young man pointed to a room with a large wooden door across the hall.. Doc went to the door and knocked.

"Come in."

Entering the room, Doc found a short, fat man sitting behind a huge desk. The man wore the collar device of a colonel.

"Are you the commanding officer of this place?"

"Yes. Who are you?"

"I'm the Doc for a group of Junk Force men we are training at the old naval base. Four of my men came here this morning for treatment and I want you to know that I don't ever want any of your staff to treat my men again."

"Who treated them?"

"I didn't get his name but he works up in that building." Doc pointed up the road. He noticed that the colonel was scowling at him, which angered him even more. He reached down and unsnapped the retaining strap that held the P38 pistol in his new holster. This got the colonels immediate attention as his eyes shifted from Doc to the holster.

"I need to show you what that quack gave my men." He laid the four vials of medication on the desk.

The Colonel picked one up and read the label, frowning. "I think there has been a mistake, Doctor."

"I know damn well there's been a mistake and your people are the ones who made it. Did I make myself clear earlier, don't ever treat one of my men again or there will be hell to pay." Doc turned and headed for the door, the Colonel jumped from behind the desk and trotted beside him saying how sorry he was. He would see that it did not happen again.

That evening after dinner, Doc told Chief Volkert and Bill about the encounter at the hospital and the medication prescribed.

"That's deadly stuff. Right, Doc?"

"Sure is, Bill. I hesitate to think what might have happened if they had taken that stuff orally, much less have it injected. While we're on the subject of trainee health, Bill, I have been wanting to ask you, is there someway we can get more protein into their diet. I'm really concerned about their level of physical activity and muscle usage."

"They will need more money in their food allowance. I can talk to their pay officer and see if we can't get them more." Bill looked at the Chief and said, "remind me to do that tomorrow, Chief."

Back at the table, Les was talking to Tom Carey and John Smith about how they might get past the gate guard at the fuel dump without causing suspicion. The plan that emerged was to fill the barrels with water. If the guard wanted to inspect them prior to entry to the dump, they would say they needed the water when they were in the field. The guard just might believe them. Once inside, they would empty the water and fill the barrels with gas along with the two tanks in the big Ford.

That next night they put their plan into action and the guard did question the barrels on the back of the truck. After checking the contents of the barrels, he passed them through the gate and the plan went off without a hitch. The team now had a regular supply of gas, which was critical to their operation.

Another day of water training added to the confidence level of the trainees as the length of their swims grew. All the team members agreed that the trainees were ready for the next phase, which was entering the water from an elevated position. Through a gradual process, they were readied for water insertion from a helicopter. This involved jumping into the water from various heights with the helicopter in motion. All SEALs were trained in this process and had successfully completed water insertion from a helicopter traveling at fifty knots at 100 feet altitude. The SEAL Team felt that this level was not possible for the trainees, but they hoped that they could accomplish insertion from fifty to seventy feet with a helicopter speed of ten knots.

In preparation for this training, Bill had spoken to a Vietnamese Naval officer in Saigon and asked what resources they had in the Da Nang area that could be used as a platform for the first phases of the training. He had been told there was an LST in the area and it could be made available for a day or two. The US Navy had given the ship, a carryover from WW II, to the Vietnamese Navy in the late 1950s. At 347 feet in length and a fifty foot beam, it would provide an elevated platform of more than thirty feet above the water for the early stages of the insertion training. The ship was able to enter a cove to the north of the Junk Force base and beach on a sand bar at the head of the cove. A shallow draft in the bow, of just over four feet, permitted it to load the trainees directly from the beach while providing adequate water depth for their jumps off the sides and stern. The ship's center deck height above the water was approximately eighteen feet and was chosen as the site for the initial trainee jumps.

The first day of eighteen foot jumps worked out well and after repeated jumps from the center deck of the LST, the trainees appeared comfortable with the jumping technique and the height. Lin functioned as the interpreter, repeatedly reminding each trainee to look straight ahead, not down toward the water. Bill, who now spoke minimal Vietnamese, was able to reinforce the instructions.

The SEAL Team boat was positioned several feet outboard of the jump site so Doc could check each trainee for injuries or other problems after they surfaced. The trainee then swam to the beach, re-boarding the LST for his next jump. On the second day, the trainees repeated the process except they now were jumping from the stern of the LST, a jump of more then thirty feet. The boat was again positioned to check each man as he surfaced. The team members were pleased that this phase had gone well. They felt the trainees were ready to advance to the helicopter jump.

Chapter Eight

Bill, Les, and Doc had taken the first flight to Saigon that was scheduled to arrive at 1030 but the flight had been delayed because of rainsqualls, that inundated the airport. Finally, arriving at a little after 1200, they managed to get a cab to MACV headquarters and go about what they hoped to accomplish in a one-day visit. Les and Doc were dressed casually wearing their green trousers with T-shirts and sneakers. Bill was dressed in his navy short sleeve khaki uniform. Les was plagued with pay problems; he hadn't been paid since his arrival in Vietnam. Doc was on a scouting mission, attempting to locate a source for medical supplies, and Bill was overdue for a meeting with Commander Rudd, head of Navy intelligence at MACV. Les headed for the disbursing office while Doc decided to stop by the dispensary to see what he could cumshaw.

Bill found Rudd seated at a conference table in his office reading a document. "Hey,

Bill, long time no see."

"Sorry I haven't been able to get down sooner but things just kept getting in the way."

"I'm really glad you made it. We need to talk about some things. First, you'll never guess who I saw yesterday entering the Vietnamese liaison office. Our beloved asshole Commander Vinh! He was wearing a sling on his right arm but otherwise looked unscathed. I haven't heard his story yet. It should be interesting, how he survived that mission up north."

"Goddamn, how could that SOB turn up here after what he did?"

"I don't have a clue. I suppose he has been spinning them a yarn about what a difficult mission it was, how he emerged as a hero in the affair."

"Well I suppose he'll be back up in our area now that he has returned from the dead."

"Yes, you can count on it. Do watch him closely. Our suspicions have been confirmed that he is VC and he'll do everything to subvert your efforts with training as well as anything else that's going on. I have spoken to several people in the command echelon about him but he is so highly connected, that they don't want to rock the boat. Gutless bustards!"

"I won't let him screw up our operations, if he does, he may come up missing again, only this time it will be permanent."

"Enough about him for now. I've been getting reports from the ARVN logistics people that they are having a problem with vehicle theft in the Da Nang region. They can't seem to figure out how it is being done, you wouldn't know anything about that would you? They claim to have lost more than half a dozen vehicles. You haven't borrowed that many have you?"

"In accordance with your suggestion, I have exercised my ingenuity and the imagination of my team members to provide essential resources for my mission."

"That's a devious answer if I ever heard one. I would expect those people to exaggerate their losses in order to get more from us in replacements, that's the way they see this situation. We give and they take. Did you hear about the warehouse fire here? It was full of uniforms. It burned to the ground. When they examined the ashes and residue, they didn't find a single trace of a uniform. Someone had emptied it before the fire, now the government can claim they need more, what the hell. You're pretty well set up now and the training is progressing?"

"Yeah, but we've really reduced the number of trainees from 120, we're down to less than fifty, lost six more in the last week, they just quit. Doc took a big toll when he did his physicals but he was right in eliminating those people. They just weren't up to the physical demands we're putting on them. We've completed the water training, except for the chopper jump, that's one thing I want to talk to you about. Can we get some chopper support?"

"We have an army helicopter squadron operating out of Pleiku, it's the 93rd squadron. They seem to be a good bunch. I'll see what I can do. When would you need them and for how long?"

"One day for sure but longer if they can make it; tell them it's worth a case of beer."

"They'll come for sure now; I'll let you know a date. On another subject, do you think your trainees would be up to involvement in some small operations at the end of their training?"

"Probably, what do you have in mind?"

"We've been watching a build up of VC down in the delta, concentrated in one small area. They're not very strong yet, but they will be before too long. I would like to give them some trouble before they get out of hand. I guess it would be something for your best and brightest. We'll talk more about it later when I have all my ducks lined up. Another reality we're facing is the existence of two Russian built gunboats operating along the coast. We think they home port in Hai Phong. The VC must have recognized the vulnerability of their coast after your ill-fated raid. They have started harassing Junk Force boats as they move up the coast and, so far, they have sunk three. Anyone who doesn't go down with the junk, they machine gun in the water, eventually they need to be taken out. Think about what you might be able to put together to accomplish that."

"I'll pass it along to the team and get them thinking about an operation that might neutralize those boats. What kind of armament do they have?"

"Mostly light machine guns and small rockets but they are fast and maneuverable, tough targets."

"Aye, aye, we'll work on it."

"Are you staying over?"

"No we're going to take the last flight tonight at 2000."

"Stay in touch, Bill."

"Yes, Sir."

"Oh, one last thing, would you have any problem with Tom Beck, my assistant, coming to Da Nang and spending a couple of days with you? He's been bugging me to get out of Saigon for weeks. It might be good for him to go to Da Nang."

"We'd like to have him, just let me know when."

Doc had better luck than he expected rounding up medical supplies. A Navy Chief had taken pity on him, led him to the storeroom saying, "Take what you need, Doc."

Doc filled two large crates with all sorts of supplies including antibiotics, painkillers, a Unit One field medical kit, stethoscope, syphgnomonometer, otoscope, lots of band aids, and several bottles of Chloroquin for malaria prophylaxis. He also found jars of topical ointment that could be useful in treating the muscle discomfort experienced by the trainees. When he finished packing the crates, the Chief told him he would see about getting them shipped to Da Nang as soon as possible.

When Doc left the dispensary, he saw Les coming across the compound toward him, waving.

"Did you get what you needed, Doc?"

"Sure did, more than I hoped for, a real haul of stuff, their going to ship it up to me."

"How about something to eat? There's a place right up the street that has decent steaks, not water buffalo."

"Good idea, I'm overdue for a good steak!"

As they left the MACV compound and started up the sidewalk, they noticed a young Marine Corps Second Lieutenant approaching them. He passed by them on the street side of the sidewalk, then turned and shouted, "stop, you two men!"

Doc and Les stopped and turned around. The Lieutenant stepped up close to Les, looked him over from head to foot, and said, "are you an American? Why didn't you salute me?"

Les, stroking his full beard, looked at him for a moment. "Fucking A, I'm an American. Who wants to know?"

"As an officer in the US Marine Corps, I want to know the unit you're attached to."

"I can't tell you, Sir."

"Who is your commanding officer?"

"I can't tell you, Sir."

"Why can't you tell me?"

"It's none of your goddamn business, Sir."

"O.K., mister, drop down and give me fifty push-ups."

Les looked him directly in the eye and held up both hands. "Which hand, Sir, I can do 100 with either one."

The Lieutenant appeared dumbfounded, he stammered for a minute, turned a bright shade of red, did an about face and continued down the sidewalk.

"I hope he doesn't have a heart attack before he can get to the dispensary." Doc chuckled while clapping Les on the back. It was obvious to Doc that Les was exerting himself to control his temper.

Locking his hands behind his head, Les made an effort to speak calmly, "I'm buying supper, Doc, they paid me on the spot. I'm up to date on pay for a change."

As they walked up the street, Les pointed out a butcher shop. "That's where we bought Junk."

"Really, they were going to sell her for meat?"

"Yes. What a waste." Les screwed up his face in disgust.

As they continued to walk toward the restaurant, they passed several department stores with large display windows. Suddenly Doc stopped in front of one large window and pointed. "Look at that, Les, a brand new 25 horsepower Johnson outboard motor with a price that's twice as much as it would cost in the states and it has the handclasp sticker on it, *Gift of the United States of America.*"

"That's common out here, Doc, we ship the stuff out and the next thing you know, the Chinese own it and it's up for sale...quite a system they have!"

"Christ, those are our tax dollars."

Les shrugged his shoulders, indicating that these things were out of his control.

After dinner, Doc and Les caught a cab back to the airport and found Bill already there. They had arrived just in time, they thought. Bill quickly told them it would be another hour or more before the plane departed, some sort of plane trouble...again.

As they waited, a man in a sport coat walked up to Bill extending his hand.

"Are you Lieutenant Evans?"

"Yes, I am."

"Good, I caught you before you left. Do you have a few minutes? I need to talk to you."

"What about? Who are you?"

"I am Herbert Slick of the Stars and Stripes."

"Yes, I know of the paper."

"I would like to come to Da Nang and spend some time with your organization. I've been told that you are training Vietnamese Junk Force personnel in jungle warfare and counterinsurgency."

"Who told you that?"

"A Vietnamese Commander by the name of Vinh, he told me I would find you at the airport."

"I have nothing to say to you, Mr. Slick, and no, you can't come to Da Nang, there is nothing for you to write about up there. The information Vinh gave you is inaccurate. I don't know what he is smoking these days but it does things to his brain."

"I will take my request to your superiors."

"Be my guest, Mr. Slick, the answer will still be no. I've got a plane to catch."

Chapter Nine

In Da Nang, the training had progressed on schedule and the trainees were now being prepared for their two-mile night compass swim. As a preliminary exercise, a short 500-yard night swim was scheduled for two days after Bill, Les, and Doc returned from Saigon.

The evening before the 500-yard swim, the team gathered around the table at dinner to be briefed by Bill on his meeting with Commander Rudd."We've some interesting things to talk about and the first is a shocker. Commander Vinh, who you have heard the Chief and I talk about, survived the raid he held on Hai Phong, unbelievably. He turned up in Saigon a few days ago wearing a sling on his arm and will probably be back up here sooner than we'd like. In all circumstances, he is not to be trusted because we are certain he is VC."

"How in hell can he be tolerated, Bill?"

"Chief, we need to for the present but I don't like it any better than you do. He will push his position until it backfires on him and maybe we can help him with that while he is up here. I am told he is well connected with top politicians in the central government, that makes him harder to get at, enough about him for now."

Shaking his head, the Chief scowled at Bill.

Bill continued, "Rudd told me that there is a buildup of VC in the Mekong delta that he's watching. He asks if we can pay them a visit in the future as a training mission for some of our trainees. Think about it and tell me what you think of the idea. In addition, there are a couple of Russian built gunboats harassing the Junk Force boats and sinking some of them. Rudd would like us to think about taking them out before we rotate out of country. That's something else for you to chew on and come up with approaches."

Bill looked around the table observing several heads nodding in agreement. "Next, the Assistant Intelligence Officer from Rudd's office will be up for a visit in the next few weeks, he wants to see what the remote areas of Vietnam are like, I guess we can show him. He's a real good man but has no experience.

We will need to keep an eye on him to make sure he doesn't do anything stupid, can you take care of that, Chief?"

"Yeah, I can but I may need some help depending on our training schedule. How about it, Doc, can you give me hand?"

"Sure can, Chief."

"O.K., crew, only one more thing. When Doc, Les, and I were waiting in the airport for our flight back, a reporter approached me from the Stars and Stripes who wants to come up and visit us. I told him to forget it. He got his information about us from Vinh! Keep that in mind if you have any contact with Vinh."

Bill started to rise then sat back down. "The 500 yard swim is on for tomorrow night. Is everyone ready?"

"I would like to check out the trainees before the swim, Bill. I need to check their lungs, blood pressure, and their general condition, I have the tools now."

"O.K., Doc, how much time do you need?"

"Not much, say two hours, providing I don't find anything serious."

"We'll do that first. Anyone have anything else?"

Everyone around the table shook their head no and left the table without further comment. Junk had entered the room during the briefing, standing at the head of the table to receive her customary pat on the head from each team member as he left.

The next afternoon the entire team was at the Junk Force base to assist in the briefing in preparation for the swim that night.

Doc took the trainees, one at a time, off to the side at an old table he had set up. He took their blood pressure and listened to their lungs and heart. He noticed the dramatic change in their average physique, compared to what it had been just weeks earlier. The change in diet, combined with the regimen of exercise and running, had transformed them. They were beginning to look tough and fit.

As the trainees finished their exams, they assembled in ranks. Lieutenant Lin came up to Chief Volkert to say something to him in confidence.

The Chief responded, "they what, they can't be in the water after dark?"

"It's what they have been taught all their lives, Chief. Maybe if I, and one or two others who haven't been taught to fear the water after dark, make the swim and come back unhurt they will follow. What do you think?"

"This is really bull shit, Lieutenant, but we'll try it if you think it'll work? I can't believe you haven't mentioned this before now."

"I knew about it, though I thought it would be solved with the training these men have had, I guess I was wrong. I don't know if me making the swim will work but I don't have any other suggestions."

Night swims can be extremely dangerous. Swimmers can get in trouble and not be seen. If swimming near surf, they can't be heard. The Chief, with Lin's assistance, explained a procedure used in most night training swims. The procedure involves the use of a tether line between swimmers. Using this technique, he hoped to dispel some of the trainee's fear of being in the water after dark.

As Lin and another trainee prepared to enter the water, the Chief explained, again, that they should swim directly toward a large buoy, which had been placed 250 yards off shore and was illuminated by a battery powered light. When they reached it, they should swim back to their original position on the beach. He reminded them that a few yards away from the buoy, the team boat was standing by with Doc and Les to help anyone who got in trouble.

Both swimmers wore web belts, connecting them was a five-foot rope tether. As the two men entered the water, most of the other trainees shrank back from the water as if it would swallow them if they got too near.

Lin and his partner made the swim in acceptable time and walked, smiling, up on the beach. This brought a cheer from the other trainees and an outbreak of chatter. Lin chose the next pair of swimmers from those he knew to have the least fear of night swimming. The 500-yard test continued until the remaining trainees had completed the swim. The Chief hoped the trainees' fear had been absolved by the experience.

The total number of men remaining in the program had now decreased from fifty to forty-two. The reason for the loss of eight additional men was a combination of family problems or inability to continue the physical demands of the training. Although this first 500-yard swim had been completed without much difficulty, the team felt that another exposure to the night environment was needed and scheduled another swim of 750 yards for the following evening.

On the way back to the house that night the weapons carrier, with most of the team aboard, took rifle fire from the hill above the road just two miles from the Junk Force base. This was the first incidence of being fired upon in their many trips to and from the base. The shots were poorly aimed and hit the shoulder of the road in front and beyond the vehicle. However, there was no question that they had been intended to hit the team vehicle.

Soule, who was driving, banged the steering wheel with his hand, "No VC activity in this area. Ha! That guy wasn't too checked out with whatever he was firing, Chief, for which I am grateful."

Back at the house, a disgusted Soule threw his gear through his room door onto his bunk and returned to sit at the table. Bill and most of the other team members straggled in and sat down.

The Chief sat down at the table and put his feet up on a chair next to him. "From now on we need to be extra careful on that road at night and never have less than two people in a vehicle, one driver and one riding shotgun."

"Since there isn't any other way to get out there we don't have much choice and avoiding the road at night will be hard to do. Shouldn't the person riding shotgun have an automatic weapon, Chief?" Doc asked, concern apparent in his voice.

"Yeah, we have some coming soon from Special Forces. I just hope it's sooner than later. The next time you drive that road look for a route around that section. If those bastards should try to block it in some way, a vehicle would be in a world of hurt. I haven't really looked at it close enough but, when driving back here from the base, you might be able to swing off the shoulder or up the bank, slam it in 4x4 and go for it."

Each team member nodded his head in agreement. Although Bill was skeptical, he went along with the approach.

The following evening the swim went on as scheduled, although two more trainees quit the program saying that they could not make a longer swim and they knew that the two-mile swim would be beyond their ability. The team members all agreed that this was an excuse and later Lieutenant Lin confirmed their suspicions. The fear of being in the water at night was the real reason. The total number of trainees remaining now numbered forty.

Later that night, the team held their usual late dinner meeting discussing the progress of the water training.

"Chief, I don't think the trainees can handle the compass swim, besides that, we are too few to monitor their safety properly. I suggest we forget that part of the training and go to something we can monitor better."

"I share your concern, Carey. Why don't we consider a two-mile daylight surface swim? We could lay it out in a 500 yard course and make it seven times around that course, it would be a lot easier to monitor and safer for the trainees."

"Yeah, why don't we do it that way? Doc and I can stay in a good location in the boat and the rest of the team can be water guards." Les got involved in his usual enthusiastic manner.

"O.K., Les, that's how we'll do it," the Chief agreed. We can do that tomorrow and move on to the next phase of training, the chopper jump.

Bill chimed in, "I got a message from the CO of the 93rd helicopter squadron and he said they could send a bird over on Monday for the day. Shall we start at ten? It would give them enough flight time from Pleiku."

Agreement was indicated by the nodding of heads as they began to leave the table.

"Hey, Vail, you got a minute?"

"Sure, Doc, what is it?"

"You told me, sometime ago, you would bring me up to speed on Combined Studies. Can you do that now?"

"I don't have the whole story," Vail called to the Chief who had moved away from the table heading for his room, "Chief, hold up. Can you help me out here? Doc has a question."

"O.K., Doc, what's your question?"

"What is Combined Studies, Chief?"

The Chief looked at Bill who was still standing at the end of the table. Bill nodded his head. The Chief acknowledged his gesture and settled back in his chair. "Combined Studies is an instrumentality of the CIA. They support special operations forces all over the world in places you wouldn't dream there were US forces. Since SEAL comes under that category, of special operations slash special warfare, they will support our efforts when there is no other support available. Our unit is covertly supported through army Special Forces by the Combined Studies unit in Okinawa. They fly all support material directly from there to here and other locations throughout Vietnam. The weapons and other items they supply to us are generally war surplus, of such a nature as to not directly identify us as a US military unit. Everything we get is in a pre-expended category, in other words, it's off the books when it goes on the plane in Okinawa, if not before. You may have wondered about the 9mm weapons, that caliber is not used by the US, as you know, which helps to preserve our covert appearance. That P38 that Vail gave you came from them and the submachine guns that are coming from them are 9mm. What we are doing and what we might be asked to do is coordinated through Navy intelligence in Saigon and the Junk Force command with the review and approval of higher authority at Coronado and Washington. I only tell you this because Bill and I think you have a need to know, your Secret clearance supports our assumption. We didn't know about this support for our unit until after we arrived. Any other questions?"

"No, that fills in the blanks for me. Thanks, Chief. I assume that this information should not be discussed with anyone outside the team?"

"Right on, Doc. I suppose, though, if asked by a superior you'd have to answer, after you knew he had Secret clearance. See you both in the AM."

Vail got up from his seat at the table and looked at Doc. "Welcome to the club, Doc. I was involved in that debacle called the *Bay of Pigs* and managed to get out with my ass in one piece, but several didn't. That was a CIA inspired operation too, but their operations generally go better than that one. I think they've learned a lot."

The following morning the team was on the beach at the base by sunrise, setting up the buoys to form a 500-yard course. They had decided to take Junk along for the day. She leaped out of the weapons carrier and raced for the beach at full speed, stopping occasionally to sniff a rock or stick.

As the first group waded out to begin their swim, Doc and Les took the boat to the buoy, which marked the end of the measured 500 yards. A rope stretched between the buoys would serve as stabilized holding points for the remaining team members to position themselves at intervals, between the beach and the 500-yard buoy. The swim went without incident for the first 2500 yards but, as the pace began to slow, Les noticed one swimmer just short of the outer buoy in trouble. With the outboard at idle, he eased the boat toward the man and when within earshot asked the man what was the problem.

"Have very bad cramps, Sir, can swim no more today," the trainee cried out loudly in a combination of English and Vietnamese.

Doc pulled the man into the boat and immediately saw that the muscles in his upper and lower left leg were in severe spasm. Doc dried the man's thigh with a large towel and began to apply a topical ointment, while he massaged the muscles in spasm. In a few minutes, the spasms subsided and the man began to move to re-enter the water.

Les took hold of the man's arm. He, as well as most team members was becoming more proficient in the Vietnamese language. "Don't even think about it, those cramps will be back in a minute once you're in the water. Agree, Doc?"

"Yeah, he needs to give those muscles serious rest. That was one of the more severe spasms I have seen, luckily it cleared fast."

There were three other cases of muscle cramps before all the trainees had finished the swim. Fortunately, they occurred within easy reach of the team members stationed along the route.

When the trainees were all back on the beach, Bill spoke to Lin asking how he wanted to handle the men who had failed. They should be dropped from the program but Lin suggested that they give the failures another chance in a day or two. Bill agreed. The trainees would be given a couple days to revive their muscles, then they could try one last time. A second failure would mean being dropped from training.

Junk had been taken to these swim sessions to give her time in the water and to bond with the team members and trainees. Emerging on the beach after an hour in the water, she drank heavily from a bowl of water given her by a team member. She suddenly lifted her head, pricked up her ears, growled, and flew toward a stand of trees at the edge of the beach. Just then, Commander Vinh emerged from the trees. Junk was barking and appeared ready to attack. Les ran to her side, taking hold of her collar, trying to calm her. Junk lunged at Vinh once, then sat eyeing him and growling.

"What were you doing hiding in those trees?" Les demanded of Vinh. Les was obviously ready to kick some ass.

Bill called out, "I'll handle this, Les."

Bill approached Vinh with a challenging look on his face."You have the right to observe our training sessions but I demand you do it openly, Commander." The word *Commander* was said in a voice dripping with sarcasm as Bill stormed off in the opposite direction. It was evident he was doing his best to control his temper.

Commander Vinh walked away with a swagger. It appeared, to those observing, he was attempting to re-establish his authority by projecting a superior attitude.

The next day the trainees were scheduled for more demonstrations and practice in methods used in hand-to-hand combat. This, along with physical conditioning, had begun early on in the program and most men were becoming accomplished in the skill. Doc watched the workout for a while, then decided to take a trot around the base. As he neared the headquarters building, he noticed six Junk Force sailors washing a pair of bright green British Land Rovers. He stopped to look at the vehicles. They appeared to be new, showing almost no wear on the tires or dirt under the fenders. Under the watchful eye of what appeared to be the senior man, Doc lifted the hood and discovered they were diesel powered. *I wonder who these belong to,* he thought as he closed the hood and walked around the vehicles. The men had finished the washing, carefully drying the vehicles with towels. Next, working as a team, they pushed the vehicles, one at a time, under a free standing roof structure about fifty yards down the road.

"Why don't you drive them instead of pushing them?" Doc inquired.

"No one drive. Belong to President in case he come to summer home in Da Nang up beach, driving wear out vehicle," one of the men answered in broken English.

Doc trotted away shaking his head, thinking, *what a bunch of shit.* As he headed back toward the beach, he heard an explosion in the distance. The Chief must be taking time out to work on his rock. Chief Volkert, a demolition expert, felt a need to stay current with his art. Outside the entrance to the Junk Force base was a huge rock about the size of a moving van. Soon after arriving in Da Nang, the Chief surveyed the rock deciding it would be a demolition challenge to split it in two. During his spare time, he continued to blast on it using surplus TNT given him by army Special Forces. Doc decided to go over and check out his progress.

"How's it going, Chief?"

"Good, Doc. A few more months and this sucker is going to be two rocks, I think. I'm not sure what's holding it together now, it's composed of two layers, the outer layer is comparatively soft but that inner core must be granite or maybe marble. There's a whole mountain of marble just outside of town, maybe that's where it came from way back when. I could have had this thing split long ago if I had the tools and more powerful explosives."

Wiping the sweat from his brow with his forearm, the Chief picked up his tools. "Have you been to the gedunk yet?" he asked Doc. (gedunk is a term used by some in the navy to identify a small store)

"No, I didn't know there was one."

"Come on, let's go get a soda."

They jumped into the weapons carrier the Chief was driving and headed toward the Junk Force base. Inside the fence, the Chief made a sharp left turn onto a small side road Doc had not been on before. Fifty yards after the turn, Doc saw a small Quonset hut next to the road. There was a wood porch out front leading to an open door. Entering the building, Doc noticed an odor similar to an old grocery store. On the sidewall was an old soft drink cooler filled with block ice and soft drinks. They each took a bottle and the Chief threw some paper "Ps" on the counter. As they stood on the front porch, the six men who had been washing the Land Rovers walked up and entered the little store. In a few minutes, they emerged. Each of them had two packages of Twinkies, a popular snack food item back in the States.

"How does this store get those, Chief?"

"I don't have a clue, Doc. Probably from the Chinese, that's where everything else in this country comes from, after we *give* it to the Vietnamese that is."

Chapter Ten

July 1962

The next evening Doc returned to the house. Entering his room in the basement he saw a wooden box lying on his bunk. The markings on the box were in a foreign language that appeared to be German. The box was closed tightly with individual nails and a heavy binding tape. He was extremely curious about the contents. He began working on the fastenings with his K Bar knife. After several minutes, he managed to pry off the cover to reveal an object wrapped in a type of oiled cloth. The object was secured with the same type of tape that was used on the outside of the box. Removal of the tape and cloth revealed a weapon that he had only seen in pictures, a German made MP38 submachine gun called a Schmeizer. Included, with the gun, were a leather pouch and six ammunition clips. This must be one of the submachine guns that the Chief said were coming from Combined Studies. The weapon was in new condition, did not appear to have been out of the box. Doc spent the next hour cleaning the grease and preservative from the gun and loading the clips from a box of 9mm he got from the gear locker. With the sling attached, the Schmeizer was a light, short, beautifully made weapon. Now he would have to learn how to fire it.

At dinner, the team conversation centered around the weapons that had been found on their return to the house. Most had received MP 38s in similar condition to Doc's but Les had gotten something different, a Swedish K submachine gun. The Swedish K was a Carl Gustov creation dating from about 1945 and was regarded as one of the finest weapons of its type to emerge after WW II. The weapon is light and short with a full-length barrel shroud. Les's was equipped with a large magazine, folding stock, and a selective fire capability that would convert it from full automatic to semi-automatic.

"How about that for a shoot'n iron, Doc?" Les held the gun up for Doc to examine.

"Never saw one of those before, how many rounds does that magazine hold anyway?"

"This one has a capacity of seventy-one. Smaller ones are available that hold thirty-six and fifty rounds. I got two of the seventy-ones with this unit. I studied this weapon in small arms school, it has quite a reputation for reliability and accuracy. You got a Schmeizer didn't you, Doc?"

"Yeah, new in the box, the date on it is 1941, surprising that it was never used."

"We have no idea where the CIA got the Schmeizers, they were probably captured at the end of the war. Yours could have been made in a factory outside of Germany…who knows. The rate of fire, in rounds per minute, is a little higher on the "K"than the Schmeizer but you won't be able to tell the difference or care in a fire fight. The secret of firing an automatic weapon and hitting a target is to initiate your fire in front of the target, then raise the muzzle to walk the fire into the target. Try it when you practice."

Bill had been listening to the conversation and now raised his hand to quell the commotion. "I have some news you all need to hear. I got word today that our Executive Officer will be arriving in about a week. He finished training a few weeks ago, is now on leave, and then will be en route. His name is, Dale Shurburn, he is an Ensign, an NROTC graduate from Florida State University. He is big, 6 feet five and 215 pounds. He will be a welcome addition to our team. In addition, Lieutenant Tom Beck from the intelligence office in Saigon will be up in about two weeks. He'll stay with us for about a week. Don't forget, Monday the chopper arrives for the high jumps, everyone needs to be there."

The weekend was restful for the team; many members had been involved in the training for as much as 18 hours a day during the previous weeks.

Over the weeks since his arrival, Doc had received a comprehensive on-the-job training course in parachute techniques from various team members. This included rigging, jump procedures, and parachute landing falls. He was not enthusiastic about the entire process but, if necessity demanded, he would make a jump.

That Sunday the team discussed the coming week of training over breakfast and the helicopter jumps that would be conducted on Monday. The conversation turned to an outing that had been planned for that afternoon. Les, Chuck Ramsey, John Smith, and Tom Carey had arranged for a Vietnamese plane to take them up over Da Nang to sky dive. Doc learned they were all accomplished in the sport. Les asked Doc if he wanted to go along for the ride. He accepted with the understanding that it was just for the ride.

When they arrived at the airport, Doc saw a dilapidated C 119 sitting in front of the hanger. Oil dripped steadily from the starboard engine and the tires were all showing bare tread.

Les handed Doc an extra parachute saying, "you better put this on, Doc, from the looks of that plane, it could be a short ride."

"O.K. I have to agree with you. Which plane graveyard do you suppose they got that one from?" Doc asked, pointing at the plane and shaking his head.

"Getting rides for sky diving isn't easy around here. As you know, this is the first one I've been able to arrange since we got here. We are all concerned about getting rusty."

They boarded the aircraft and sat along the sides waiting for the engines to start. Fortunately there was a four-man ground crew standing by. On the first attempt, the port engine let out an ear-shattering backfire. Everyone reacted to the noise. At the next attempt, the engine started but only briefly then died. On the third attempt, it started and amazingly continued to run. The starboard engine let out the customary backfire, belching an enormous cloud of white and grey smoke, then died. The next attempt was fruitful, accompanied by the same smoke but this time there was fire in the black smoke and the engine was shut down. The ground crew went to work extinguishing the small flame while covering the engine with CO2.

Doc looked at the team members. "Are you guys sure you want to take this flight, even if it is a short one?"

"Yeah, it'll be O.K. This is not uncommon for a Vietnamese plane. It was probably worn out when they got it," Les answered Doc with an unconcerned look on this face.

After a brief cooling off period for the engine, the pilot attempted to start it again and, miracle of miracles, it started. After a rough taxi to the end of the airstrip, the plane started its takeoff run, slowly rising into the clear sky. The day was hot, sunny, and humid. As the plane gained altitude, the cooler air felt good. Relief from the ever present heat and humidity was welcome.

The crew chief, a Vietnamese Air Force Sergeant, came aft in the plane and asked Les, in garbled English, at what altitude he wished to jump. Les looked around at the other members, holding up five fingers, meaning five thousand feet. The crew chief nodded and headed for the cockpit. The plane continued a circular climb until the ground had faded behind some thin clouds. The crew chief returned holding up his thumb followed by five fingers. He then activated a lever, on the rear bulkhead of the cockpit, and the rear ramp began to lower, the team members moved toward it. Les looked at Doc and gave thumbs up, then winked at the other three jumpers. A gesture Doc did not see. After they had bailed out, Doc stood well back from the open ramp to watch their parachutes open, after a substantial free fall. He went forward to settle into a seat when the crew chief came up to him.

"You jump now?"

"No, I don't jump, not now."

"Oh, you go Saigon with us."

"No, not go Saigon, go back down to Da Nang."

"Plane not go back to Da Nang, our orders say Saigon. We go there now."

Doc was in a fix, he really was not ready to make a jump but he certainly didn't want to go to Saigon, it might take days to get back even if he could explain it to Bill.

With a very shaky hand, he grasped the handle on the ripcord of his parachute and moved toward the open ramp. He stepped to within a foot of the end of the ramp, holding on to an overhead static line, looking at the crew chief who smiled. Doc took one-step forward and pushed off with the second step. He was in the air, falling faster than he ever imagined he would. He was counting to himself and at the pull count, yanked violently at the ripcord handle. It seemed like a lifetime. Suddenly the chute furled out above him and he felt the violent jerk as the chute opened fully. As his decent slowed, the air whistled by his head but he heard loud laughter coming from below. He managed to steer the chute toward what seemed to be an open area next to the runway. As he neared the ground, he tried to remember the parachute landing fall lessons he had received. Before he could remember all the details, his feet hit the ground. He did a roll over, ending up on his butt. The team members were now standing around him having the laugh of their lives.

"You sons a bitches, you knew that damn plane was going to Saigon, goddamn it." They helped Doc up from the ground asking if he was O.K., as they began to gather his chute.

"Well now you're jump qualified, Doc. If we should have to jump into somewhere, it will not be a problem for you to go too. We knew it was a dirty trick but would you have jumped just for the hell of it?"

"No damn way, Les, but I am glad it's behind me. You guys had months to learn that in jump school. Was your first jump scary?"

"Nah, we just ate it up, Doc."

"Bull shit, Les, my legs were shaking on my first jump and I'll bet yours were too." Carey clapped Les on the shoulder as they all headed up the field toward the hanger and the weapons carrier.

Les looked at Doc, "I did have one scary jump on a weekend right before we came out here. We were jumping out of a private plane in Bakersfield and I was the last one out. It was routine until I pulled the cord and nothing happened. This came as a surprise because I packed the chute myself. I looked up and saw that I had what is called a streamer, the chute just streams out above you but doesn't catch any air. I reached up into the shrouds and started shaking them. It was sort of touch and go for a while, but they finally let loose and the chute opened with about fifty feet to spare…too close!"

"How many people outlive a streamer, Les?"

"I don't think there are any stats on that, Chuck, the people who could count them are the ones who don't shake them out."

Monday morning came bright and early with the entire team on the beach at the Junk Force Base just after sun up. As some of the trainees limbered up for the day, the Chief and Bill discussed the coming jumps. After a short deliberation, it was decided that the small bay up the coast, where the LST jumps had been conducted, would be a good location for the free fall chopper jumps. It would be only a minute or two flight time from the beach to transport the trainees to the bay in groups of eight.

The HU-1A (HUEY) helicopter approached the beach by flying low over the base before making a landing. The engine dropped RPMs. A US Army Sergeant wearing an olive drab flight suit jumped from the side door of the helicopter and saluted Bill. "We are ready if you are, Sir. Where are we going for these drops?"

"There's a bay up the coast about two miles, Sergeant."

"We can load up anytime, Lieutenant."

The Chief called Lieutenant Lin and told him to have the men break up into units of eight. The first group boarded the HUEY. The chopper lifted off and headed up the coast.

Doc and Les had left earlier, heading up the coast in the team boat. The rest of the team took the two weapons carriers over a primitive road to the bay, parking near where the LST had previously beached. Bill and the Chief accompanied the first group of trainees on the helicopter.

As the HUEY approached the bay, Bill spoke to the pilot, Jim Deal, an Army Warrant Officer, about the speed and altitude. "Let's try fifty feet with no forward motion, Jim"

"O.K. I'll position us just downwind from your boat down there."

The chopper arrived over the site and the trainees prepared to jump. None of them had ever been in a helicopter, much less jumped out of one. Lieutenant Lin stepped up to be the first out. The tension was obvious.

While Les and Doc watched from the boat below, Lin stepped into the door. Bill stood close and yelled in his ear, repeating instructions that had been given repeatedly in Vietnamese and English during preliminary training for this exercise.

"Keep your arms at your side, legs straight, eyes straight ahead…don't look down."

Lin jumped from the HUEY entering the water in a vertical position with almost no splash.

The remainder of the first group followed suit, after receiving the same instructions from Bill about body and head position. The jumps were successful. Each man returned to the surface with a smile on his face, indicating a sense of accomplishment. After completing the jump, each trainee swam to the beach and took up a position around the weapons carriers. Doc noticed the building of comradery among them. As the training progressed, they were showing a strong personal bond for their peers and a sense of team unity and pride.

The HUEY continued to ferry groups from the Junk Force base to the jump area. In less then three hours, all five groups had completed their first jump with success. On the beach of the jump bay, Bill drew Lin aside. "We should now progress to a jump with forward motion, Lei."

"I think they're ready, Bill."

"O.K. We'll go for seventy-five feet with ten knots forward speed."

The chopper had landed on a small stretch of beach and the trainees re-assembled in groups of eight for the second jump. After taking off, the HUEY made a sweeping turn over the bay, approaching the drop zone. Lin was again first to jump. As the chopper approached the drop zone, he jumped through the door landing in the center of the drop zone. He entered the water in a slanted position, caused by the forward motion of the HUEY.

Jumps by the first group were accomplished flawlessly and the chopper returned to the beach for the second group. The same flight pattern was followed, with the HUEY making a wide sweeping turn to approach the drop zone after each man executed his jump. In each instance, the chopper would wait until the previous jumper had cleared the jump area.

The last group was in the chopper as it approached the drop area. The first trainee exited the aircraft, entered the water, and quickly came to the surface. The second and third followed in quick succession, the fourth man to jump did not come to the surface.

Doc looked at Les. "We got a problem."

Doc quickly put on SCUBA gear and jumped into the water. There was no sign of the trainee. He took a last look at the water trying to fix the exact area where the trainee had entered. He looked at Les and pointed down, Les nodded his head.

Doc descended as quickly as possible trying to make out the trainee in the poor visibility. Nearing the bottom, he saw the outline of a body lying on the bottom about fifteen feet to his left. He dove down as fast as he could. The man lay motionless with his neck in an unusual position. Doc immediately felt his neck for a pulse, there was none. He grasped the body around the chest and headed for the surface. When he broke the surface, he saw Les heading for him in the boat. Together they lifted the trainee's body into the boat. While Les re-started the motor, Doc slid in over the side and they headed for shore.

The HUEY had landed on the beach. As the boat approached, Bill and the Chief ran toward the area where the boat would beach.

"What's the story, Doc?"

"He's dead, Bill, broken neck. You can tell by the bulge in the back of his neck at the level of the third and fourth cervical vertebrae."

"Damn, we sure didn't want that to happen, he was a good man."

"He must have looked down, Bill. I was watching closely. I didn't see it."

Less was quick to agree, "I was too, Chief, and I didn't see it either."

Just then, Lieutenant Lin ran up to the scene and knelt in the water beside the boat. He took the dead trainees hand in his and looked at Bill and the Chief. He had tears in his eyes but he quickly wiped them away on his forearm, shaking his head in disbelief. This was the first death of a trainee in the program but it would not be the last.

Chapter Eleven

The crew of the HUEY opted to stay over that evening so Bill invited them to the house for dinner. The mood around the table was somber. The death of the trainee had a sobering effect. Questions were repeated as to what could have been done to prevent the accident. Junk improved the mood of those present, sensing something in the team attitude, she circulated around the table giving each member a warm nuzzle and eye contact. She seemed most attentive to Doc as she made an extra effort to hold his attention. He rewarded her with a scrap of meat left over from the meal, although she was seldom fed from the table.

After dinner, most of the team members drifted off to their rooms or out into the backyard. There were always chores to be performed maintaining the vehicles and particularly, keeping them refueled. This was a slow process since it involved siphoning gas either from the barrels in the bed of the big Ford or directly from its tanks. When fueling from the barrels, the vehicle being fueled could be parked next to the Ford and gravity did the rest. When it was necessary to siphon directly from the truck tanks, it first had to be transferred into a gas can and then poured into the tank of the vehicle being refueled.

Doc and Vail were in the bed of the Ford operating the input to the siphon while Les and Chuck Ramsey directed the output. Standing by the backyard gate, a crewmember from the chopper was watching the process with interest.

"You guys got a regular gas station going here, how much do you charge per gallon?"

Vail looked up. "The gas is free but the personal service is ten dollars a minute."

They all laughed, the first time for any of them that evening.

Fueling of the vehicles was finished for another day. Doc got off the Ford and walked over to the man who had now moved into the parking area behind the house.

"These weapons carriers look just like pictures of ones I have seen used in WW II. Where did you get them?"

Doc looked at him and smiled. "You don't really want to know but it was a covert exercise." He extended his hand to the man who took it with a firm grip.

"We didn't have time to meet earlier today, you were very busy and I didn't want to get in the way. My name is Andy Kraft; I'm the paramedic in this HUEY crew."

"Nice to meet you, Andy. I'm Chris David, the paramedic in this outfit. I am glad you stayed, the opportunity to talk shop is a little limited around here."

The conversation between the two men continued for a few minutes and got around to the weapons carriers.

"What kind of an engine do these things run, Chris?"

Doc walked to the nearest one and lifted the hood. "You won't believe this but they appear to be an exact copy of the old Chevy overhead valve six cylinder. Not a whole bunch of power for their weight but they get the job done. Even more interesting is where they appear to be made, look at this tag on the firewall, looks like Japanese writing to me."

"Sure does. The body is an exact copy of the old Dodge weapons carriers with a Chevy engine."

"Looks that way, Andy. How about a beer?"

They walked across the street to the small store for the beer and then stopped on the way into the house to feed and play with Junk.

"She is a beautiful dog. Where did you get her?"

"The team got her at a butcher shop in Saigon before I got here. She would probably have ended up on someone's dinner table otherwise."

Andy shook his head in disbelief.

"That was a tough break with your trainee today, Chris. I'm not sure what you guys are doing and I guess I don't want to know. I hate to see people die, sort of contrary to our training, isn't it?"

"Yeah, that's the first one we've lost but we have to move on."

"It's been good talking with you. It looks like the others are ready to head back to the airport so guess I better join them if I don't want to walk."

Andy walked out the driveway to where the Jeep the HUEY crew had borrowed was parked; he waved as they pulled away from the curb. Doc felt a comradery that he had been missing. He could tell by Andy's demeanor that Andy felt the same.

The following morning the team drove all the vehicles to the Junk Force base in order to transport the trainees to the rifle range set up at the army Special Forces camp. This would be the fifth training session for the trainees using the M 1 Carbine. About mid-morning, they saw a man dressed in camouflage fatigues walking across the field heading for the shooting range.

Doc recognized him immediately and trotted to Bill's side behind the firing line."Our friend Mr. Slick, of the Stars and Stripes, is heading our way."

"Shit, how did that son of a bitch get up here?"

Slick walked toward them and flashed a condescending smile, "Lieutenant Evans, isn't it? Good to see you again. I was looking around in Saigon and ran into Commander Vinh who said he was coming up and offered me a ride. He knew I was anxious to do a story on your group."

"Is that so? Well there's no story, Mr. Slick, and you have no right to be here. Did you get this visit approved by Naval Intelligence?"

"Why should I get their approval if what you're doing is routine training?"

"That's where your information is flawed, Mr. Slick, what we're doing and how we do it is not for publication, you get it, Mr. Slick?"

"You killed a Vietnamese trainee yesterday, Lieutenant, that is NEWS as far as I'm concerned and needs to be reported."

"You can write it as you see it but it will not be published until I personally approve it. In the meantime you had better get out of here and don't even think about writing anything until I get instructions from Saigon on what to do with you."

"I don't care for your attitude, Lieutenant. It will be reported when I return to Saigon."

"If you return to Saigon should be the question, Mr. Slick. This is dangerous territory."

Slick wheeled around and headed toward the Special Forces compound.

Bill looked beyond Slick toward the compound and saw Commander Vinh standing near the headquarters tent. When he realized Bill had seen him, he began walking toward the rifle range.

Vinh walked up to Bill and nodded at the range. "How's the training with the M1 going?"

"I've been waiting for the opportunity to ask. Who brought you back from the dead, Commander? You never filled me in on the details. I'll bet it's quite a story. Did the people in Saigon buy it?"

"You are being insolent, Lieutenant, I won't tolerate it. You are in no position to question me or my activities."

"Yeah, that's what you said a couple of months ago and several men died. How do you explain that, Commander?"

"As I said, I owe you no explanation. How are the trainees doing with their marksmanship?"

"I can't believe you give a shit, Commander. If you want a training progress report, submit your request in writing with copies to Commander Rudd in Saigon."

"Commander Rudd, that idiot, he wouldn't know what to do with it."

"I'll be sure to share your opinion of him the next time I'm in Saigon. Now, if you have nothing else to do, why don't you go away and let me get back to work."

Commander Vinh walked away heading toward the Special Forces compound.

Then he veered from that direction and headed for Bill's Jeep parked under a nearby tree.

Doc quickly alerted Bill. "Oh, oh, Skipper, Vinh is heading for your Jeep."

Bill ran toward the Jeep just as Vinh crawled into the driver's seat. Bill could see him fiddling with the controls as he walked up.

"Get out of my Jeep, Commander," Bill demanded.

"This is my Jeep, I ordered it months ago and would have picked it up but you stole it before I could."

"This is not your Jeep and never was. Get out!"

"I will not. I intend to leave this compound in my Jeep."

"You will leave this compound in a body bag, Commander. This is the last time I'm going to say this, get the FUCK out of my Jeep."

With this statement, Bill reached to his belt and pulled his Browning High Power 9mm-automatic pistol from its holster. Stepping close behind Vinh, he placed the muzzle directly beneath Vinh's left ear. "I won't hesitate to blow your brains all over the place, even if I have to clean it up myself. Out Commander."

Bill got Vinh's attention. On shaky legs, Vinh gently stepped from the vehicle and walked toward the Special Forces compound. He never looked back.

"Are we in trouble, Skipper?"

"No, Les. I should have shot that goddamn traitor two months ago."

That evening, dinner was short and simple and most of the team drifted off to do other things. Les had left the table but Doc stayed behind to finish off a cup of coffee. When Les returned, he had his hands full of paper and pencils. He spread them out on the table and began drawing on the sheet in front of him.

"What's up, Les?"

"Oh, it's a design for a SEAL emblem, Doc. I've been working on it for a while and it's starting to come together. We've discussed the components several times and have decided that it should have an eagle, an anchor, some sort of weapon, and a trident. The tricky part is fitting them into a compact design. Take a look at what I've come up with so far."

Les slid the sheet of paper toward Doc and leaned back in his chair.

"Looks good, Les. Where's the weapon?"

"None yet, but I'm pushing for a dueling pistol, something that won't go out of date."

"Have you thought about the finish on this design? Will it be in silver or gold?"

"I think it should be gold, but it will probably be differentiated by rank, silver for enlisted and gold for officers."

Just then, Junk, who had been lying next to the balcony door, jumped to her feet and growled. She moved slowly through the open door and walked out onto the balcony. Les and Doc looked at each other and followed her without saying a word. It was a dark night but there was a small light in front of the store across the street and a porch light, next to the front steps, on the house next door.

Les leaned close to Doc. "Turn those lights off." Doc reached around the door jam and flipped the switch.

They heard muffled Vietnamese conversation coming from next door and then the light over the front steps was turned off. They heard footsteps going down the walk and saw a figure in the shadows. As the person passed under the light across the street, they both recognized it to be Commander Vinh. Without a sound, they went back inside. Junk followed quietly and lay back down on her pile of blankets near the balcony door.

"What do you make of that, Les?"

"I don't know, but I think we had better watch our conversation around this table. We may have VC sympathizers right next door, somehow tied up with Vinh."

Les sat down at the table and wrote a note, folded the sheet of paper and wrote Bill's name on the front then looked at Doc.

"Bill is out this evening at Madam Chang's but I thought we should get news to him of our next door visitor ASAP. I'll put this note on his bed."

"Just another problem to add to his list, what is he going to do about that Stars and Stripes guy?"

"I don't know but he sent a message to Commander Rudd this afternoon, I'm sure that's what it was about."

The next morning, Bill questioned Les and Doc about their sighting of Vinh the night before. "Are you sure it was him?"

"No question, Skipper. He was dressed in slacks and a shirt but there was no mistaking that cocky walk of his. Right, Doc?"

"Unless he has a twin, it was Vinh, Bill."

Training on the rifle range continued for the next three days. The trainees were developing into expert marksmen and were handling the M1 Carbine as if it were part of them. Everyone in the team felt confident of the trainees' shooting ability, they were better than most trained infantrymen. They should hold their own against the Viet Cong. The training then shifted to some exposure to handguns. The trainees would not be receiving any but it was important that they know how to shoot one, in case the need presented itself.

Doc got involved in this phase of the training by acquainting a group of trainees with the P38, its operation, field stripping, and cleaning. Then he accompanied the group to a shooting position on the range and had each trainee fire two clips of ammunition through the weapon. Although the weapon was from another war, the men were impressed with its simplicity, speed of operation, and accuracy. Other team members used their handguns for the same purpose. By the end of the day, the trainees had been exposed to and fired the Walther P38, the Browning Hi Power, and the German Luger.

Back at the house, the team was gathered around the table sipping coffee and beer when Bill entered the room.

"I've some good news and some bad news, the bad news is that Commander Rudd did not authorize Slick to come up here. He is furious that Vinh brought him to Da Nang and we have been instructed not to cooperate with him in any way. Rudd has taken steps to get him sent back to Saigon immediately. The good news is that on July first, the President signed an executive order establishing the US Navy SEAL Teams. We are the first increment of SEAL Team One, the East Coast Team will be Team Two. Right now the plan is for that team to relieve us sometime in October."

"Now we is official but not for publication."

"That's right, Chief, but the name will still carry the same security classification of SECRET. In some instances that may expand to TOP SECRET, depending on the circumstances."

"Yeah, that TOP SECRET means you have the best chance of getting your ass shot off. Right, Chief?"

"That could be, Boats."

"Take it from me, it is. I was on one of those TOP SECRET parties a while back and we just about didn't make it. We got involved with those people, you know the ones on Okinawa. They had this plan that required someone who could speak Russian and handle themselves around explosives."

Doc looked at Les with raised eyebrows as they both got up from the table and closed the windows and the balcony door.

"I have Russian in my lineage and went to the navy language school in Monterey to polish up on my Russian pronouns. There was another guy in an east coast UDT team with similar qualifications so we were linked up for the job. The plan involved a nuclear enrichment plant construction project in Siberia, cold damn place in the winter. Anyway, the Ruskies were building this plant to process uranium and that takes a tremendous amount of electrical power. The plant couldn't run without the power so they were in the process of installing this big ass generator."

By this time all the team members were leaning toward Boats, listening attentively.

"Well, to make a long story short, we were dropped in with credentials of agriculture inspectors from the Kremlin. Now don't ask me what an agriculture inspector is going to do in Siberia in February but no one seemed to mind. Those Combined Studies forgers are top notch. The final stage of the generator installation required an overhead crane to move this enormous generator, from one end of the building, to its foundation at the other end. We were to make sure that they didn't do that."

Boats looked at his fellow team members to make sure he was still holding their attention. "We went about our business during the day in the vicinity of the power plant checking bushes and shrubs. We made it look as good as we could and even took samples to take back to Moscow. No one bothered us. On the second night, we played sneaky Pete and moved into the generator plant. The overhead crane ran on rails supported from the roof of the building. We simply put C4 charges on those rails to cut them in three places. That left nothing to support the crane, so it would come tumbling down like Humpty Dumpty. We put sixty-minute timer caps on the charges and beat feet. No crane, therefore no generator, and as a result, no power for their new nuclear enrichment plant. We were told it would take months for them to replace all the gear that we displaced."

"How did you get out, Vail?"

"We slowly made our way to the coast, damn near froze to death in the process. A sub picked us up on the Siberian coast. What a great sight to see that sucker surface!"

Chapter Twelve

August 1962

Training resumed the next week with an introduction to the use of explosives in various maritime and clandestine settings. During this phase, there were classes on C4 plastic explosives, TNT, satchel charges, and Claymore antipersonnel mines. A greater variety of explosives had become available as the SEALs' relationship with Combined Studies grew. Chief Volkert lead the discussions about explosives, having one third of the trainees watch and listen closely as he demonstrated fusing, placement, and detonation techniques. The remaining trainees were engaged in counterinsurgency and weapons maintenance lectures conducted by other team members. After the initial presentations, groups rotated so that each trainee began to build a basic understanding in all three subjects. Lieutenant Lin circulated among the groups to add interpretation of the material.

Many trainees were becoming more familiar with English and some were beginning to have limited conversations in English It had recently been discovered that some of the trainees spoke limited French. Les and the Chief had studied French in Monterey so, sometimes using all three languages, an essential point was eventually understood.

During breaks, the trainees voluntarily engage in hand-to-hand combat practice in a sort of game playing activity. The SEAL Team members recognized the behavior from experiences during their training, a sure sign of comradeship and team spirit. The trainees were beginning to think and function as a team, with strong commitment for what they were being trained.

That evening, Bill took Doc aside telling him that he could move upstairs. A space in an alcove off the center room had been cleared out and now held a bed and a metal locker.

"You mean I have to desert my rats?"

"I didn't know we had rats in the house."

"I've never seen any up here but I can guarantee they are down there. The first night I heard noises inside the back door. There was a bright moon and I could see them silhouetted against the open doorway. They're big, I've seen harbor rats in the Philippines and Japan but none as big as these. One night three of them got on the same side of that big trash can and it tipped over. You can understand why Junk sleeps upstairs at night and I keep the Walther under my pillow."

"Sorry about that, Doc. I suppose we need to keep the back door open so Junk can go out. You can move up anytime you're ready."

Doc went downstairs immediately and began to gather his gear. Junk wandered in during the packing and watched.

When he was ready to make the first trip upstairs, Doc looked at Junk. "Do you want to help me move?"

She stood and waged her tail so vigorously that the tail wagged the dog. Doc knew he was becoming more attached to Junk than he should, but it seemed beyond his control. "You can carry my laundry bag." He nudged it with his foot.

Junk walked over and picked the bag up in her mouth then followed him up stairs to his new room. She dropped it at the foot of the bed and stood looking at Doc.

Doc dropped his load on the bed and gave Junk a thorough rub behind her ears. "That's all for now, girl, thanks."

Junk turned and walked to her pile of blankets inside the balcony door. Her tail was still wagging when Doc returned to his task.

The move complete, Doc wondered out to the table where there was a discussion concerning how best to destroy the Russian gunboats operating out of Hai Phong. Vail and Les had been engaged in how best to lure the boat into range of what weapons could be acquired. Les felt that rockets disguised and mounted in bamboo tubes would be effective, although the angles would be critical. Vail agreed with the firepower they would deliver, however, was bothered about the ability to aim them.

"We need to have something that will sink those suckers and do it quickly, while we suppress the return fire. Do we know what their armament is?" Vail asked.

At this point, the Chief entered the conversation. "We think they have heavy machine guns topside and maybe rockets. The real problem is that we have no first hand information; there haven't been survivors from the junks taken out. They kill the entire crew even shoot them in the water."

Les threw up his hands. "Nice guys we're dealing with."

Everyone looked up when they heard heavy footsteps coming up the stairs. The large figure stopped at the head of the stairs and smiled. "I'm Mr. Shurburn, didn't have a chance to meet any of you earlier. I got in late this afternoon and Bill has been showing me around."

The Chief stood and extended his hand. "Welcome aboard, Ensign." He then introduced everyone around the table ending with Doc.

"You guys talking about the Russian gunboats Bill told me about? I guess we're gonna take them out, right?"

"Yeah, that's the current topic." Les took a sip from the coffee sitting in front of him.

"I had some exposure in the foreign weapons portion of our small arms training classes. I would guess that the boats are carrying the Russian 12.7 mm NSV heavy machine gun. It's a mean sucker; it would do a job on a junk."

The Chief quickly glanced around the table and everyone acknowledged by gesture or eye movement that they were impressed with the new Ensign's knowledge.

Vail, who had been deep in thought leaned back in his chair. "What about a recoilless rifle. I had a chance to use one when we needed to take out armored personnel carriers, they worked like a charm and should do a number on a thin skinned gunboat."

"That's great for punching holes on the hull but the VC aren't going to stand around while we do that." Les slapped the table for emphasis.

"I know that, Les, unless we are able to equalize the crew in short order. We don't have anything handy to do that but maybe we could get a couple of M60 machine guns from Sergeant White.? Another thing we need on our side is the element of surprise."

The Chief was beginning to see the possibilities. "Yeah, we might be able to beg a couple machine guns for a good purpose."

"This is a very good purpose, Chief. What about a recoilless rifle? Maybe we could hit up Combined Studies.. The recoilless has been around since WWII."

"I hate to ask stupid questions, but maybe you can cut your Doc a little slack. What the hell is a recoilless rifle?"

The Chief welcomed an opportunity to educate Doc. "It's a shoulder fired weapon that has the power of an artillery piece and has almost no recoil. Just two men can operate it. It's available in a variety of calibers, our forces have used the 57mm round most recently in Korea, with the HEAT rounds, and it did a hell of a job on the Russian built T34 tank."

Doc looked at the Chief inquisitively.

"I got the message, Doc, the HEAT round is a special shell fired from the 57mm. It stands for high explosive anti-tank."

Doc nodded his head in understanding, "I got it."

Vail leaned forward. "That's what we need, Chief, a 57 with a case of HEAT rounds. You can fire those things fast, with a little practice, we should be able to punch a major hole in that Russian built tub before the VC know what hit them."

"That's true, Boats. Providing we can sucker them in close enough to get our licks in before they realize the score."

"We don't need them too close, Les, the 57 mm has a range of over 4,000 yards, although the closer we are the more damage we'll do."

"Sounds like we are on our way, men. I'll check with Sgt. White tomorrow and see how much of this stuff he can get." The Chief was anxious to finish the job.

Ensign Shurburn re-entered the conversation, "before you guys run off, I should tell you that I met a Lieutenant Beck in Saigon and he said he would be up to spend some time with us day after tomorrow. He also said it was his first time out of Saigon so he's really looking forward to the trip."

"Yeah, we knew he was coming, just not when. Tomorrow is another day team and it's getting late."

"Yes, Mother Chief, we can tell time," Les retorted with a grin.

The next day the trainees were back at the Special Forces range for grenade training. Surprisingly, soon after they arrived, Commander Vinh showed up to oversee the training. The Chief led the discussion demonstrating the technique for proper grenade throwing while Vinh stood by. After a round of questions, the group moved up to the throwing line. The grenade range consisted of an embankment about four feet high with a shallow ditch behind it. Mock enemy emplacements, simulating pillboxes, were located in front of the embankment at about fifty feet. The procedure was to crouch in the ditch, take a grenade in your throwing hand, pull the pin with your free hand, extend the throwing arm behind you, and throw the grenade at the emplacement, then get down behind the embankment.

The trainees practiced this procedure with rocks they had picked up in the area. Then, one by one, they moved up to the throwing area for the live grenade throw. As usual, Lieutenant Lin chose to be the first to throw. Commander Vinh moved up beside him.

"Do you plan on throwing a grenade, Commander?" Chief Volkert asked with a note of sarcasm.

"No, Volkert, I want to instruct the Lieutenant."

"He needs no further instruction, he's ready," was the Chief's curt reply.

"Are you questioning my authority, Volkert?"

"No Sir, I'm not, I just think it unwise to have two people side by side in this situation." He turned and saw Bill standing back at the rear of the group talking to Shurburn. He motioned to Bill, who trotted up to the throwing line.

"What's the problem, Chief?" Bill asked frowning at Commander Vinh.

"The Commander wants to instruct the Lieutenant on grenade throwing by standing next to him; I don't think it's safe."

Bill stepped up and took Vinh by the arm pulling him backward. "Step back behind the Lieutenant, Commander."

Vinh looked at Bill with a glare and hesitated. He then looked at Lin, speaking Vietnamese in a low voice, "after you throw the grenade, you must stand and watch the deployment of the shrapnel, it will give you an idea of their effectiveness. That is an order."

Bill and the Chief had taken several steps back, too far to hear the order Vinh gave Lin.

Lin crouched in the trench, picked up a grenade, pulled the pin and threw. He remained standing as the grenade flew through the air landing dead center in one of the mock emplacements. The grenade exploded, doing considerable damage to the mock up. Lin immediately grabbed his right arm.

Bill rushed to him and saw blood streaming down his forearm. It was obvious he was in severe pain.

"Where's, Doc? We need him right now," Bill shouted.

"He's at the other end of the line, I'll go get him," the Chief called over his shoulder as he ran.

Doc was sitting with a small group of trainees talking about first aid when the Chief ran up shouting, "Doc, Lin's been hurt."

Doc jumped to his feet and ran up the line to where Lin was setting, under a tree, with a handkerchief wrapped around his forearm.

"The bleeding has let up, Doc, but it looks like there's a hole in his arm," Bill told Doc as he relinquished his hold on Lin's arm.

Doc carefully removed the handkerchief to reveal a puncture wound about the size of a dime in the mid-forearm. After careful examination of the arm, he determined that there was no exit wound. He quickly opened his Unit One pack and got a medium size battle dressing, applying it to the wound.

"I need to get him over to the army Special Forces Aid Station where there are things I'll need to treat this. I'll use your Jeep, Bill."

"Have at it, Doc. Do you need any help getting him there?"

Lin responded for Doc, "I can walk O.K." When he began to stand he added, "I do feel a little faint."

Doc supported Lin and helped him into the Jeep. He drove to the Aid

Station pulling up in front and he helped Lin through the open tent flap. As they entered, two army medics got up from a table.

"I have a man who is injured. I need to use some of your equipment."

"All right, what do you want?"

"First, I need some sterile normal saline to irrigate the wound channel. I need a minor surgery pack, a sterile drape, gloves, a probe and groove director, an irrigating syringe, for openers. I'll need more, I'll let you know."

The medic began to assemble the equipment without comment while Doc moved Lin to a small surgical table and helped him lie down. He looked around and saw a scrub basin and towels in the rear of the tent. After scrubbing, he returned to Lin and removed the dressing he had applied. As he worked, one of the army medic stood looking at Lin.

"What happened to him?"

"He got a piece of grenade shrapnel in his arm."

"How did that happen?"

"I don't have time to explain that now. Please finish getting what I asked for." Doc was becoming impatient with the medic.

"O.K. O.K." After getting the gloves laid out, the medic went back to the front of the tent and sat down.

Doc drew up a syringe of sterile saline and began to irrigate the wound until the outflow was blood free. It was curious how the shrapnel had entered below the elbow leaving no exit wound. The chunk of metal must still be in the arm somewhere. "Are you in much pain, Lei?"

"Not bad, Doc. Do what you have to do to get that metal out."

Doc inserted the probe into the wound channel and slowly moved it up the arm until the probe was inserted to the hilt. *That chunk of metal went a long way*, he thought as he withdrew the probe.

Doc called, "do you have a longer probe?"

"I don't know, I'll look around and see," the medic answered with obvious disinterest.

In a few minutes, he returned unwrapping, a sterile probe that was twice as long as the first.

Doc inserted this into the wound and traced the channel to the limit of the probe. By now the probe was passing the elbow joint, how could that be with no apparent damage to the joint?

Doc rotated the arm and began to examine the back of Lin's elbow. With careful palpation, he discovered a lump about four inches above the elbow. It was obvious that the shrapnel had traveled almost twelve inches up Lin's arm, through the elbow joint and lodged in the triceps muscle.

Lin was obviously experiencing increased pain when he asked, "did you find it, Doc?"

"It's here, above your elbow, on the back of your arm, don't ask me how it got there without wrecking your joint. You're very lucky. I'll have to remove that shrapnel chunk. I'll give you a local anesthetic. It shouldn't be too painful."

After irrigating the wound channel again, Doc asked, "do you have some Zylocaine, and a syringe with a 21 gauge needle?"

When the items he requested were delivered, Doc injected the area around the lump and the entry wound then returned to the scrub sink for a brief surgical scrub. After gloving, he removed the scalpel from the sterile minor surgical set and inserted a blade. He called out to the medics lounging in the front of the tent, "I'll need some 6-0 plain gut suture and 4-0 Dermalon with a-traumatic needle."

"O.K. O.K., hold your horses." The medic threw down a magazine he was reading and shuffled into the main part of the tent. "What was it you need?"The other medic also got up and moved about the tent collecting what Doc had asked for.

Doc now asked if one of them could clean the area around the location of the lump.

"You mean a surgical prep scrub?"

"Yes, if it's not too much trouble."

The medic scrubbed the area with sterile 4x4s and Phisohex soap. Doc placed a sterile drape over the area of the lump. With the scalpel, he made a two-inch incision over the chunk and spread the tissue open with a small retractor. The shrapnel was imbedded in the triceps muscle tissue just below the fascia. Doc expanded the incision, exposing the shrapnel; it was jagged and had seared the tissue around it. With a pair of rat-toothed tweezers, Doc worked the chunk and was able to slowly remove it. He repaired the muscle with a 6-0 gut suture then closed the skin with the Dermalon. He sutured the entry wound and applied sterile dressings to both areas. With a sling in place to immobilize the arm, he gave Lin a quantity of strong oral antibiotic capsules to ward off infection. He would need to be followed closely for the next few weeks to make sure his recovery was complete.

Doc returned to the grenade range and left Lin to rest at the aid station until he could be driven back to the Junk Force base.

Bill walked up to Doc. "How's Lin?"

"I think he'll be O.K. That shrapnel went all the way up his arm and lodged in the muscle above his elbow. He has full range of motion in the elbow, I can't explain it, just lucky I guess. What went wrong?"

"Vinh ordered him to stand up to see the deployment of the grenade shrapnel."

"What the hell is that guy trying to do, Bill?"

"It should never have happened. I think Vinh is trying to kill off his own people, one by one."

That night, Doc was putting away his clean clothes and overheard a conversation among a group of team members who had gathered for a beer. The individual comments went like this:

"Damn, looks like we got ourselves an honest to god corpsman."

"Did you see the hunk of grenade he took out of Lin's arm?"

"Big as a marble."

"Lin's gonna be O.K."

Doc couldn't help the smile that spread across his face. He felt like he had finally been accepted into the team.

CHAPTER THIRTEEN

THE FOLLOWING DAY TRAINING IN the use of explosives continued. Chief Volkert was now explaining techniques for the use of TNT, as an anti-personnel charge in ambush and beach placements, to repel covert force landings. In this exercise, the trainees were being taught the value of placing the charges in a staggered format and random detonation cycles to avoid predictability of detonation, which would contribute to the confusion of the landing force.

"Listen up," motioning to Lieutenant Lin that he was ready to start the lecture, "a critical issue in arming charges in this fashion is fuse timing because it can vary according to the length of fuse you use. The variation in the burn time of the fuse material is also very important. A sample of fuse from each lot needs to be timed in seconds of burn time per foot, only then can you figure out how much fuse you need to give the desired delay before detonation. Do you have any questions?"

Lieutenant Lin indicated that he did. "I was wondering, Chief, if a batch of fuse has been timed and recorded on the coil, is it necessary to re-time that same batch of fuse? Also, would you routinely use a timed fuse for this type of application or might you use electric detonation?"

The pleased look on the Chief's face would have been detected only by someone familiar with his serious nature. "I think timing burn rate should be a matter of practice, Lieutenant. It's not that you don't trust the first timing but that may have been done sometime before you want to use the fuse and burn time does change as fuse ages. The answer to your second question would depend on the planned use of the charges. In an ambush situation, electric detonation would be the method of choice. It might be the best for beach placement as well. I chose the fuse method today because you need to know how to work with fuses and this is a simple exercise to use them. Any other questions? O.K., we'll break up into our usual groups and start learning how this exercise is done."

The four groups of trainees began experimental fuse burning and timing, at the same time, began to plan their scattered distribution of the charges. In order to achieve the random detonation desired, each group had to coordinate with the others in determining their fuse burn time. These exercises promoted planning with fellow team members while contributing to the team objective. The plan called for all the charges to be placed no more than fifteen meters from the water, with a beach span covering 100 meters.

While the training progressed, Junk wandered among the groups looking for a pat on the head or a word of recognition. She enjoyed the time at the base since it gave her the freedom to roam and explore, that she didn't have at the house. Several times during the afternoon, Doc had noticed groups of birds had landed on the beach and in every instance, Junk chased them away. Her actions indicated that this was her beach, she didn't want any intruders.

The trainees had worked out their plan for charge distribution and detonation and were preparing to plant the charges on the beach. Doc watched the activities, saw a complex pattern emerge that would be very confusing to a landing force. After the charges were placed, fuse material buried, and fuse igniters activated, the trainees walked back to the head of the beach, well away from the explosives area.

The first explosion was at the far end of the designated area, the second at the opposite end followed by a series in between. There was a lull and during that brief pause, Doc saw something streak by him out of the corner of his eye. Junk was racing toward a group of birds that had just landed at the waters edge in the middle of the explosives area. He quickly evaluated the area deducing that, since the center of the explosives field charges had detonated just seconds before, it was unlikely that more would explode soon. It would be safe to pursue Junk. Doc dropped the Unit One medical kit he had over his shoulder and raced after her, hoping that he could turn her back before the next series of blasts started. Junk stopped just short of the flock of birds as they took flight over the water. He called to her and she turned and ran to his side. He knelt alongside her grasping her collar as he started to rise, there was a blinding flash and an explosion boiled up out of the sand off to his right. He felt a rush of hot air against his body, accompanied by a razor sharp pain on the right side of his head. Everything went black.

The Chief and Les saw him run after Junk, they rushed to his side. Junk seemed unharmed, Doc would take a few minutes to come around. When he did, he found himself back up the beach with Les, Bill, and the Chief leaning over him.

"That was a dumb thing to do, Doc. Are you O.K.?"

"Is Junk O.K.?"

"Yeah, your body shielded her from the blast but it moved you both about six feet. What the hell was she doing down there?"

"She was chasing birds; she's been doing it all afternoon."

Bill took hold of Doc's shoulder. "Are you sure you're O.K.? I can send a message to the 93rd and have a chopper fly you to Nha Trang to see a doctor."

"No, I'll be fine. I'll just have one hell of a head and ear ache for a few days. In fact, I can't hear anything in that ear, probably broke the drum."

Back at the house, Doc spent more than an hour picking grains of sand from his face, shoulder, and right arm. He realized he was lucky that no rocks or other debris had been mixed with the sand. Many months later, Doc would be told he had suffered permanent nerve damage, he would never hear more then twenty percent through his right ear.

After a dinner of mystery fish and more eggplant, John Smith pushed back from the table. "Does that cook have any imagination, how many ways can you fix eggplant, do we have to try them all?"

As Doc looked around the table, he noticed most plates still held eggplant including his own. He silently told himself, *when I get back to the states, I will never eat eggplant again.*

Tom Beck, the Intelligence Officer from Saigon, had joined them for dinner, after settling in Doc's old cubicle downstairs. He planned to visit Da Nang for about six days and wanted to see everything. Les pointed out that their training schedule was heavy but they would all make an effort to show him what they could. Since Doc was not directly involved in the explosives training, he told Tom he would act as his guide. They moved to the end of the table, began discussing a schedule, and soon had one that covered the next four days.

"Is it always this hot up here, Doc?"

"From what we have been told, the answer is yes. Central Vietnam is warmer in the summer than any other region in the country but the humidity makes it even worse. The average humidity nationwide is eighty-four percent but most of the time we're pushing ninety percent, I hope there will be a break when the rains come later on."

Bill had been absent from supper but now made an appearance with a scowl on his face and hatred in his eyes, he held a newspaper at arms length in front of him."Anybody want to read the goddamn headlines? I'll do it for you. SECRET U.S. NAVY TEAM TRAINING JUNK FORCE COMMANDOS IN DA NANG, son of a bitch. If I ever get my hands on that Mr. Slick, I'll kill the bastard. I sent Commander Rudd a flash message about this; he didn't authorize the release of the story. Do you know anything about this, Tom?"

"No, I sure don't. No one in our office was aware the story had been written and, if we had known, we would've killed it on the spot."

"I guess we can thank Vinh for this one, again. We've managed to stay under the radar since April, I'm sure that will change and the VC will become part of our everyday life."

"This puts a different face on our operations and security," the Chief voiced with concern.

"Yes, it does. I suspect we'll see more activity at our ambush site by the base. We should try to avoid making that trip after dark."

"I'm not sure that the activity will be restricted to the base, Bill. We have always had interest shown in our activities in the neighborhood but it has seemed more curiosity than malice. The other afternoon I saw a few young men prowling around your Jeep, when you parked it out front; they got bold enough to pop the hood to look at the engine. You know they've been getting bolder so I decided to give them a surprise. I wired a smoke grenade under the hood and attached the trigger to the hood latches. None of them was around, when I did it, so I thought it might just catch them off guard. I wrote you a note and put it on your bunk so you wouldn't lift the hood, for some reason, when you came back from Saigon. Just before dark they returned, sat in the seat, manipulated the gear shift and one decided to have a look under the hood. About half way open, the grenade blew, it was a red smoke type. They made record time running in all directions. I thought I would laugh my ass off. Sorry more of you weren't around to see the show," Les barely managed to speak through his laughter.

As the laughter spread around the table, Bill wasn't sure he agreed with Les's approach. "That's a great way to build community relations, but I agree, we'll need to keep a closer watch on the house and activity on the street. We're vulnerable, from now on, we need to keep the back gate and door locked. I doubt that the VC would openly hit us here but we can't be positive."

Doc made a mental note to ask the cook to let Junk out into the backyard several times a day when the team was away.

The Chief, as usual, was ready to take action. "I have an M60 machine gun coming from Sergeant White in the next few days; I thought we might find it useful in future activities. Why don't I set it up behind that drape in my bedroom front window. From there I would have a 180 degree field of fire."

"Do it, Chief."

"Is there any word on the recoilless rifle?" Boats inquired.

The Chief answered, shaking his head, "not yet, but it looks like we have a chance of getting one in the next few weeks."

The conversation then shifted to include Tom Beck in a discussion of the current situation surrounding life in Da Nang.

"How's your sex life up here?" Lieutenant Beck asked unexpectedly.

"What do you mean? If it is what I think, we haven't had much time to build any lasting relationships. How's yours in Saigon?" the Chief asked with a grin.

"Non existent, I never feel comfortable fooling around in Saigon because of my job, I'm too visible at MACV, if you know what I mean."

"I guess my question was, are you looking for some action up here?"

"That would be something to consider, Chief."

The discussion continued for several minutes culminating in the admission by Tom Beck that he had never been sexually involved with a woman. The team members took issue with this statement but Tom finally convinced them that he was telling the truth. None of the team members, except Bill, had spent time with Tom but his demeanor served to reinforce his claims, he was clearly an intellectual but a good-looking man, nonetheless.

Les looked at Beck. "We'll have to do something about that, Lieutenant. Maybe we can fix you up while you're here." He glanced at the Chief who nodded discretely and smiled.

The following morning, Doc crawled out of bed with more aches and pains than he could ever remember. The blast from the explosion had obviously bruised more muscles and tissue than he had realized.

When he dragged himself to the breakfast table, Bill looked at him and said, "take the day off, Doc, you look like hell warmed over. We won't be doing anything heavy today and you look like you can use a little extra rest."

Doc took a bite out of a roll the cook had baked the day before and headed back to his bed.

That evening, feeling a little better after the day of rest, Doc joined the team for dinner. The Chief was telling the team about an ambush operation being planned by Special Forces as a training exercise for their Vietnamese Ranger students. He indicated Captain Marz was willing to include some of the best Junk Force trainees in the operation if they thought they could handle it.

Tom Carey spoke up, "if they can handle it, you gotta be shitting me. I'd put our guys up against those so called Rangers any day of the week. Our men get better by the day and think like a team more than the Rangers ever will."

"Do you think we can come up with a few of the best, Carey? Say, about six or eight?" the Chief asked.

"Hell yes, I can think of a dozen off the top of my head."

"Put together a list and we'll make the selection in a day or two."

"Will do, Bill."

"While on that subject, Chief, what kind of an operation is going down?"

"An ambush, Les, there's a village about twenty clicks out to the north of town that Special Forces have been visiting for several months. You know, trying to help with their basic medical needs and supplementing their food supply. The local VC got wind of their visits and started raiding the village at gunpoint. They take food, kick the village elders around, and rape some of the young girls."

"It sounds like they need to be ambushed and erased."

"That's what it's about, Boats. Special Forces plans to take out the entire VC block, or as many as they can."

"What's the plan, Chief?"

"I don't know all the details yet, Doc. We should have them in a day or two. In the meantime, for planning purposes, they'll hit the VC on the only good trail into the village, the one they always use when they come in."

"How many usually show up, Chief?" By this time Les was on the edge of his chair.

"The average has been about twenty to thirty. They are well armed with AK47s and some small explosives. They blew up a hooch on their last visit because the man and his wife who lived there didn't contribute any rice. They took all the couple had and then blew up their home. The explosives they used were described by a couple of villagers, the description sounded a lot like our TNT blocks."

"Where are they getting TNT and AK 47s?"

"Not sure, Mr. Shurburn, but the Special Forces people think the 47s are Chinese made, the TNT would be from the VC sources tied into the black market. Maybe Mr. Beck could give us some info on that?"

Shurburn looked at Tom Beck. "How about it? Do you have any insight into the black market operations in Saigon?"

"Yeah, I can't go into detail but it exists and it's big. It ties to the Chinese who, in turn, market their goods to the Vietnamese insiders, who in some cases are VC sympathizers. That would explain some of the equipment the VC have. The AK 47s are probably a direct shipment into Haiphong along with some other equipment we've run into."

The Chief asked, "are the Chinese supporting this undeclared war directly through their politics, as well, or is it from a fractional group up there?"

"I can't answer that question directly. For the record, the Chinese government won't support either side as they claim, they are opposed to war and revolution. In reality we know different and I'm sure our government understands their position well."

"If they don't," Les added, "the CIA does."

The next day, after breakfast, Doc and Lieutenant Beck left for a tour of Da Nang and the surrounding area. First was a visit to the harbor and downtown, where they walked through many of the shops. Doc pointed out the shop where he bought his ring and Beck took a liking to a silver bracelet with some small rubies that he purchased for his mother. Later they drove out to an area called Monkey Mountain, a huge deposit of marble. The area was surrounded by an encampment of workers who cut and processed the marble. Many beautiful objects were being produced including statues of animals. Doc was fascinated by a small grey marble elephant statue that stood about three inches tall and purchased it for about two dollars. Of great interest to Beck was the process of cutting the marble, which was accomplished by workers each using a steel blade in a groove filled with sand. One worker, cutting a three foot block, said he would finish the cut in another month. A trip to the Junk Force base was the last stop of the day.

On the road, leading to the base, Doc slowed the weapons carrier and pointed to his right."See that ravine leading up that hill?"

"Yeah, I do. What about it?"

"That's the VC ambush point. As you can see the sides of that hill look right down on the road, we've been fired on at this spot in the road several times. The problem is, they only do it at night so there's no way to tell where they are. They're local VC, they come out for a little sport shooting at us when we head home. We try to avoid making the trip at night as best we can."

As they entered the gate area, Tom jumped at the sound of an explosion. "What the hell was that, are we under attack?"

"Not to worry, that's Chief Volkert working on his rock. He has a goal of splitting a rock, the size of a house, in two, before we leave; he's been working on it since they arrived in April."

"But why is he trying to split it?" Lieutenant Beck stammered.

"That's what he does; he's a demolition expert and feels he needs to keep a hand in it."

Prior to heading out to the base that morning, Chief Volkert had stopped at the little store across the street from the house to ask the proprietor, Mr. Chi, a favor. That favor concerned the availability of young women to carry out a joke on their visitor that evening. Chi understood the situation and assured the Chief that he could handle the arrangements. The Chief slipped him a 1000 Peastrie note and went on his way.

That evening at dinner Les looked at Doc. "How's your head and ear?"

"Not bad, but I still can't hear anything in my right one. My hearing has had a number done on it since I've been assigned to the Submarine Escape Training Tank. We run all the pressure test for submarine school and diving school for the Pacific Fleet west of California. That can amount to many hours per-month in the recompression chamber with noise levels at 130 decibels or more. The blast on the beach didn't help any." Doc appeared disgusted with himself.

The Chief changed the subject. He didn't like to dwell on anyone's injury."Say, Doc, we were talking today and wanted to ask you about propellers, how do you change them on say, an aircraft carrier? I know how they do it in dry dock but how about when the ship's in the water?"

"It's not too complicated; you blow them off with prima cord. It takes two to three divers and a big crane for a carrier screw. Just like changing one on an outboard motor only bigger."

"Sounds complicated to me," the Chief said emphasizing the *me.*

"Hey, Mr. Beck, when's your birthday?" The Chief was determined to keep the conversation moving.

"It's in November, why, Chief?"

"Well, the team and I have been talking about your virginity and we've decided to give you an early birthday present. Just stand by for a few minutes and we'll get your presents."

Chapter Fourteen

Les, Chief Volkert, and Vail left the room and went to their bedrooms. In a few minutes, they returned armed with their submachine guns and, without a word, hurried down the stairs and out the back door. Doc noticed that none of the weapons they carried had ammunition clips but Tom apparently didn't notice.

"What the hell is going on, Dale? They look like they're going on a combat mission," Tom asked urgently.

"No. It's routine around here when we go out of the house at night and particularly now, with the Stars and Stripes headlines."

The team members, who had not gone along, struck up a conversation attempting to convince Lieutenant Beck that what he had seen was routine.

"Do you guys do this often?" Lieutenant Beck wasn't convinced.

"Do what, no big deal," Dale answered with a straight face.

In less than ten minutes, there was a commotion downstairs and several female voices could be heard crying and pleading. Next, there were multiple footsteps on the stairs as a column of girls ascended and moved to the far end of the room. At the head of the column was Vail, with his gun at the ready, behind him was Les. The Chief brought up the rear. When all six young women had filed to the end of the room, the Chief, brandishing his weapon said, "you all line up so the Lieutenant can have a look at you."

All of the girls were faking tears and letting out gentle sobs of terror. They were all attractive young women. Doc guessed their ages at between eighteen and twenty-four. One of them, apparently the oldest, did have a look of the street, as she postured herself to display a full figure. Lieutenant Beck was obviously completely taken in by the show and looked as though he wanted to turn and run down the stairs to his cubicle. With a little encouragement from the team members, led by Vail and the Chief, he approached the line of girls and introduced himself as Tom Beck. They acknowledged his introduction by whispering their names in Vietnamese.

When he got to the girl, who appeared to be the oldest, she stepped forward and took hold of his hand. "My name is Pearl. I think you and I could have a great evening together."

Lieutenant Beck looked long at her, saw her full figure, and took both of her hands in his. He turned to the other girls and thanked them for coming, as he led Pearl toward the stairs and down to his cubicle.

The room remained silent until the sound of the couple going down the stairs faded away. The silence was followed by a round of hilarious, yet suppressed, laughter and backslapping.

"We pulled it off, Chief. I think he really thought we brought those girls up here at gunpoint, hot damn." Les could be serious but he also appreciated a good laugh.

"I'm pretty sure he did, Les, but if not, he is one hell of an actor."

The Chief then turned to the remaining girls, who were giggling and chatting with each other. He thanked each one, shook their hands, and gave each of them a 500 Peastrie note. Leaving his submachine gun on the table, he ushered them down the stairs and back across the street to the store where he had collected them.

When he returned, Doc clapped him on the back. "The one he picked is the real prostitute, isn't she?"

"Yeah, it was rather obvious, wasn't it? They were all good looking heads though but Pearl didn't have the typical Vietnamese figure. Wow, did you see the tits on her?"

When several team members said, in so many words, that they really hadn't noticed her figure that much, the Chief exploded, "bull shit, troops. If any of you knew she was in the neighborhood, well we all know the rest, don't we? She was imported for this job, I am not sure where from."

The next morning, Saturday, the team gathered for breakfast. The cook had appeared and said he was there to cook for the guests, word gets around in a small neighborhood even in Vietnam. The cook prepared omelets from eggs of unknown origin but they looked like real eggs.

"Has anyone seen Tom or Pearl yet?" Les asked with a sly grin.

"I saw them come up to the head at about 6:30 this morning, they went back down stairs," Doc said, raising his eyebrows.

"Uh ha, well true love has a way of capturing you, doesn't it?"

"How would you know about that, Les?"

"I've had many true loves. Some lasted for as long as a week at a time."

"No longer than a week?"Doc asked, shaking his head.

Les assumed his serious expression. "No, beyond that it gets too dangerous, they start thinking about matrimony."

The team went to work on routine vehicle maintenance, which included oil changes, tune-ups, and refueling. Doc spent time helping with the refueling and then, before lunch, reorganized his medical kit.

At lunch the subject of Tom and Pearl arose."How long can they go at it?" Doc's question was presented in an insincere tone.

"One never knows. For us married types, that first go around can last a while," the Chief assured.

"Do you think we should call them for lunch, Chief? I think you're the expert on this," Les chided.

"Nah, hunger is secondary to the basic sex drive. I'd give them another twenty-four hours anyway." The subject was dropped for the moment.

"Did you get any more information on the Special Forces ambush plan?" Doc asked the Chief.

"Yes, and this is a good time to talk about it. Did you guys come up with a list of trainees that would go along?"

"Yeah, we talked it over with Lin and we agreed on six, the top six. All the trainees are very good, these guys are the best," Chuck Ramsey said with pride.

"Let me see it."The Chief studied the list for a minute. "They will work just fine. I see Lieutenant Lin's name at the top of the list."

"Yeah, Lin wasn't comfortable having his men go without being there. He also feels he owes the VC a lick or two," Chuck was quick to respond.

The Chief leaned back in his chair. "All right, here's the plan so far. The VC, usually come in during the late evening, load up on food, rape, steal, and whatever. They overnight in the village and leave early in the morning. Captain Marz wants to hit them in the morning as they come out of the village. You know, when they're still foggy and not fully awake. That means being onsite very early to get set up. It's gonna be tricky, but he assured me the village people were all behind it and would keep the secret."

"So, how do we take these guys out, Chief?" Les asked.

"Special Forces will set up Claymoors along both sides of the trail about 300 yards beyond the village. The kill zone will be about fifty yards long and there will be automatic weapons people at the far end of the trail, to turn them back. After the Claymoors are detonated, another group will move in at the head of the trail and they will be boxed in, unless they take off into the jungle which is really thick all along the trail."

"There will be no warning, just blow them away?" Les wanted every detail.

"No, they will be given a chance to surrender prior to the Claymoor detonation. Captain Marz say's they seldom surrender. These are hard core VC mostly from up north, surrender is not in their vocabulary. Often their superiors will shoot them if they try to surrender."

"Nice guys," Boats said shaking his head.

"That is what we are dealing with, Boats. These guys are playing for keeps. As the VC move into the ambush zone, they will be warned and given a chance to surrender. If that doesn't get their attention, next come the Claymoors and, as they charge ahead, there will be a kill zone of automatic weapons fire at the head of the trail. The second team will cut off the ones who turn and head back to the village. There may be a few who try to head out through the jungle. Special Forces will have some of their men fanned out in back, at about 200 yards, to be out of the reach of the Claymoors."

Les leaned across the table looking at the Chief. "O.K. Where do we and our men fit into this scheme? There will be six trainees plus three or four of us."

"Our component will be the trainees, me, Les, Vail, the XO, and maybe Doc. What about it, Doc? You want in on this party? Bill thought it would be a good idea in case there are casualties, but left the decision up to you."

"Sure, count me in, Chief."

"Good. We'll be in position two hours before sun up. That means walking as silently in the dark as possible. Special Forces will lay out a route for us marked with white tape at ground level; we just follow the yellow brick road, so to speak. We will take up positions at the far end of the kill zone with five men on either side of the trail. Special Forces will also mark the maximum range for the trajectory of the Claymoors. We need to stay well back from that since they cover about a sixty degree arc. Any questions?"

"Yeah, how do we get out there, by vehicle? How do we know when to go?" the XO inquired.

"We can get within about a half mile and we hike in from there. Special Forces will have two of their trainees on site, they blend in well, in fact, and one of them is from that village. They have a communications link set up to get the word back to Captain Marz when the VC enter the village."

"So we really won't know when to set up, will we?" The XO, Ensign Shurburn, wanted to be sure he understood the plan.

"No, it will be short notice, no more than a few hours. Be ready to go. Les, give Lieutenant Lin a heads up on this tomorrow so he can have the selected trainees ready to go on short notice, any other questions or comments?"

"Yeah, how long can those people downstairs screw anyway?"

"You're asking the wrong person, Les, I suggest you go down and ask them in person." The Chief was grateful to Les for changing the subject.

"Sure, I'm gonna do that right now, in a pig's ass."

"Is there any chance Pearl could be VC?"

"What do you mean by that, Boats?"

"Well I just thought she might be trying to screw Tom to death. Whadoya think, Chief?"

"Not likely," the Chief responded.

In late afternoon, Doc headed out to a weapons carrier to check on his gear. As he passed through the basement, Tom peeked from behind the curtain, covering the door to the cubicle. "Hey, Doc, do you have any rubbers? I ran out. I had one pack of six but I've used them all."

"You mean condoms. I wear rubbers on my feet when it rains, just kidding. Sure, give me a minute."

In a few minutes, Doc returned. "Here you go Lieutenant. There are more if you need them." Doc looked at his watch. It was now five PM. *Wow, that IS endurance*, he thought.

Chapter Fifteen

Early Sunday afternoon, Tom Beck emerged from downstairs looking well rested and eager to continue his tour of the Da Nang area. At this time, the Chief was the only person in the house.

"Well I see you finally made it back to the land of the living. Where's Pearl?"

"She headed out early this morning, Chief, said she wanted to head back home for some fresh clothes. We made arrangements for her to come and visit me in Saigon in a few weeks."

"Is this the start of a relationship, or shouldn't I ask?"

"I don't know but she is quite a woman. I got to know her over the last thirty-six hours, there's a lot more there than meets the eye."

"Take your time, Lieutenant. First encounters tend to be like this, just give it time. If there is something lasting, you'll know."

"Thanks. I take that as advice from someone who knows."

On Monday, the daily routine of training continued while those who were to be involved in the ambush operation waited with impatience. The trainees, seeing this as a new experience, had many questions and responded positively to the encouragement and information offered by team members.

Les encouraged the group, "just play it the way you've been taught. It may get intense but that's why we devoted the time training you to handle stress. Your physical and mental abilities are proven, you will have the edge in any situation."

Lieutenant Lin got up from the bench and addressed the trainees scheduled to be in the ambush. "You've heard Petty Officer Barter. He has been there and knows well what to expect. What he is telling you is keep your head and do exactly as you've been taught. Let's break now and come back at 1500 hours."

That evening, the team gathered after dinner to again discuss the plan for participating in the Special Forces village ambush.

Boats spoke as he sat down at the table, "can we depend on those trainees that Captain Marz is putting into this operation, Chief?"

"I don't know, he claims they are the best in the group and they're motivated because these raids threaten family members. Family means a lot to most Vietnamese. We will have some separation from them, being that our position is at the far end of the ambush site. All we can do is hope for the best. I don't care much for joint operations but, if we want our trainees to get some experience in close combat, we don't have many choices at this juncture."

"Do you have any idea when the VC will come into the village?" Doc asked the Chief, as he sat down at the table.

"No, we don't, there isn't a pattern. They rotate from village to village with no schedule but they seem to hit this one every week. There is a question about how much these villagers can give up. They live on the edge as it is, so giving up a large portion of their food supply makes it especially tough for them."

"If we don't get all of them, I've heard they'll be back and do as much damage as they can. Andy Kraft from the 93rd told me that in many cases, they kill everyone in the village and then burn it to the ground."

"I've heard that too, Doc. The ones that aren't killed in this ambush will be captured and turned over to ARVN authorities. There's some hope that will keep them out of circulation for a long time, at least, that's how it's supposed to work."

Late the next afternoon, most of the team was back at the house well before dinner. Les, Vail, Ensign Shurburn, and Doc gathered around the table to talk over the pending operation. They sat close together, speaking quietly, as they hesitated to close up the room and shut off the minute breeze.

"We should be hearing from Captain Marz pretty soon. The Chief went out to Special Forces camp early this afternoon to get an update. I don't know if the village gets any advanced warning of a VC visit but, if they do, we should know about it soon," Mr. Shurburn leaned back in his chair as he spoke.

Just then, they heard a vehicle entering the driveway followed in a minute by the slamming of the back door. Guessing the Chief had information about the ambush, Les motioned to Doc and they quickly closed the windows and doors to the balcony. When the Chief hit the top stair he hollered, "tonight is the night, crew. The VC sent a scout into the village this morning to check things out, he had never been there before therefore, apparently, he did not notice the new faces in the population. The new faces being the Special Forces Vietnamese Ranger trainees."

"Any changes in the basic plan, Chief?"

"None yet, Les. We'll head out from here, pick up our men at the Junk Force base and head for the Special Forces camp. We need to be there by midnight, then we'll head for the village and make the last segment of our way in on foot. The Special Forces folks will wait until the VC are in the village before they plant the Claymoors then meet us partway back up the trail to lead us in."

Doc looked directly at the Chief. "Do they know how many VC are coming into the village?"

"No, but we should have sufficient numbers if they send thirty or less. Take plenty of ammo. Everyone will use face black, should put that on before we leave here, much easier than in the field."

"I've never used the stuff, Chief."

"Les, give Doc a hand with the process when he gets to that stage."

"O.K., will do, Chief."

"Anything you want to add, Mr. Shurburn?"

"No, Chief, I think you covered it. Is that rain I hear?"

Boats spoke up, "sure as hell is. That should make this little party even more interesting."

The Chief was quick to chastise Boats. "Come on, Boats, it will strengthen our position and cover our sounds, if it keeps on."

"Are you kidding me, didn't you say, 'if it keeps on'? Hell man, this is Nam, it will keep on." Boats took no offense at the Chief's earlier tone.

After collecting Lieutenant Lin and the other trainees, the entire group rode in one weapons carrier to the Special Forces base and followed their two vehicles out into the country. The road was poor and became increasingly muddy as they went through water and mud up to the hubs of the vehicles. The three vehicles churned away in four-wheel drive low range for what seemed like thirty miles. It was raining harder now, but they finally arrived in a clearing and slid to a stop. The men crawled silently out of the vehicles; Doc was impressed with their stealth. Hand signals were the means of communication. Captain Marz, the army Special Forces CO, took control of the entire group. He led the way heading for a small opening in the thick jungle canopy. The trail was crude and littered with brush and vines. The white tape placed at strategic points along the trail made the hike possible, without it, the darkness would have engulfed them. In a few minutes, Captain Marz froze in his steps and pointed to his ear. Off in the distance, to the right of the trail, loud voices and a woman's scream could be heard. So far, they had not been detected. The noise from the village would cover their advance.

As the rain continued to fall, the group worked their way up the trail, the first of the Special Forces team headed toward the head of the trail outside the village to take up positions. Les, Doc, Vail, Chief Volkert, Mr. Shurburn, and the Junk Force trainees headed for the far end of the trail to become the "stopper force" to turn back Viet Cong who might charge ahead after the Claymoors exploded. By using shielded flashlights, Captain Marz and a contingent of Vietnamese Ranger officers went about planting four Claymoors on the ground, using the spike legs attached to the device. The devices were positioned two on either side of the trail about fifty feet apart. Wires were then laid from their electric detonating caps to a safe distance toward the head of the trail and out of the angle range of the explosives. Next, two of the Vietnamese officers carefully covered the wires with debris and leaves so that they were invisible. The SEAL group, along with their trainees, reached their position and settled into concealed positions on either side of the trail. The SEALs had cautioned the trainees to hold their concealed positions during the encounter to provide maximum protect from VC return fire. They would be in an ideal location to establish a cross fire with the M1 carbines. Once everyone was in position, they settled down to wait while the rain continued to pour down..

It was still an hour before daylight but the noise from the village continued as if a big party was in progress. The rain was coming down harder now, everyone was soaked to the skin, it was a relief from the humidity and heat, and it felt almost cool. In spite of the calming effect of the cool rain, the tension in the group was obvious. This was the first combat encounter ever conducted with a SEAL component. Doc looked around him. The darkness prevented seeing anyone but Les who was only a few feet away. Les returned the glance and patted his Swedish K submachine gun as he gave a tense smile. Doc leaned against the tree he had been kneeling by and, while he kept his senses alert, he thought about this group called SEAL. His experiences during the last three months had been unique, although, he wondered about the lack of support this team had been shown. Maybe it was because they were the first SEAL Team assembled and deployed, well in advance of their official formation by the president. Yet, this was the greatest group of men he had ever served with. They showed a high degree of commitment, intelligence, and exemplary dedication to the task of training a Vietnamese version of SEAL with nothing but their own initiative and resourcefulness. He did not know about the future of this concept called SEAL. *If these men were representative of future teams, SEAL would undoubtedly emerge as the premier covert fighting force in the world.*

There was a slight hint of daylight to the East, barely visible through the thick jungle foliage. Over the noise of the pounding rain he heard low-pitched voices up the trail toward the village...the VC were moving out. The voices grew louder. He could see faint outlines of men walking in tight formation further up the trail.

At that moment Doc felt a searing sharp pain in the back of his neck. He slowly moved his hand up to determine the cause. He couldn't move quickly for that might attract the attention of the VC coming down the trail. He discovered that the back of his neck was covered with some sort of insect. He grasp one and brought it in front of him, there was just enough light to see a small red bodied ant; there must have been dozens of them on his neck. He swept them away with a subdued motion of his hand...what a time to be attacked by ants. They must have come from the tree he was leaning against. He continued to be bitten but there was little he could do to prevent it, he could not chance being seen. The VC were drawing closer by the minute.

As had been previously agreed, he heard a Vietnamese Ranger Officer Trainee shout, in Vietnamese, a warning to the Viet Cong. The VC on the trail froze, paused just a moment, dropped on one knee and began firing in the direction of the voice. Next came the sound of men running, followed almost immediately by a double explosion, first on the side of the trail to the left then to the right. Doc saw bodies falling, those who did not fall were on their feet running. Some of the group turned to flee back to the village, the rest charged ahead toward the SEAL position. When the VC were within a range of fifty feet, the SEAL group initiated the cross-fire pattern with the SEAL weapons set on full automatic, while they maintained their concealed position.

The Chief was the first to fire a short burst at the figures, the rest followed his lead and bodies began falling. Now there were muzzle flashes from the VC, Doc heard a bullet wiz by his shoulder and slam into the tree he had been leaning against. The fleeing VC stopped about twenty feet from the SEAL position as the automatic weapons fire continued. They heard firing and another explosion from the other end of the trail; it was assumed that a similar attempt to escape had been made by the VC headed back toward the village.

Doc, without changing his position, could see several bodies in the Claymoor kill zone. There were seven bodies on the ground where their escape had been cut short by the SEAL Team and trainees. His first urge was to see if any of the injured men could be saved and he stepped from cover to check them. Out of the corner of his eye, he saw one of the VC roll over and lift his gun pointing it at one of the trainees, getting off one shot. As Doc raised his Schmeizer from the shoulder sling, he heard a rapid-fire short burst from behind him and saw the VC fall forward over his AK 47, dead. Doc glanced behind him, saw Les lowering the Swedish K, he nodded to Doc.

The trainee the VC had fired at was on the ground on his back. Doc rushed to him and immediately saw a pool of blood on his chest. The 7.62x39 round from the AK 47 had hit the man mid-chest just to the left of the sternum, an exact heart shot. The man was already dead when Doc got to him.

Lieutenant Lin organized the other trainees to carry their comrade back up the trail to the weapons carrier. The trainee's body would be returned to his family by the Junk Force command.

The SEALs circulated among the fallen to insure they were all dead. The team members gave nods to one another and started the hike back to the weapons carrier. The Special Forces medics would check for VC wounded. The bodies of the dead would be turned over to ARVN for disposition. The wounded VC would be taken to the ARVN hospital outside Da Nang. Doc hoped none of them would be given a strychnine injection.

On the hike back to the weapons carrier, Vail raised a question about the welfare of the people in the village, suggesting that someone should check on them. Captain Marz, who was walking with the SEAL members, assured Vail that two of his men had been sent to the village for that purpose.

The ride back to Da Nang was in total silence. Apparently no one wanted to verbalize his feelings.

Chapter Sixteen

The next morning, after closing windows and doors, the team members, involved in the ambush, gathered around the table in an informal debriefing. Bill joined them and sat at the head of the table. "O.K. Dale, give me a rundown on our part in the operation. I've just been out to talk to Captain Marz about how they did."

"Well, Skipper, things went pretty much according to plan except that we lost a trainee and that's a goddamn shame. It was unavoidable though, all the VC we encountered were down and out, as best anyone of us could tell. We hadn't had an opportunity to check them when one son of a bitch rolled over and began firing, Les stopped that, but… to late," the XO, Dale Shurburn, explained.

"How many VC were there?"

"We didn't do a body count but I would estimate there were around twenty-six or twenty-seven in the group that came out of the village. Did Captain Marz lose any men? He said nothing during the walk out or the ride back," Dale spoke in a concerned tone of voice.

"Yes, he lost one."

"How did that happen, Bill?"

"It was a screw up, Chief. As I understand it, they had a few men stationed near the village facing down the trail. Those men were to launch a grenade attack against any VC that made it through the Claymoors and tried to head back toward the village. I guess there were some VC that went back that way, the Captain's men did what they were told. The problem was that one of them dropped the grenade with the pin pulled. He got down on his hands and knees to look for it. Before he found it, the grenade went off under his chest."

"That explains the second explosion after the Claymoors went off."

"Yeah, Chief, and it also points up inadequate training. Marz feels terrible about it. I guess it's the first trainee he has lost to an accident. What about our trainee's body, Doc?"

"Lieutenant Lin had him taken to the ARVN hospital for the kid's family to claim. He was pretty broken up about the death, although he seemed to be handling it well."

"There was nothing you could do for the kid?" Bill questioned.

"No, he was dead when I got to him, shot in the heart."

Bill started to get up from the table then sat back down. "While I have you together, thanks for a great job out there. I'm real sorry we lost a trainee but you did give the VC something to think about. I hope what has been done benefits the village. If any of the VC got away, the village will suffer."

"We don't think any of them escaped, Skipper."

"But we don't know, do we, Chief?"

"No, Sir."

"I was meeting with Commander Rudd, that's why I was away when this operation went down. He wants us to go look at the suspected VC buildup in the Mekong delta. He had suggested that we stage it as a raid a couple months ago, now the intell is indicating much more of a build up than he thought. He wants us to go down to have a look, just a look."

"Who goes on this 'turkey shoot'?"

"We need you, Chief, Doc, Dale, and most of the crew here to carry on the training. I will take Les and Vail with me, shouldn't take more than a few days. We need to get in there and out without leaving any footprints but Commander Rudd really needs to know what is going on down there."

"Where exactly is, 'down there'?"

"The Mekong is a big ass river, Les. It flows into the South China Sea south of Saigon but the headwaters are in China. It branches east and west before entering the sea. The activity Rudd is interested in is up the east branch north of a settlement called Vinh Long. He doesn't know much more than that except there seems to be a buildup of VC in the area and he needs to know how big the force is."

"What does this have to do with our activities in Da Nang?" Les asked.

"Nothing, right now, it may be the VC position that will pose a threat to Saigon in the future, you know, if this thing goes on that long."

"If we keep it on the scale it is now and train men, like our trainees, to fight the VC the way the VC fight, it can be contained. If we escalate the process and start bringing in heavy armor like the old wars, it could go on for a long time."

"You're right, Boats. They don't leave those decisions to the folks fighting wars now do they?"

"Not in any history book I've read," Boats responded.

Les leaned toward the table and looked at Bill. "How do we get into this Vinh Long and points north?"

"We fly to Saigon and catch a small cargo ship that runs the lower part of the Mekong up to a town called Tra Vinh. There we pick up a smaller craft that will take us the rest of the way up river. The cargo ship belongs to an Aussie sailor who retired here after the war…we can trust him. The second boat has good credentials, it belongs to a covert operation controlled by Combined Studies."

"These VC up river are going to welcome us while we inspect their camp and count noses…oh yeah?" Boats Vail looked at Bill with a smirk on his face.

"I doubt it. However, there are dozens of boats similar to the boat we'll be on running up and down the river past our point of interest every day. We should be inconspicuous and able to get a handle on their operation with a little after dark snooping."

Les, with a disgusted look said, "that sounds like fun, Skipper. Nothing challenging about it, just go look, maybe take a few pictures, write a few notes."

"O.K. I hear you, Les, but we need to give it a try. Maybe what we learn will save other troops from being shot up, or worse, and we have a sort of cover. Rudd had some credentials cooked up for us as part of his planning for this operation. It seems the United Nations has been planning several hydroelectric projects for the Mekong since the mid-fifties. I know we may not appear to be what the credentials say but, for the time we will spend on the river, we will be Canadian engineers working for the U.N to advise them on actual dam construction sites."

"This must have been in the works for some time, why are we hearing about it now?"

"I did mention it a while back, Boats, but our training schedule and the ambush pushed it down in priority. Rudd mentioned it months ago but things kept getting in the way and his early information was real spotty, it's clearer now."

"O.K., we'll do it. What about the Combined Studies guys. They're on the scene, why can't they tell Rudd what he wants to know?" Les questioned.

"Their cover is so good he doesn't want to jeopardize it at this point, that's why!" Bill's abrupt answer silenced Les for a moment.

"O.K. O.K. I just don't want it to turn into another wild goose chase and end up with no goose grease. So what do we know about the weapons these guys have?" Les countered with one of his usual get to the point questions.

"The best intelligence Rudd has puts their numbers at less than 100 bodies armed with nothing larger than the .30 caliber AK 47s."

"Can you tell us the source of that intelligence?" Boats Vail asked.

"Yes, it's ARVN."

Les and Vail looked at each other and Vail said, "oh brother, now I know we're in trouble, who would take anything those bastards say as accurate. I'm disappointed in Rudd."

"Boats, you need to understand that his intelligence sources are very limited, he works with what he's got. The intelligence network in this country is very weak and he has a tough job to do."

"What weapons should we haul along?" Les wanted more information.

"Side arms only, there won't be room for anything else. If we get in a pinch, I imagine the crew of the Combined Studies boat will have some weaponry, they should anyway."

Vail asked, "when do we leave, Skipper?"

"We can fly down to Saigon early next week. We'll need to coordinate with the cargo ship after we get there. It might be few days before it comes in."

The rest of the team had drifted off early in the three men's discussion, knowing that the conversation was one that they did not need to hear, as they were not involved. The Chief and Dale had moved onto the balcony, closing the door behind them, and were talking, in low tones, about the training schedule. After a few minutes, they noticed, Chi, the shopkeeper from across the street come out of his store with bottles of beer cradled in his arms. They looked at one another, shrugging their shoulders, when they heard hurried footsteps on the stairs.

As Chi reached the top stair, he headed directly to the Chief.

"You not order beer but need talk to you."

"O.K., in my room," the Chief pointed saying, "the door on the left."

Inside the Chief's bedroom, with the door closed, Chi sat on the edge of the bed and looked directly at the Chief."Many new faces in neighborhood, Mister Chief, I think they VC, they watch your house very carefully, all day, all night. I see out my store window, can see now. Look next to store doorway."

The Chief slowly eased the curtain back and saw a Vietnamese man standing where Chi said he would be. He was dressed in the typical black pajamas and had something around his neck. He did not appear to be armed. However, he was taking long glances across the street and up and down at the house.

"Just thought you should know, Mister Chief. You good customer and I not like VC. Brother killed by them year ago."

"Thanks, Chi, I am very glad you told me. Will you be safe now that you've told me?"

"Yes, Chi dumb storekeeper. VC not cause him trouble if he not get smart."With that statement, Chi jumped to his feet and grasped the Chief's arm, smiled, and headed for the door.

"Chi let me pay you for the beer. How many bottles did you bring?"

"Not matter. How you say, 'on the house', right?"

"Right, Chi, thanks for both the beer and the information."

Chi quickly departed down the stairs, the Chief heard the back door slam behind him as Chi hurried across the street.

The men involved in the Mekong operation were still seated around the table. Chief Volkert stepped behind Bill, leaning over to speak to him privately.

"What did you say, Chief?"

"We need to get everyone here and keep the windows and doors to the balcony closed, we have big ears next door. Remember, Skipper?"

"Let's get everyone up here, Chief."

The other team members, who were scattered about the house, were around the table in short order.

"Everyone's here, Chief, repeat what you said to me."

"Chi, from across the street was just up here to tell us that we are being watched by people he thinks are VC. I've noticed more activity on the sidewalk in front of the store recently, wasn't sure what to make of it, now we know. In fact, that guy standing next to the door right now is one of them."

Doc shook his head, "damn, I noticed Junk has been restless. She's been going out on the balcony growling and looking across the street. I should have paid more attention to her."

"I guess there isn't much we can do about it right now but keep an eye on them and don't do anything, that can be seen through the windows or doors, that might give them something to go on. Everyone needs to keep a low profile when you're up here. Make sure the windows and doors are closed before any important conversations are carried on. I really don't trust those missionaries either so we need to watch out for them as well...damn that Stars and Stripes article!" Bill was still steaming about that newspaper article.

Chapter Seventeen

September 1962

The following week, Ensign Dale Shurburn drove Bill, Les, and Boats to the Da Nang airport to catch the plane to Saigon. The remainder of the team headed to the base to begin the preliminary briefings on the next phase of training; escape, evasion, and survival. Since there was some paperwork to wrap up recapping the ambush operation, Dale decided to go back to the house prior to heading for the base.

As he drove into the yard, he saw a man in a business suit walking away from the back gate, Dale drove the Jeep up beside him as the man walked down the driveway. "Can I help you, Sir?"

"I stopped over to have a chat with your leader about some important matters. I am Reverend Devout from next door."

"I'm in charge right now, you can discuss whatever it is with me, I'm Mr. Shurburn."

"Well, Mr. Shurburn, we've heard some disturbing rumors about your group's activities in this area and I felt it was my Christian duty to discuss them with you."

"Maybe, if you would tell me those rumors, I could dispel them. What are they?"

"Well, we had our suspicions when your group rented this house," he gestured with his hand toward the house as he spoke. "Then we read a disturbing article in the Stars and Stripes. We are Americans you know and we subscribe to that newspaper to keep up with what's going on. After we read the article and conferred with a close friend who is a Vietnamese Junk Force officer, he confirmed that your group is the one mentioned in the article."

Dale looked at the pudgy little man in the black business suit. He could see the sweat running down the man's forehead and dripping off his nose.

"What you say means nothing to me, but what concern is it of yours?"

"As I said initially, I felt it was my Christian duty to attempt to dissuade your group from any activities that would assist the illegal military force that is active in this country."

"And who would that force be, Reverend?"

"Why, the army that is supported by that corrupt government in Saigon and the United States, of course. You must see the error of your ways and offer your support to the true peoples' army, the army that is trying to unify their country under one legitimate government in Hanoi. After all, you are nothing but a group of paid mercenaries, even though you claim to be in our navy. The United States Navy would never harbor a group such as yours. Your group lacks the regimentation and discipline of a military organization, not to mention the heavy beards and slovenly dress. Just ask Jesus for his guidance and join us in prayer whenever you like. In fact, Commander Vinh will be at our meeting this evening."

"You've got all the details wrong, Reverend, but I don't have time to discuss it with you, good day!"

"You can't brush me off like that, young man."

"Reverend, you can take your preaching, and whatever else you acclaim, next door and keep it there."

"I've been in Da Nang for four years, you don't know what you're doing, Mr. Shurburn."

Dale re-started the Jeep and drove to the backyard-parking place. When he got out of the vehicle, he saw the reverend walk up the driveway and turn into the sidewalk that would lead him to the house next door. The team had accomplished one of its goals; a nondescript appearance, along with the physical image of a group of mercenaries, would divert most peoples' attention. It would cause them to question the military bearing of his team, just the ticket for the activities SEAL would possibly undertake in the future. As he entered the house, he was joined by Junk who greeted him with her typical enthusiasm and a jump into the air. He headed for the front room and looked across the street, Junk came up beside him growling deep in her throat. There, sitting on his heals, was a man with his back against the front wall of the store looking up at the house. Dale went onto the balcony and looked around nonchalantly then looking at the man, waved at him in greeting, the man quickly looked away, got to his feet and entered the store.

Those guys must get tired of watching this house, I hope that's all they do is watch, he thought, as he went to the room he shared with Bill to complete the ambush paperwork.

Later that day at the base, Dale drew a group of the team aside and told them of the conversation with Reverend Devout.

The Chief listened carefully, thought a minute and then said, "well, we've accomplished two things with that conversation. First, it leaves no doubt that Vinh has been cavorting with our neighbors and second, our identity seems to be covert."

"Mercenaries, how about that, a year ago I couldn't even spell it and now I is one." Doc kicked the sand and shook his head as he spoke.

Ramsey, Smith, Soule, and Carey had spent the early morning going over escape and evasion techniques with the trainees.

When they had finished their lectures, the Chief asked Lin to bring the trainees together so he could brief them on the next phase of the training. "O.K. The actual field application, of what you've heard earlier today, will start today. We're going to ferry everyone up to our training bay and let you set up camp. You will need to put together some sort of shelter because you will be there overnight or longer. You'll also need to think about what you're going to eat. We'll send enough rice along for two days but the remainder will be up to you to forage. Once you're set up, we'll divide you into two groups with designations of red and green. Then we will position the two groups at some distance from each other, but neither will know the location of the other. Your mission will be to find the other group and capture as many of that group as you can. Bring them to the command center, which will be at the original base camp. The strategy of how you accomplish these things will be up to each team leader. You'll choose team leaders once we start the exercise. Any questions?"

"Yes, Chief. How do we capture members of the other team?"

"That's a good question, Lieutenant; each man in each group will have a cloth band on his arm depicting his team's color. Once that band is removed he will be considered captured. Let's not have anyone getting hurt in this exercise, just physically capture them and bring them to the command center for holding. The team, that captures the largest number of their opponents, wins. There are boundaries for this exercise and they are clearly marked with flags, the area is about a square mile. Any more questions? When we shut down this part of the exercise there will be additional training in interrogation tactics."

One of the trainees stood and asked the Chief, in broken but understandable English, "how do we know when the exercise is over?"

The Chief pulled a gas powered marine signal horn from his backpack and let out a loud blast, which caused the trainees to jump to their feet; it was probably the first time any of them had heard such a horn. "We will sound four blasts on this horn every five minutes for fifteen minutes, that should bring you all in."

The trainees quickly returned to their barracks to gather up some miscellaneous items of clothing and personal items, each trainee would be permitted to carry a belt sheath knife only, no other tools or weapons. When they returned to the beach, they were ferried up the coast to the training bay by Doc and John Smith in the team boat.

"What did you have in mind for the interrogation phase of this exercise, Chief?" Dale asked.

"I thought we could push them around a little, maybe tie their hands behind them and give them the third degree about their activities and unit. A little time on an Apache pole might give them something to think about in terms of their ability to resist questioning. What do you think, Dale?"

"That sounds good but let's not get too hard on them."

"You mean like the VC might treat them...right?"

"I get your point, Chief."

When Doc and Smith arrived at the bay with the last group of trainees, they were amazed at what they saw. The first three groups that had been brought to the site had organized quickly with each group going about the necessary activities as though they had done it many times before. There was a framework for a thatch structure that would house all of the trainees. Several fish had already been speared, cleaned, and were on cooking sticks by a huge fire. Other members of the group had created a clearing twenty yards square and, when Doc asked about the men who were not on the scene, he was told they were hunting in the jungle. It didn't appear that these men needed much training in survival. Most of them had been surviving all of their lives under similar circumstances. The key to all these accomplishments was, of course, Lieutenant Lin and his organization of their efforts.

Within two hours, the hunters had returned. Although game was scarce, the group returned to camp with two adult monkeys, several frogs, and a cat-like animal about the size of a small dog. The hunters went about dressing their prey and shortly thereafter, the game was on cooking sticks by the fire. They had killed the game with long spear pointed sticks made from a scrub bush that grew tall and straight in the area. Late that afternoon, Ensign Shurburn and the Chief called the team together to lay out what they should do next.

Shurburn spoke, "we have decided to give the two groups of trainees the rest of the day to check out the area and plan their strategy for tomorrow. Later on, we'll assemble the red and green teams and identify each member so that they can begin to know who they will be working with."

"What do you want the team to do now that we have the trainees out here, they seem to be doing a great job so far," Doc asked as he looked at the Ensign.

"I want Carey and Soule to stick with the green team, Smith and Ramsey to go with the red team. You four can function in an advisory role but don't make suggestions. If they come up with ideas and want your opinion, give it to them but keep it simple, I don't want either team to have an advantage because of your input. Doc and the Chief can go back to the house tonight; I'll stay out here with the troops."

Lieutenant Lin approached the team huddle, "Mr. Shurburn, I think we need to warn the men about what they might find out here after dark. One of the men, who was hunting, told me that he saw fresh signs of tiger activity to the east, about a thousand meters, and many of the deadly snakes are nocturnal. Men do get up during the night. Most of the men know of these hazards but it would be well to remind them."

"Glad you mentioned that, Lieutenant, I didn't think of it. You can give them the word, it was your suggestion. I have a question though, how do you identify tiger activity?"

"Tigers mark a territory with urine, by scratching on trees, and by leaving their droppings. The man who told me, found scratching and droppings, some were fresh. Tigers range over a large territory, it may not even be around now but we shouldn't take a chance. Where I grew up, on a plantation, we had regular visits from tigers and even had one on our front veranda, my father shot it, and we had a rug in front of the fireplace."

Shurburn smiled thinking about a fur rug in front of a fireplace. "Sounds right cozy to me." Then he got back on track, "I think it would be a good idea to have men on lookout duty during the night, Lieutenant. I'll let you assign them, why don't we have three men per shift for two hours at a time, that should get us through until daylight and not deprive them of too much sleep. Have you thought about the red/green team selection?"

"Yes, I have the men picked for each team. Do you want me to tell them?"

"Yes, why don't you."

"I'll take care of it. I was going to suggest that we keep the fire burning high all night anyway, for several reasons and now we can add tigers to those reasons."

Lin headed back to his men while the team members chatted about the next day's activities.

"If those big cats are around, I wish we had something a little heavier than a 9mm weapon."

"Yeah, Chief, why don't you see if you can get us a couple of M14s, they might come in handy in other situations."

"I'll see what I can do. Are you ready to head for the house, Doc? I think we should motor back to the base before total darkness."

"I am ready, Chief."

As they boarded the team boat, the Chief went to the stern and started the motor while Doc shoved off. It was later than either of them realized. It was pitch black before they arrived at the base beach. As they hauled the boat onto the beach, they saw a figure walking toward them, it was Commander Vinh.

"Good evening, gentlemen, you're out late tonight. Up to no good, I would guess. I understand that your neighbor had a little talk with Ensign Shurburn recently, did it do any good?"

The Chief glared at Vinh, "I'm not aware of any conversations Mr. Shurburn had with, who did you say?"

"Come, come, Chief, I'm sure he briefed all of you about it. The reverend is a good man; I've known him and his wife since they arrived in Da Nang over four years ago."

"Really, Commander, well we know now who else to watch in the neighborhood. Goodnight."

Doc and the Chief piled into the weapons carrier, that had been left at the base, and headed for the house. It was a dark night and the headlights on the vehicle illuminated only a short span of the road.

As the Chief drove, he commented on the poor lighting and the dangers it posed. "Sure glad I don't have to drive this thing in Coronado with all the people who walk on the streets at night. It wouldn't be long until you hit one of them."

The road surface was poorly graded gravel and the heavy off-road tires threw rocks against the inside of the fenders in a constant hail of noise and thumps.

Doc looked at the Chief, "Did you hear that one? It must have been a real boulder, sounded like it came all the way through the truck."

"Yeah, I heard it, bet it made a dint. I wonder if any of the boys are out to shoot at us tonight, have your Schmeizer handy, Doc."

"I got it, Chief."

As they pulled into the yard at the house, Doc looked at the Chief, "We made it through again, must be doing something right."

"Yeah, maybe the boss gave the VC a night off."

"What do you think Vinh was trying to accomplish with his remarks about our neighbors?"

"He is testing us, trying to see if he can get a response that he can use in some way, the SOB."

Junk greeted them at the back door with her usual enthusiasm. They both patted her and let her out into the backyard. She only stayed a minute and was back at the door to come in.

Doc rubbed Junk behind the ears while talking to the Chief, "she wants to be back in with us tonight, maybe it's our friends across the street she doesn't care for. Dale told me that he checked out the scene earlier today, before he came to the base, there was a guy standing in front of the store. He even waved at the guy before he scurried into the store. They know we're watching them now so they may get more aggressive...who knows."

"That's probably it; I do feel better with her in the house."

The cook had left a cold plate of food for them, after eating, they both headed for bed, tomorrow would be a long day.

In the morning, they found the cook had prepared a stack of hot toast, fresh fruit, and coffee. After eating, the Chief headed out to fuel the weapons carrier while Doc checked the ammunition supplies and fed Junk. As he walked out the back door and into the parking area, the Chief had just finished the fueling job.

He looked up gesturing to the vehicle, as Doc approached. "Remember that *rock* last night?"

"Yeah, I do, did it make a dint?"

"It made more than a dint, come here."

Doc walked around the vehicle to where the Chief stood and looked at the area where the Chief pointed. In the rounded panel, on the passenger side of the cab, was a distinct bullet hole about half way up the panel.

"Looks like .30 caliber to me and right about waist high on you," the Chief said with emphasis.

"Shit, that's too close. Where did it go from there?" Doc apparently had not yet fully absorbed the fact that he had come close to death, judging from the tone of his response.

The Chief opened the passenger side door and looked at the hole from inside the cab. Located in each rear corner of the cab were racks designed to secure a rifle in a vertical position and within easy reach of the occupants.

"It went right on through and hit the weapons rack which deflected it down." The Chief lifted the cushion on the seat and saw the course of the bullet after being deflected; it had passed under the seat and lodged in the wood frame on the lower seat structure.

"That rifle rack saved your ass, Doc. If that bullet had been three inches higher, it wouldn't have hit the rack and you would've gotten it in the chest." The Chief wanted to drive the point home regarding how close Doc had come to being shot.

Doc nodded at the Chief to indicate he got it, then in his usual cool manner commented, "I like the design of this vehicle after all, I'm sorry I ever said anything bad about it. You wouldn't have known what was wrong, I would have just fallen over and that would have been the end of my tour."

Shaking his head the Chief said, "we really need to watch that area along the road, I'm sure that's where it came from. We've been fired at before but never any hits, they must be getting better."

"It must have been from something other than an AK, the range is too far from the top of those hills for that round, unless it was just a lucky shot. Don't you think?"

"It could've been one of our rounds, coming back at us. Anyway, yesterday was your lucky day, Doc."

They drove out to the base and took the boat up to the training bay to see how things were progressing. When they arrived, they saw the other team members seated around a big fire drinking from tin cans.

"Whats ya drinkin, troops?"

"Coffee, Chief, you won't believe this, the trainees chipped in and bought coffee, smuggled it in, cooked it up, and served it to us when we got up this morning. I guess they appreciate the training and other stuff we've done," Chuck Ramsey spoke with a smile and pride in his voice.

"A good bunch of men, where's Lieutenant Lin?" the Chief asked.

"He's out with Mr. Shurburn positioning the red team; the green team is in the shelter so they can't see which direction they went. They'll come back for the green team and then we'll start the exercise," Chuck chimed in.

The Chief was anxious to share the latest incident. "Sounds like everything is on track. I need to tell you that we took fire last night on the way back to the house, missed Doc by about three inches. We heard it but thought it was rocks hitting the bottom of the vehicle, the rifle rack deflected the round down and under the seat, too close. We also had another encounter with Vinh. He questioned us about the lecture Mr. Shurburn got from our neighbor, news travels fast around here."

Chuck looked directly at Doc. "Sure glad that round missed you, Doc; I wouldn't want to be out here without a Corpsman. Were you fired on at the same place in the road?"

"Thanks," Doc said with a grin, "yeah, same place, about, it was real dark."

The group began talking about the ongoing exercise when they heard voices coming from behind the shelter. It was Lieutenant Lin and Mr. Shurburn returning from positioning the red team.

"Doc, Chief, glad you made it back. We were wondering if you took the day off?"

"No, Dale, we're here as scheduled."

Lieutenant Lin walked to the door of the shelter and told the men of the green team to get ready to move out.

"Do you want me to come along, Lieutenant?" Shurburn asked.

"No, I'll position this team and we can get started with the exercise."

As the Lieutenant led the men out of the camp, Ensign Shurburn spoke to the team members, "I would like the Chief and Doc to hang out here. The rest of you can fan out and observe. Ramsey and Smith join up with the red team, Soule and Carey the green. We will commence as soon as Lieutenant Lin gets back. I'll show you on the chart where we positioned each team to save you time hunting for them. We told the team captains to take the arm bands of the men they capture and send the men captured back here, it will simplify the process."

The day progressed and within two hours some of the trainees, covered with mud, began showing up at the base camp. Some of them had serious scrapes caused by encounters with thorns and brush. They were all in high spirits even though they had been captured early. Doc examined each man as he returned, cleaning, dressing, and treating any wounds or injuries. As evening approached, both officers agreed that it was time to call in the men before it became too dark for them to find their way back. When everyone was accounted for, and the arm bands tallied, the exercise was a tie; each team had captured seven men from the opposing team. As the trainees prepared their dinner and ate, various team members began explaining techniques that might be used by the VC to extract information. Techniques the SEAL Team members had been taught in their own survival, escape, and interrogation training. During the afternoon, two poles, about four inches in diameter and eight feet long, had been gathered. They planted the poles firmly in the ground to a depth of two feet.

Ensign Shurburn explained, "these are called Apache poles. They are a very effective method of torture. Once secured to one of these, the prisoner can neither set nor stand and the muscle pain becomes intense. I want each of you to have a go at it to demonstrate how effective they can be. Who wants to go first?"

Lieutenant Lin stepped forward.

"No, Lieutenant, I want you to be the interrogator of the men on the poles."

Another trainee stepped forward immediately and while Soule and Carey secured him to the pole, the Lieutenant began shouting at him and asking questions in Vietnamese.

The next trainee was motioned forward and he stepped up to the second pole. To secure him, Ramsey and Smith first had him kneel in front of the pole facing away from it. Next, they had him extend his legs backward past the pole and, once in position, they securely tied his ankles together. Seizing the trainee by both shoulders, they raised him up with his back against the pole and had him extend his arms behind him. They now secured his arms with the pole between his arms. This placed the man in a forward leaning position from which he could neither stand nor sit. The strain on the leg, back, and arm muscles is intense and can't be tolerated for an extended period of time.

The torture process continued until all trainees had a turn on the pole. Most tolerated the experience well, but none left the pole without tears in their eyes and a new respect for this type of torture.

Soule walked over to Doc, who was standing at the edge of the group, put his arm over Doc's shoulder, and began his account, "I went through survival training with Les at Pickle Meadows, it was rough. The interrogators were part of the marine staff that ran the place. They all spoke fluent Russian and so the interrogation was realistic. When they turned us loose in the survival phase, we had a sheath knife and a parachute for equipment. We spent three days trying to avoid being captured. Eventually we were all rounded up, but they had five groups of marines looking for us, which made the odds about ten to one since there were ten men in each of their groups and only five of us. We all spent some time on the pole and in cages but Les really gave them a hard time when they captured him, he even hit one of his captors, hit him hard. The marine was bleeding from his nose and mouth when they brought Les in. Les was the last to be captured."

"Did the marines slap you around?"

"Yeah, they did just about everything in the rule book trying to get us to divulge information about our unit. Les didn't cooperate so they really zeroed in on him. They put him on the pole after about six hours in a cage that was so small you couldn't turn or lay down. When they took him out of it, they put him directly on the pole and he was on it for the rest of the night, probably five hours or more. They didn't take him off the pole until we secured from the training. He couldn't walk but he never broke. Two of us carried him back to the training headquarters. By the time we got to that stage none of us cared much about anything. We just wanted it to be over!"

Chapter Eighteen

Following their flight from Da Nang to Saigon, Bill, Les, and Boats met with Commander Rudd to coordinate the Mekong reconnaissance mission. The information Rudd provided added little to what had already been discussed, except the arrangements for their passage on the costal freighter that ran from Saigon up the Mekong to Tra Vinh. The second leg of the journey, aboard the CIA scow, had also been cleared. The boat would be standing by to take them aboard in Tra Vinh for their continued trip up the river to Vinh Long and beyond to the suspected VC encampment. Rudd volunteered that the mission, by necessity, had been cleared through ARVN.

"Are you kidding me, Commander?"

"What do you mean, Bill?"

"ARVN knows about this look and see trip?"

"We can't avoid that protocol. Remember we are in an advisory capacity in this country. We just can't run operations in their country without their input, review, and approval."

"I understand, Commander, but do you trust ARVN?"

"In a word, No! We have no choice in the matter. Your freighter ride leaves the wharf at 1800 tomorrow night. The skipper's name is Olaf Madson, the Aussie I told you about earlier, he's a good man and knows a little about what we are up to."

Les turned to directly face Commander Rudd, "How many other people know about this operation, Commander?"

"Not very many, Petty Officer Barter. Lieutenant Beck, the top dog at ARVN, Madson, and those in this room. Check in with me when you get back, Bill…I hope everything goes well for you. Good Luck! Bill, would you stay a minute? I have something I need to run by you."

"Sure, Commander, see you guys back at the hotel."

Les and Boats got up from the conference table where they had been sitting, nodded to Commander Rudd, and left the room, closing the door behind them.

"Bill, I need to ask you about your choice of men for this mission. Primarily, why Barter and Vail?"

"There are several reasons. First is experience. Vail has had considerable exposure with east coast UDT teams. He was in the Bay of Pigs debacle and involved with CIA operations in Siberia. He is focused and a skilled close combat expert. He will kill without hesitation, when required. He is vindictive but totally dedicated to the team. Barter has many of the same qualities but a different mind set. He, too, is the best in personal defense but views killing an opponent as unavoidable, part of the job. He's not vindictive. I thought they made a good balance. I think we'll need that on this operation."

"You've convinced me. I think you looked for the right qualifications in your team, although a small team it is. I agree with the decision not to involve the trainees."

Rudd came from behind his desk to take a chair next to Bill. "The folks over at Combined Studies have been asking questions about you and I thought you might want to have a chat with them soon. When you get back from the Mekong, I'll schedule one of their aircraft to pick you up here and fly you to Okinawa. The trip will take you no more than a day. They can ask the questions directly to you and not through me."

"What's this about?"

"I don't want to spoil their fun but I think they might be trying to recruit you."

"How can that be, I still have two years of obligated service before I can even consider getting out or doing something else."

"That can be taken care of; you really wouldn't need to resign from the navy. The navy can 'loan' you to the CIA indefinitely, if you get my drift."

"Got it, but why me?"

"You'll have to ask them."

Later that night at the hotel Les and Boats sat down with Bill to discuss the coming days.

"I'm not nuts about all these people knowing what we're about to try, Bill, in particular, ARVN. My impressions of that outfit fall somewhere between zero and none."

"I share your concern, Boats, but we'll have to be even more careful than we thought. Unless there is an informant close to the senior ARVN liaison officer, we should be O.K."

"Yeah, cross your fingers," Boats responded, a deep frown on his face.

Before noon, the following day Les and Boats made a trip to the waterfront in Saigon to check out the location of the freighter they would ride part way up the Mekong. They found it in an isolated berth next to the main road leading into the area, judging from her appearance, the ship looked rather disheveled but seaworthy. As they walked along the pier looking up at her, several of the crewmembers stood by the rail looking down at them.

"She looks O.K.," Less observed still appearing concerned. "The crew looks to be mostly Chinese but I did see a couple of white men on the bridge."

"Yes, probably the captain and first mate. They hire the Chinese for the heavy labor but maintain control through command, they save money that way. That name painted on the stern tells me she was probably built in Japan, 'Mekong Maru'. She might be a leftover from WW II. The Jap navy used similar ships to transport supplies to their bases in this area." Boats, as usual, enjoyed sharing his knowledge.

After a brief dinner at the hotel, the three men caught a cab and headed for the waterfront to start the first leg of their journey. Captain Madson greeted them at the head of the gangway and welcomed them aboard. The first mate escorted them to a small cabin just aft of the bridge on the second level. The cabin was furnished with two sets of bunk beds and a small metal sink. A porthole looked out over the starboard railing. The cabin was clean and the bunks were made up with fresh sheets and pillowcases.

"This cabin is an oven, it must be 100 degrees in here, even though the sun is going down. Looks like we'll be spending most of our time on deck," Bill moaned.

"That sounds good to me. We won't get much air through that porthole anyway." Boats smiled, he would always rather be on deck taking in the sea air.

A few minutes later, there was a knock on the door. Les opened it to find a Chinese crewmember standing there. In very broken English, the crew member informed them that the Captain would like them to join him in his cabin. He then lead the way and they followed him up a ladder to a level above the bridge. After knocking on a heavy wood-planked door, the crewmember left them and ran down the ladder.

Captain Madsen opened the door, his demeanor was cordial. "Come in, gentlemen. I hope you found your accommodations to be satisfactory. It's the best we have on this old girl. She was built in Yokohama in 1942 and has been running in these waters ever since. I bought her after I retired from the Australian Navy in 1954 and started hauling cargo to the cities up the Mekong. It had never been done before with a ship of this size but she makes it up the river just fine. I understand you are all Canadian engineers. Are they really considering damming the river?"

"It will be a long time in coming, Captain. Our job is to make a preliminary survey for potential dam sites up river but it will take years to get the projects underway, even if they are approved and funded by the UN," Bill spun the cover-up story.

"That's good news, Mr. Evans; dams would put me out of business. Will you excuse me? I'm needed on the bridge." The captain took a bottle from a bedside locker and sat it on a small desk in the corner with three glasses. "Help yourself to a Scotch and enjoy your trip, we will be underway in about fifteen minutes. We should arrive at Tra Vinh after dark tomorrow."

On their way back to their cabin, Bill stopped for a moment and leaned on the rail as the others joined him. "I don't think he has a clue about us and that's good. Rudd did a good job arranging this trip…so far."

The Mekong Maru encountered heavy seas on the trip south to the mouth of the Mekong and, by early morning, had made less then half the distance to her first port of call at Tra Vinh. After a sleepless night, the three men headed for the galley for breakfast and some strong coffee.

As they entered the galley, Les said, "I'm glad I signed up for UDT, I couldn't take a life at sea."

Boats countered this statement, "I had six years of it before I came to the teams. A Boatswainmate is destined to spend most of his career at sea unless he gets some rinky dink job on shore duty like base security." He had enjoyed his years at sea.

The ship's arrival was delayed even further by some minor engineering problems and, by the time they put the lines over at Tra Vinh, it was early morning and pouring rain.

"Your second boat was here to pick you up hours ago but had to leave, it'll be back this afternoon," Captain Madsen informed them. Looking at the three of them he suggested, "why don't you go below and catch up on some sleep, I'm sure you didn't get much last night."

Bill, looking tired, responded, "O.K., Captain, we'll do that."

After a lunch of beans and biscuits, the three men were on deck watching the ship unload pallets of boxes when they saw a shallow draft scow approaching from up river. It looked like a miserable little boat of about thirty-five feet, the decks looked slimy and the crew unkempt.

As it eased beside the Maru, Les looked at Boats, "I'll bet that's our ride up river. It's so covert it stinks."

Boats agreed, "I can smell it from here and they got 100 feet to come, what did you say about the arrangements Rudd made, Skipper?"

As the scow pulled alongside, the three men looked on. The decks appeared to be littered with gear, with a large hatch cover amidships. Aft, the boat had a small pilot station and some seating with a bowed canvas cover over the entire stern. A small man was at the wheel as the craft made fast to the Maru. Two deck hands on the scow passed lines to the crew of the larger ship where they were soon made fast. The man at the wheel looked up at the three men standing at the rail and said, "come aboard." The deck of the scow was ten feet below the rail of the Maru and a small rope ladder had been dropped for their boarding. With their gear thrown down to the crew of the scow, Les was first down the rope ladder, followed by Bill, then Boats.

Once on deck, the man who had been at the helm walked forward and extended his hand. "My name is Joche Flambeau. I skipper this craft, welcome aboard."

The three men introduced themselves and stowed their gear under the seats in the stern of the craft. On the very stern of the scow, suspended on davits, was a boat with an outboard motor. The entire assembly was covered by a canvas tarp so only the shaft of the motor was visible.

"What is the purpose of this craft, Mr. Flambeau?" Bill asked.

"We ply the river buying fish from the resident fishermen and then bring them down river to sell at the major ports. A good cover, don't you think?"

Bill was surprised to hear Flambeau discuss his cover so openly but guessed he knew what he was doing. Bill decided to play dumb.

"Cover, what sort of cover do you refer to Joche, if I may call you by your first name?"

"By all means, Mr. Evans, you know what I refer to but if you would rather not discuss it, that's fine with me. I went to work for the 'organization' two years ago after they approached me to carry out a few little jobs for them."

"Are you French?"

"Yes, I'm a hold over from a few years ago before my country was expelled from Vietnam. I was a fisheries agent for our foreign affairs office trying to teach these people how to farm and market their fish. The entire program fell through, after our expulsion from the country, but I managed to stay on through my contacts with the Saigon government. I bought this boat and decided to take advantage of my own teaching."

"How about your crew, can they be trusted?"

"They are all employees of the 'organization' and battle proven. They were fighting against the VC before your country ever knew there was such an organization."

"Where is this VC outpost, how far up river do we need to go?"

"North of Can Tho, about fifty kilometers from where we are now. It's been a while since we were up that far, maybe three months. There was substantial activity at that time and it's probably heavier now...we shall see. Our trip there will take about two days since we must stop and bargain with fishermen as we go and we must maintain a schedule because our ice in the hold will last only five to six days. When we get underway we will pick up ice before we head up river."

During this conversation, Les and Boats had made a preliminary tour of the scow. There was not much to see; the stench obviously was coming from the hold of the vessel even with the hatch cover in place. They discovered a small compartment in the forecastle of the vessel with the access hatch well hidden, the hatch was locked. As they walked aft, they saw Flambeau had seen their discovery and wondered if they had exceeded their welcome.

"May we ask what's in that forward compartment?" Boats asked.

"Yes, of course. It contains items we don't want visible."

"That's not much of an answer, if you'll pardon me, Mr. Flambeau."

"If we need them you'll know its contents soon enough."

Boats looked at Les and decided to let the issue drop. They walked aft and sat next to Bill as the small craft edged away from the Maru and headed across the river toward a large metal building. The boat was pitifully slow and the small single diesel engine labored to overcome the downstream current.

"Where would you put the flank speed of this rowboat?" Les asked Boats.

"Probably about seven knots with a good tail wind."

After taking on a load of ice, the scow headed up river passing dozens of hand propelled craft and powerboats. It was now early evening and the men assumed that many of the boats carried workers heading down river to their homes.

Bill, squinting into the late afternoon sun, said, "can you get us close to the encampment, Joche?"

"Yes, there is a small tributary stream just up river from where the camp was three months ago. We can put in there out of sight; it shouldn't be more than a few hundred yards from there. We can keep the boat hidden from view quite easily; the underbrush on the banks is very thick. If you go in after dark, you can probably avoid detection."

Bill looked at Les and Boats for their comments, they offered none except looks of skepticism.

After a mostly sleepless night, the men awoke to a smell of fish and the presence of two small craft on the port beam of the scow. Crew members, using long handled nets, were dipping fish from a well on the craft and dumping them into the hold of the scow. After several minutes of this activity, the hatch cover was replaced and the scow was underway up river.

Several fish buying stops punctuated the next two days and, by evening of the second day, they had passed the village of Can Tho heading north up river. As they rounded a bend in the river, the VC encampment came into view on the right bank. They passed it on the far side of the river and headed into a stream just north of the VC location. They had seen little at the encampment to reveal the nature of the site except a large concentration of makeshift huts and the presence of many men.

"I didn't see any weapons, Skipper," Boats stated, his concern coming through in his voice.

"No, I didn't either however the foliage is thick enough to hide artillery. It's going to be tough to get close enough to see much but we'll give it a try. Sure are a lot of people milling around though." Bill's concern was evident.

Les leaned back on a makeshift seat back and looked at Bill. "I think we would be wise to make our penetration in early morning. We would have some visibility and we might catch them groggy."

Less looked at Flambeau. "How is the river bank along the route to the camp?"

"It's shallow and muddy, that may be your best route of approach."

"What do you think, Bill? I'd feel better in the water than walking through that maze of brush."

"That'll be our route," Bill agreed. "As they say in BUDS, the water is our mother."

As the evening progressed, Flambeau produced swim fins, masks, and face black for the three SEALs. It was after three AM when they went over the side of the scow into the water. Half-swimming, half wading, they moved down the river bank until they were at a point where they could climb up the bank without much noise. Once they reached the crest of the bank, Bill used hand signals to direct Les and Boats to do a sweep of the perimeter. Their plan was to make mental notes of what they observed and return to the river at the same point on the bank. As the two men moved off in opposite directions, Bill worked his way toward a group of small buildings near the center of the compound. There wasn't a sound and, once the others had moved out, Bill had no indication of their position or direction. As he approached the buildings, he heard a low-pitched conversation between two men standing in front of one of the buildings. Although they were speaking in Vietnamese, his command of that language had become sufficient to understand the basics of what they were saying. Apparently, there was a supply barge headed up the river bringing in more weapons and basic supplies. As he reached the corner of one of the buildings, he stopped and crouched down, listening intently. At that moment, he heard a metallic click from behind him and felt a cold round object pressed against the back of his neck. **It was the barrel of a gun.**

Chapter Nineteen

The HUEY made a soft landing on the runway apron near the airport terminal in Saigon. Les, with his arm in a sling, was helping Boats. Using a rough stick to support his weight, Boats hobbled down from the helicopter hatch. Bill limped off unassisted.

"Why don't you guys come back here after you see the medics at MACV and catch the first flight to Da Nang?"

"O.K. You don't want us to help you brief Rudd?" Les asked.

"No, I can transmit the bad news well enough. Hey, there's a Jeep coming across the runway, maybe it's a ride?"

As the vehicle approached they recognized Lieutenant Beck behind the wheel, he had a big grin on his face as he greeted them. "You guys are a sight for sore eyes. Good god, what happened to you two. He noticed the bloody bandage on Les's arm; he noticed Boats was having difficulty walking. We must get you people to sickbay. Hop in, next stop after sick bay will be for a shower, clean clothes, and some hot chow."

"How did you guys know we needed a ride? Boats asked, then added, as he hobbled into the Jeep, "that helicopter sure was a welcome sight."

"The scow skipper managed to get off a message, through a closed channel communications link he has with Okinawa, they passed the message on to us and here we are. You guys had a rough time getting out of there, so we heard," Lieutenant Beck's face reflected his concern.

None of the three men said anything but Bill nodded his head and looked at the other two seated in the rear of the Jeep.

After a furious drive across Saigon, the Jeep pulled into MACV; Beck parked near the entrance to naval intelligence. Tom told Bill that Commander Rudd was waiting in his office as he escorted the others to Sick Bay. A shower and change of clothes was to follow.

Bill limped through Commander Rudd's open door as Rudd jumped to his feet and extended his hand. "You're a hard man to kill, it seems as though you ran into a bit of trouble getting out of that VC nest. How about some coffee and a soft seat?"

"I'll take both. I really need to clean up. Can that be arranged?"

"Let's talk briefly first, and then we'll take care of that."

Commander Rudd suddenly realized Bill was limping. "Are you alright? Do you need to go to Sick Bay?"

Bill responded, "no, I pulled a muscle getting into the Zodiac, I'll be alright."

After they were both seated at the conference table, Rudd continued, "give me a rundown on how it went."

"Well the rides up the river were O.K. I will say the fish scow leaves something to be desired. After we penetrated the VC compound, I had Barter and Vail do a recon around the perimeter. I zeroed in on some buildings more toward the center of the compound and that's where I ran into trouble. I didn't see anyone but the next thing I knew there was a gun barrel pressed into the back of my neck. I thought I had 'bought the farm'. The VC allowed me to turn around, probably to get a look at me. That's when I saw Les sneaking up behind him; the next thing I knew, the VC was on the ground with a whole lot of blood coming out of his throat. Les put a K bar through his lower neck, no sounds, no struggle. We made our way back to the scow, but it was now full daylight. We knew it would be tricky to get out of there but we couldn't sit around and wait for night. We came out of the little stream and headed down river toward Can Tho. As we entered the main river, the fifty caliber machine guns in the VC compound opened up. The crew of the scow had broken out two M60s, that they had in the forward compartment, so we did return fire. A .30 caliber is no match for a fifty, as you know. The scow was being hit hard because it was so slow and one of the crewmembers took a round in the chest. He went overboard before we could get to him."

"The VC had 50s?"

"Yeah, lots of them. They're probably the Russian ones but I never got close enough to be sure. That's not all they have, Commander. I got a quick look into one of the buildings before that VC stuck a gun in my neck. It was full of rockets and launchers."

"Give me your best estimate of the VC strength."

"From our observations, I would put it at no less than 200, possibly more. They have fifty calibers around the entire perimeter, with mortar emplacements in between. I didn't see any gunboats but they are being re-supplied by barge traffic up the river. The only thing they seem to lack is nighttime security. I'll bet that improves real soon."

"Well, you and your men did a great job. That's valuable information we couldn't have without your help. How are Barter and Vail?"

"I sent them to sick bay and then to catch a flight back to Da Nang. They both had minor injuries but they should recover in a couple of days. Our Doc in Da Nang will take care of them."

"Was the boat destroyed?"

"Yes, she sank just south of the compound. We ran her into shallow water. She had too much damage to be of any use. We took off in the auxiliary boat they had suspended on the stern, a Zodiac with a 25 horsepower outboard, fast! We ran down river to Can Tho, you know the rest of the story. I saw the scow skipper fooling with an electronic device right before we left the scow but I had no idea he was communicating indirectly with you. We were sure glad to see that HUEY waiting for us when we got to Can Tho, thanks! I can't help but think the VC knew something was in the wind. We were lucky they didn't figure it out before we got there. With the weapons they have, they could have blown us out of the water before we could land. They might have expected more then a recon, maybe a landing force."

"You may be right. Our intelligence has denied any presence of weapons the size you've told me about...damn lousy information."

"Where is you information coming from, ARVN?"

"In some cases yes and also from the Junk Force command leaders."

"With all due respect, Commander, your sources suck!"

"I can't argue the point with you but it's the best we have."

There was a knock on the door as Lieutenant Beck entered the office.

"Come in, Tom, have a seat. Bill was just bringing me up to date on the situation down in the Mekong. We got a real mess on our hands down there."

"Yeah, I had a brief chat with Barter and Vail while we waited in sick bay. You guys are good, also lucky to get out of there in one piece. They are both going be all right. I have arranged a ride for them out to the airport, there's a flight for Da Nang in about an hour. They had showers and I found them some clean fatigues. When I left them they were chowing down on fired chicken and fries."

"Do you feel up to a trip to Okinawa, Bill?" Commander Rudd asked.

"Yes, I guess so. Is it really necessary right now?"

"Yes, they want you over there ASAP."

Bill leaned back in his chair. "Before we break up this discussion, Commander, can you tell me how you got a chopper to Can Tho from Pleiku in that amount of time?"

"The 93rd has a unit temporarily stationed at Saigon, you know, to haul the generals around on site seeing tours. The unit that collected you was just waiting for something to do."

"We've become good friends with those guys out of Pleiku, they've been a big help in our training activities. We'll have to have them over for another buffalo steak dinner soon," Bill added with a grin.

"I'll try to set up your flight to Okinawa tomorrow. Tom, can you check on that for me?"

"Yes, Sir. Bill, why don't you hang out with me for a while until I can get the details for your trip."

As Bill and Tom prepared to leave the office, Commander Rudd put his arm around Bill's shoulders, "I am glad you made it back, we have a lot to do before your tour is up in October."

In Lieutenant Beck's office, Bill asked if there was somewhere, he could take a shower and cleanup. Beck directed him to an officers' locker room with showers. He also provided him with a clean set of civilian clothes. After a shower, shave, and a change of clothes, Bill returned to Beck's office for more coffee.

"How's your friendship with Pearl coming?" Bill grinned at Tom.

"She was down two weekends ago, I haven't heard from her since, I'm a little concerned. Things are getting so crazy in this country I'm not sure I can trust anyone. I don't suppose there is any connection but, she was with me here on the compound for an hour or so. Vinh saw us together and made a big fuss over her, he's an obnoxious sun of a bitch and even worse around women."

"Is there anything I can do to help?"

"Not that I can think of, if I do come up with something, I'll let you know. On a different subject, those gunboats from up north are taking a toll on the Junk Force inventory. They lost four in the past two weeks. They're getting more aggressive by the day and running down to within fifty miles of Da Nang; we gotta put an end to those bastards."

"The team has developed a plan to deal with them; we've been waiting for the ordinance to accomplish it. It may be in by now. If it isn't, we'll juice up Combined Studies for it. I'll address those needs when I am in Okinawa. How about something to eat? I haven't had anything for two days or thereabouts."

"Just give me a few minutes to make a couple calls and we'll head out."

Back in Da Nang, Les and Boats found part of the team waiting for them when their plane landed. Les had noticed one of the 93rd helicopters sitting on the runway apron as they landed.

The Chief was the first to greet the pair as they descended the ladder from the aircraft.

"You guys look a little beat. What's with the bandage, Les, and Boats with a cane? I assume it was a rough trip?"

"About as rough as you would want, Chief. We did get out in one piece, a little damaged," Les did his best to respond calmly.

Doc and Andy Kraft from the 93rd held back while the Chief greeted the two.

"Hey, Les, whats with the bandage on your arm?"

"I'll tell you later, Doc. I think Boats needs your help more than I do."

Doc had noticed that Vail was limping as he walked away from the aircraft."What's up, Boats?"

"I got the edge of one of those pungy stick holes, just one spike. It went through my boot and got me in the ball of the foot. The medic on the chopper that picked us up cleaned it up and put a bandage on it, I told him our Doc would fix it up when we got back to Da Nang. The medics at MACV looked at it and gave me some kind of a shot, an antibiotic, I think."

"I'll take a look at it when we get back to the house. In fact, I want to work on both of you."

The group, including Andy, headed for the weapons carrier for the drive back to the house. As they drove through Da Nang, the Chief leaned toward Boats. "Where's the Skipper?"

"He had something to do in Saigon, said he would be up in a couple days. How's Junk doing? How did the escape and evasion training go?"

"Junk's doing fine but she becomes more restless everyday. We think it's those VC, roaming around across the street, make her nervous. The training went great those guys could have taught us a few things. You should have seen the way they established a base camp and put together food and shelter. We introduced them to the Apache Pole. I think they were glad to get through that phase. We have them doing advanced water work this week, we're getting close to the end of our training schedule. They now have an official name, the Biet Hai Commandos. We got the word from Junk Force command. We didn't know who they were talking about at first then figured it out. The trainees seem to like the name. The pride in their accomplishments is really showing."

"I was glad to see the 93rd chopper. We owe you guys a big thanks, Andy. It was great that one of your units was waiting for us in Can Tho," Les said as he slapped Andy on the back. His way of saying thanks.

Andy acknowledged Les's thanks, "yeah, we have one unit that rotates to Saigon to haul VIPS around. It's horse shit duty so we pass it around, everyone gets their share of the misery."

"What have you guys been doing?" Doc asked Andy.

"We've been looking for potential landing sites. There isn't too many the further north you go and we figure the day is coming when we will need to go in and out fast. You can't do that and look for a spot to sit down. We break off as often as we can and come see our friends in Da Nang. By the way, we brought steak this time, enough for everyone."

"Where in the hell did you get it, the steak I mean?" Les displayed the biggest grin he had managed since their return.

"One of our admin types took R&R for five days and went to Japan. He went to a town called Kobe, supposed to have the best steak in the world. Anyway, he brought back 20 T-bones and we saved some of them just to have with you guys."

"That is what I call true friendship, Andy," Doc said with a big smile.

The weapons carrier pulled into a space behind the house. Doc and the Chief gave Boats a hand getting out and up the stairs.

"Make yourself at home, the 93rd is always welcome. Hey, Chief, order the beer while I check these two guys out," Doc said as he grabbed his medical kit.

"Will do," came the Chief's reply.

"Need any help?"

"Yeah, Andy I can always use a second opinion, I'm really concerned about that arm wound that Les got. However, let's take a look at Boat's foot first. You're up first, Boats."

Doc followed Boats into his room and sat down on a chair while Andy stood by the door. "O.K., buddy, let me see that hoof of yours," Doc said as he got on one knee to assist Boats with his boot.

"It hurts like hell, Doc. The pain runs up my leg, I heard they put shit on those sticks."

"Yeah, they mix feces with water and dip the sticks in it. You've got the beginning of a real bad infection there, Boats," Doc said as he examined the bare foot. "Do you know what the antibiotic was they gave you in Saigon?"

"I'm not sure; it was one of the cillins, like penna, amxo, something like that."

"They gave you an injection, right?" Doc needed to know.

"Yeah, it was white and looked like about a syringe full."

"I'll assume it was penicillin and I have some in my bag, but you'll have to take it by mouth, it's not for injection."

"That's fine by me, Doc, the less shots the better."

"Anything you want to add, Andy?"

"I would suggest some hot soaks for a few days, at least four times a day for thirty minutes at a time."

"Good thought, you heard the man. There are pans big enough for that paw downstairs, I'll bring one up."

Next Doc and Andy went to examine Les. They found him in his room, on his bunk."Hey, buddy, can I have a look at your arm?"

Les brought his left arm across his chest and Doc removed the dressing that had been applied earlier. The wound was on the front surface of his forearm, about five inches long and very deep.

"It looks like they got some muscle, Les. Knife wound?"

"Yeah, the son-of- a- bitch slipped one past me before I neutralized him with my K bar."

"Who sewed it up?"

"The medics at MACV, a Navy Doc was on duty so I got a good job, don't you think?"

Doc agreed, looking at Andy. Andy shook his head, nodding he concurred.

"Yes, it's good." Doc went on to caution Les, "we'll have to watch it close for infection. I think I'll give you an oral antibiotic just to make sure you don't end up with one. Be careful when you take a shower; try not to get it wet until it begins to heal."

"You are the Doc."

"How did the recon go?" Doc asked.

"We had a slow ride up the river in two slow boats. The VC compound is big with at least 150-200 men. We ran a recon around the perimeter, Bill took the center. Boats and I circled the place looking at what they have. They have plenty; heavy machine guns, some light portable field machine guns, and mortars. The heavy's look like the Russian ones we know about, the light ones I didn't recognize, probably Chinese. The Skipper found rockets before the VC found him."

"He got caught?" Doc was alarmed.

Les quickly reassured him. "For a short while, a VC had him at gunpoint when Boats and I saw him. We were on the outer perimeter circling back to our insertion point and saw this VC pointing an AK 47 at the Skipper. Boats covered me while I did a sneaky Pete on the guy and planted my blade in his talking box, he never knew what hit him. We collected the Skipper and started out with Boats covering our back. That's when he hit the bungy stick hole, which slowed him down. One VC jumped him and he did a neck break hold on him. Two other guys came out of the trees just before we got back to the river. Boats used his K bar on one without a sound. The other one got me before I could neutralize him."

"So you got back to the boat?"

"Yeah, we made it to the scow that brought us up river, a real slow SOB. It was daylight by then, but we couldn't wait around for tea time so we started down the river, ever so slowly. We came abreast of the VC base and they opened up on us with the heavy guns, tore the shit out of that old scow. The scow had some .30s on board but they weren't very effective, the VC heavies were placed behind logs. The damn boat started taking on water and we knew we would have to develop an alternate plan," Les said this with a smile and a twinkle in his eye."We beached her on the far shore downstream from the VC's. The scow had a Zodiac on the fantail and we took to that real quick, minus one of the scow crew who took a fifty in the chest, not pretty. Down the river we went, as fast as the 25 horsepower would push us and got to Can Tho, the first little village down river. There, low and behold, was a 93rd chopper waiting for us next to the bank. Somehow, helicopters look a lot like angels. They flew us to Saigon and here we are, safe and sound."

Chapter Twenty

The following Monday, Doc was surprised to see Andy ascending the stairs."You guys back so soon?"

"Yeah, we have to make a run a little ways to the south but we have a day layover. Where else better to stop than Da Nang? How are Les and Boats doing?"

"They seem to be healing slowly. The infection Boats had in his foot is clearing up, so that's a blessing," Doc informed Andy, then added, "thanks again for your help, Andy."

"Happy to be of assistance." Andy assumed a cocky grin and bowed. He then asked, "where's the skipper? Haven't seen him around yet."

"I really don't know. Boats said he would be up in a couple days, had some business in Saigon. What is your trip to the south for?"

"Aw, we go into these villages from time to time with Special Forces, primarily their medics, and see if we can offer assistance with their sick or injured."

Les entered the room and pulled a chair up to the table. "What's up, Andy? You guys were just here a couple days ago."

"I was just telling Chris we make these medic runs up in the highlands from time to time, have one tomorrow."

"Are they Montagnard villages?"

"Usually, I know the one tomorrow is. They are great people and real friendly. They make lots of neat stuff; I bought some for my kid the last time we were up there."

Doc looked puzzled. "Would you guys mind bringing me up to date here, who or what the hell are Montagnards?"

Andy was quick to respond, "I don't know much about them, they are a group of native people who live in the highlands. They aren't Vietnamese, they hate the Vietnamese. President Diem has been very hard on them since he took office in '54. He would be happy if they all moved to Pasadena."

Les re-entered the conversation, "I had a briefing on these people in Coronado before we deployed, Doc. I've since read and studied their history. They go back a long time; they've been in Vietnam forever. Originally, they were costal people but the Vietnamese drove them out of that region into the highlands, about 900 AD. Seems like they have been resisting outside authority ever since. They helped drive the French out of the country and they don't tolerate the VC, who have been really hard on them. Same story, cooperate or we'll clean you out, food, women, and what they don't take they destroy. The Montagnards are diverse, five major tribal divisions and several dialects in each group. They are proficient at living off the land and have done so for over a thousand years."

Doc wanted to know more. "What's their origin?"

"I don't think anyone knows for sure, their language has it roots in Malaysian and Polynesian so they may have come from the Malay Peninsula. Their true name is Degar but the French renamed them Montagnard meaning 'mountain people'. The word Degar is derived from the Chinese word Thuong, which I think means 'new people'. What region are your guys heading for, Andy?"

"We'll be heading south west. The Montagnard village is west of a hamlet called An Khe, about a forty-minute flight. I was going to ask Chris if he wanted to tag along, we can always use another opinion and set of hands."

"Got room in your bird for another passenger?"

"Sure, Les. You want to come, Chris?"

"Absolutely, our training is winding down. I could use a change of scenery."

"Just where is it you guys think you're going?"

"Oh hi, Chief, with Andy. He's taking a couple of medics from Special Forces out to a native village for medical assistance and asked me to come along; Les is coming too. Naturally, we would run it by you or Mr. Shurburn before we went."

"You got room for one more, Andy?" The Chief was always looking for a new experience.

"Yeah. The passenger compartment in these birds can hold eight comfortably so, no problem. We'll probably lift off shortly after daylight so we get there with a full day and get out in time for a daylight flight back."

"What time are we talking about?"

"Oh, probably 0600, Chief."

The lift off was smooth and the sky was clear as the HUEY headed southwest toward the Montagnard village in the Bahnar district. Onboard, in the troop compartment, were Andy, Doc, the Chief, Les, and two Special Forces medics, Tim and Jeff. They flew at 1000 feet and the deep green of the forest below them spread out like a giant blanket. The leaves took on a special hue as they caught the first rays of sun, as it rose above the horizon. The Chief moved forward to talk with the chopper pilot, Chief Warrant Officer (CWO) Deal, while Doc and Andy tried to talk over the roar of the rotor noise. Les sat wedged in the corner of the troop bay with his ever present book and occasionally glanced out the open door. Tim and Jeff leaned back against the hard seat and tried to sleep.

"What happens next, Andy? I mean when we get there," Doc asked Andy.

"We'll find a place to sit down close to the village and go in and introduce ourselves. Those guys," pointing toward the army Special Forces corpsmen, "have been to this particular village before, so there shouldn't be any trouble with the Montagnard village chief. In some cases, he resents strangers."

About thirty minutes into the flight, Andy pressed his headset tight against his ears in order to hear what the pilot was saying to him.

"Oh shit! We're taking ground fire from our right flank."

Doc looked out the door and saw muzzle flashes coming from the edge of a small clearing off to their right.

Andy took a pair of binoculars from a pocket on the side of his seat and looked toward the ground in the direction of the flashes."It's a damn little kid shooting at us, can't be more than ten years old. Someone must have given him an AK 47 for his birthday and he's trying it out…on us." He relayed this information to the pilot.

"O.K., will do."

Les closed his book. "What's going on?"

"Some kid is shooting at us with an AK."

Andy swung an M60 machine around on its bracket and pointed it out the hatch.

"Jim wants me to be ready to return fire but only if he continues shooting at us. We'll be out of range in a few more seconds." Andy hoped it wouldn't be necessary to kill a child.

"Kill the little bastard, otherwise he will get one of us the next time we penetrate this area." Jeff leaned forward with his fist clenched and looked Andy in the eye.

"The boss says be ready, that's the way it will be."

Doc watched through the binoculars, Andy was ready to fire with the M 60. Doc saw the boy lower his weapon and move back under the trees. "He's had his fun for today, Andy. He's headed back into the trees, for now."

"Good, I'm not into killing kids…yet."

Tim glared at Andy. "You haven't been here long enough, fly boy. We've had more casualties caused by kids than adults during our tour. They're so brain washed that they think they're doing a great service for their country... striking a blow for freedom."

"Does this happen very often, Andy?" Doc shouted over the rotor noise.

"No, only once in a while but most often over these highlands. The VC are developing a trail from the north to supply their troops... it'll be a big problem in the near future."

Doc showed his concern. "Are these choppers armored in any way?"

"Yeah, the floor has some armor plate but none in the bulkheads or overhead. I guess they figured that most people would shoot at us from directly underneath, that hasn't been the case often though. If we took a round or two in the rotor transmission we would be in a world of hurt."

The chopper gradually decreased altitude as they approached a large clearing covered by neatly placed huts. The pilot headed for a small clearing just south of the village after making a complete circle around it. As the chopper began the last fifty feet of decent, a dark skinned man ran into the clearing and began waving his arms. The man pointed to the ground shaking his head, pointing to another clearing just east of the village. The pilot eased up the decent and headed for the area indicated by the man on the ground. The clearing to the east was smaller but adequate for the clearance needed. As the chopper settled to the ground, Tim and Jeff stood in the door; their landing site was now a popular place and villagers ran toward the helicopter shouting. Jeff jumped from the door and was mobbed by children and young adults.

"You can tell he's been here before, quite popular isn't he?"

"It would seem so, Les, but I don't care for his attitude about killing kids," Andy said as he eased out the door.

The entire group moved through the clearing and into the village, with the exception of CWO Deal who felt he must stay with his 'bird'. As they walked, villagers crowded around them, holding their arms and trying to befriend them. Doc noticed the vast difference in the villagers' appearance compared to the Vietnamese population at large. The Montagnards were somewhat larger in stature and very dark in skin color with fine features, more like the people of Polynesia. The village was composed of small thatched huts built on short stilts about three feet in height. The huts were arranged in neat rows, which showed a good sense of organization. In the center of the village was a large hut that seemed to be the central focus point of the village. Tim and Jeff led the way into that hut where an elderly man was seated on a series of woven mats. He nodded to them as they entered and extended his hand. Doc noticed that to his right was seated a woman he would guess would be about twenty-five years of age. She had long black hair and a pleasant smile. She rose to her feet as the group lined up in front of what Doc surmised to be the village chief.

The first words out of her mouth were spoken in clear distinct English with almost a mid-western accent. "Welcome, gentlemen, we are so pleased to see you again. I assume these other gentlemen are here to assist you in helping us with our medical needs?"

Jeff introduced Doc and Andy, and explained that Les and the Chief were along as visitors, not medical people. The woman repeated, what had been said, to the man seated on the floor in a dialect that sounded more Philippine than Vietnamese. The old man nodded his head, and smiled at the group.

The woman then resumed the conversation with the group."My name is Son Lie. I will take you to a place where you can examine our people who need your help. The rest of you are free to roam about the village and meet our people. Some of them speak a little English and will try hard to understand your questions, if you have any." With that, Son Lei patted the old man on the shoulder and led the way out of the hut.

Les addressed Son Lie, "can I ask you a question?" Son Lie nodded and Les continued, "why were we waved off from landing in the first clearing?"

"That clearing is reserved for some of our planting. It was recently hand planted with a special herb that we use in cooking."

"That makes sense, thanks, Son Lie."

They walked toward a larger than usual hut at the north end of the village; Doc was impressed with the neat appearance of each of the huts and the cleanliness of the children and adults. Down the row of huts on the right, he saw something that shone in the sun, reflecting light like a new automobile bumper. As they drew near, he could make out the object, it was a portable Singer electric sewing machine with a bright blue body and chrome trim. The machine sat on a small woven table in front of the hut, as if it was on display. He quickened his pace slightly and caught up with Son Lie. "Can you tell me about that sewing machine? It seems a little out of place."

"Ah, the sewing machine, yes. If you look closely at it you will find that, it is a gift from your country. The woman who lives there received it from the civil aid office in Saigon on a recent trip to that city. She is quite impressed with it and wants to share her good fortune with other people in the village."

"But there is no electricity here, is there?" Doc questioned.

"No, the nearest is many kilometers away but it is an object of beauty... she can't understand its use but that hasn't mattered. Our people appreciate the handcraft ability of others because we have made all we need for ourselves for a thousand years."

The group entered the larger hut at the end of the road and found it to be a sort of hospital. In it were small woven cots arranged in neat rows along three walls. Most of the cots were empty but a few were occupied.

By this time Les and the Chief had moved on to explore the village.

Tim approached the first cot while the others waited to be brought into the effort. "I saw this man the last time I was here, he has terminal tuberculosis. I thought he would be dead by now."

Doc looked at the man, who was probably in his late sixties and very thin. He was dreadfully ill but still had the ability to smile. He smiled at Doc and the rest of the group and shakily raised a hand in greeting. On the next cot was a teenage boy with a large bandage on his left arm.

Son Lei walked to the boy's side and spoke to the group, "this young man fell from a tree where he was planting an animal trap. Our people do this quite often and a fall is quite unusual, occasionally they do happen. As he fell, a jagged branch caught his arm, he suffered this massive laceration. We have been treating it as best we can and he is somewhat better now, I would appreciate it if you could examine him, maybe there is more we can do."

As Andy removed the makeshift dressing of cloth and leaves from the young mans arm, Tim and Jeff moved on to examine the other villagers, who were lying on the cots.

The wound on the young man's arm was deep. Its edges were ragged and badly infected. The wound depth went through the mid arm muscle, almost reaching the radius, one of the two primary arm bones.

"What do you think, Chris?" Andy asked as he examined the wound.

"Wow, that is one bad laceration and badly infected. I think the wound edges need to have the debris removed and sutured shut. Do you have a sterile minor surgical kit with you?"

"Yeah, there's one in the chopper, I'll go get it." Andy hurried off.

Upon his return, Andy looked at Doc. "Do you want to do it? My surgical skills are a little rusty."

"Sure, I'll take a shot at it. Let's get Tim and Jeff's opinion first," Doc suggested.

In a few minutes, Jeff and Tim had examined the other patients, returned to the cot of the young man, and examined the arm. They concurred with Doc and Andy's analysis of the wound; neither of them was willing to attempt the cleaning and closure procedure.

Doc knew that the best technique to be used at this point would be a thorough irrigation of the wound with sterile saline solution, of course, none was available. He was not comfortable using local water for this purpose so the best he could do was to wipe out the wound with sterile gauze taken from the minor surgical kit.

After a hand wash, with alcohol, and putting on sterile gloves, Doc began the slow and tedious procedure of removing the ragged tissue along the edges of the wound. Andy assisted Doc by passing him the instruments he needed while Son Lei stood by to interpret for them with the young man.

Doc had used multiple injections of a local anesthetic to lessen the pain of the procedure and the boy seemed to experience little discomfort. It took Doc an hour to remove the damaged tissue from the wound edges and clean the wound, using sterile gauze. The wound now had smooth tapered edges that could be drawn together with simple sutures. Left jagged and un-sutured, the wound would have healed with a terrible scar and possible long-term arm damage.

"I have some oral penicillin in the first aid box, Chris. I figured you'd probably want to put him on a seven day course after this procedure."

"Thanks, Andy, that's just what the doctor ordered."

After suturing the damaged muscle with absorbable gut and the soft tissue of the wound edges smooth and straight with 4-0 silk, Doc applied a sterile dressing and used a sling to immobilize the arm.

"That should do it for now," Doc turned to Son Lei as he spoke. "The dressing should be changed every day. The stitches in the skin should be removed in about seven to ten days. They need to be watched for evidence of infection, if they show any, take them out. Do you have small scissors to take them out?"

"Yes we do, I have removed stitches in the past. I think I can manage his care and do as you have instructed. Thank you so much, Chris. He might have lost the arm without your help."

Doc smiled in a self-conscious manner, he always felt embarrassed when thanked for doing something he considered his job."You're welcome. Thanks for your hospitality in allowing us to visit your village. I'm curious about your background. Where did you learn to speak English? Not in the highlands."

"No. The French had a program to 'educate the savages' when they were in power. I am not a Bahnar Montagnard, I am a Koho. That is the region of our people just north and west of Saigon. The French came into our village looking for young people that would benefit from education; I was selected to go to school in Saigon. I did fairly well and at first, I thought I would be sent to France to further my education. It was then that I heard of scholarships available in your country. I applied for several and won one at UC Berkeley. I majored in Asian History and continued for a graduate degree in Sociology. When I returned to Vietnam, the French were gone but I was still looked upon as a 'savage' from the highlands. I thought the best thing for me to do was to return to my people and try to help them. Since my own territory is so close to Saigon, they really didn't need my help so I came to the Bahnar region where

I could do the most good. Incidently, the father of the young man you worked on wants to meet you before you leave. I'll take you to his hut."

As they walked back through the village, Doc thanked Son Lei for sharing some of her history with him. Soon they arrived in front of a hut not unlike the dozens of others. A man, who appeared to be in his forties, came out of the front opening and extended his hand in greeting.

He spoke no English so Son Lei interpreted for him. Addressing Doc, "he says he thanks you for helping his son back to health and wants to give you a small token of his appreciation."

"Oh, I couldn't take anything for doing what I've been trained to do."

The man left them shortly and emerged from the hut carrying a small wooden object. It was a crossbow carved from a species of wood Doc had never seen before. With the crossbow was a small bamboo quiver full of bamboo arrows sharpened to needle thinness. The fletching on the arrows was made from some sort of hardy leaves. The string on the bow was made from a strong, but thin vine, the quiver had a loop tether made from the same material.

"This is beautiful, but I couldn't accept it."

"If you refuse this gift you will dishonor him, it's our way."

Doc gave a slight bow. "Thank you, Sir. I'll treasure it."

Son Lei interpreted Doc's answer to the man who smiled and returned to his hut, waving as he passed through the door opening.

It was getting well into late afternoon and the entire group began to work their way back to the HUEY for the flight back to Da Nang.

After boarding the chopper, Andy sat next to Doc and looked at him."That was a beautiful sewing job you did on that kid's arm, Chris."

"Thanks, but I would have no excuse not to do acceptable work, I had the opportunity to work with some of the best surgeons in the navy when I attended Operating Room Tech School at Great Lakes."

"What do you plan to do when your hitch is up?"

"Start another one, I'm career navy, Andy; hope to get a commission in the near future."

The flight back to Da Nang was uneventful with the HUEY touching down just before sunset.

"How about a beer at the house, Andy?" Doc was anxious to spend more time with Andy.

Chapter Twenty One

Bill knocked on Commander Rudd's office door and entered. "Back so soon. I thought you would overnight with our friends in Okinawa."

"No, Commander, they offered me a quick flight back and I took them up on it. Nice people though."

"How nice? Did they offer you a job?"

"Yeah, in a way, I doubt you want to hear it…need to know?"

"Not really. I imagine you're anxious to get back to your troops. A couple of men from your team, along with the Corpsman, made a little trip with the army to a Montagnard village yesterday and saved a boy's arm, I am told. The 93rd keeps me informed on all their operational flight reports."

"I've got a great bunch of people up there. What about the assignments of our trainees after graduation?"

"From what I've been told, Bill, they plan to split them into ten man teams and attach them to three major Junk Force units to do what you've trained them for, counterinsurgency, maritime surveys, and things like that."

"I hate to see them split up but I guess it makes sense, one more week until graduation. Do you think Vinh will be there to take credit?"

"I don't think so, he's been missing for about a week. His boss tells me he is on a special assignment…some where."

"Up to no good probably, well, thanks for the coffee. Is Tom around these days or is he on a special assignment too?"

"No, he's here, but sometimes I wish he would get out of the office, he's too much of an analyst for me…makes me nervous with all the figure juggling. He is in love, no thanks to you guys," Rudd said with a subtle smile on his face. "See you later, Bill."

Bill was on his way out of Rudd's office when the Commander stopped him. "How about those VC gunboats? Let me know about your plan ASAP."

"Aye. Aye., Sir. Should have the details worked out in a few days."

"Very well. I look forward to hearing about it."

Bill went next door to Tom Beck's office and knocked on the door.

"Come in, Bill."

Bill opened the door and stuck his head in. "How did you know it was me? That's a stupid question, you're an intelligence officer."

"I don't feel too damn intelligent these days, have a seat and I'll tell you a little story."

Bill took a glass from a tray on the office credenza and poured himself some ice water then took a chair across from Tom's desk."I'm all ears, is this story classified?"

"Yes, as a mater of fact, at least confidential and very personal."

"O.K., shoot."

"It has to do with Pearl, you remember Pearl? Well anyway I told you a couple of days ago that I hadn't heard from her for quite a while."

"Yes, I remember…go on."

"I had a note from her yesterday asking if I could meet her for a drink after work at the Continental Hotel bar. I didn't have time to answer but I assumed she would expect me so I showed up at the appointed time. We had a nice chat; I wanted to know where she had been. Are you ready for this? She was in Hanoi. Seems her family lives in a small village just outside of Hanoi and she went up to pay them a visit and tell them about me."

"Tell them what about you?"

"She's in love with me and I'm in love with her. Isn't that just crazy?"

"Not really if you're sure about your feelings and you're not going off the deep end because of your relationship, you know lose your head over a piece of…"

"I haven't told you all of it yet. She's been working for the North Vietnamese Army (NVA) since she came down from the north three years ago, an agent no less. She had to tell her family because she wants to stop but she doesn't want to cause them trouble."

"You have a real problem, mister, the Assistant Naval Intelligence officer in a relationship with a NVA spy…wow! Have you told Commander Rudd about this?"

"Hell no, he'd have a stroke. I've been keeping to myself a lot lately."

"Yeah, he mentioned that you're too involved with analysis…that's some kind of analysis you're into."

"I don't know how to handle this. I do care about that woman. That's my problem. How was your trip?" Tom seemed anxious to change the subject.

Bill took the cue, "quick and hot. As I'm sure you know, they offered me a job. I haven't committed to anything yet and I can't say much more…

you understand. Back to your situation, you don't suppose that some of the information Vinh got hold of came through her, do you?"

"I've never mentioned my work to her, she's been on the compound but never in this office."

"She could have pieced things together though, just enough to give Vinh a direction to go with his other sources. He found out about our Mekong operation, I'm convinced. Those people on the Mekong knew something was coming, just not what or when."

"You could be right, but I don't think so. Do you need a ride back to Da Nang tonight?"

"Tomorrow would be fine, first flight in the morning?"

"I'll take care of it. How about dinner, I'll buy?"

"You got a deal. I need to clean up and change. I'll be back about 1700."

Bill's plane landed in Da Nag at mid-morning.

"Hey Skipper, thought you might need a ride. Get all your business taken care of in Saigon?" As usual, the Chief was waiting for him.

"For the time being, Chief. How are things here?"

"The whole crew is out with the trainees doing some last minute lectures and Doc wanted to run a quick physical on all of them before we turn them loose next week. Any idea how Junk Force is going to use them?"

"They're going to split them into ten man teams and disperse them to major Junk Force commands, to use in covert operations. It's a good use of their training but I hate to see them split up."

"I do too. Guess that's not up to us to decide though. Oh, I need to tell you; Doc, Les, and I went with the 93rd to a Montagnard village south of here yesterday; it was a medical assistance effort. Doc fixed up a kid's arm, did a good job."

"Commander Rudd already had a report from the 93rd, he told me about you guys goofing off."

"It was real interesting, Bill. Those people are something else. There's a woman up there, probably in her twenties, who has a masters degree from Berkeley. The father of the kid, Doc worked on, gave Doc a crossbow; it's amazing what those people do with that weapon. I watched two of them do some target practice. They can hit a piece of fruit no larger than a tomato at fifty meters, three out of four shots. The arrows, they use to hunt with, are tipped with some stuff they cook up, it's some sort of poison and deadly."

It was late afternoon when the team returned from the base. In a few minutes, the entire crew sat down at the table and launched into a lively discussion concerning the attack on the VC gunboats. Bill and the Chief joined the group, each grabbing a beer from an ice-filled bucket in the center of the table.

"Welcome back, Skipper. Have a nice trip?"

"It was busy, Les. You guys talking about those gunboats brings to mind a fact we need to know. Commander Rudd told me those boats, at least two of them, are ranging south to within fifty miles of Da Nang. In fact, the last Junk Force boat they sank was less than forty miles north of here. He wants us to lean on them hard and soon. Do we have what we need to pull it off, Chief?"

"I picked up the recoilless rifle the other day; it's down in the gear locker. What we need is a Junk Force cover boat, you know, one we can outfit and yet be low profile."

Bill looked at the Chief, "I'll send a message down to Rudd and see if he can arrange for one through his Junk Force contacts down there. I don't want to try it locally because that would involve Vinh."

Boats leaned toward the table and looked at the Chief. "That recoilless came in and you didn't tell me...why?"

"Because the first thing you'd want to do is take it out and play with it. We have to keep that sucker under wraps, I don't want the locals to know we have anything like that, it's an anti-tank weapon...seen any tanks running around here lately?"

Boats was quick to respond, "no, but if one does come down the street we'll be ready for the fucker."

A round of laughter erupted from around the table following this remark.

Bill got up from the table and leaned on a chair. "Do we have the beginnings of a plan to take out those boats, or at least, one of them?"

"We do,." the Chief responded with emphasis.

"Good. Let's hear it."

"We take a Junk, set it up to appear to be a fishing vessel, crew it with folks armed with machine guns and the recoilless rifle and go look for the sucker."

"That sounds too simple, Chief. I think you're missing something." Bill looked skeptical.

"Yeah, what we're missing is good hard intelligence information about the operating areas and schedules of those boats. Can we get that?"

"I'll do my best. In the meantime, work out the details of your plan, this is a team effort so let's think like a team. Next topic, are we ready for graduation next Monday?"

Ensign Shurburn spoke for the first time, "yes, Bill, all the ducks are in a row. We managed to get some new uniforms for the trainees so they will look sharp. There won't be any announcements made about the event, we don't want to compromise the group before they ever get off the ground."

"Good. Thanks, Dale. Anything else for now?" When Ensign Shurburn answered in the negative, Bill headed for his room. "O.K. I'm gonna call it a night, had a long two days in a row."

On Monday, the entire team loaded into the vehicles and headed for the Junk Force Base, graduation was at hand. Functioning as instructors had been a new experience for most of the team. Throughout their preparation for SEAL, they had been the trainees. They felt an enormous pride in what they had accomplished, knowing that the new warriors were among the best in Vietnam. Doc rode with the Chief and Bill in the Jeep leading the caravan.

"We received an advanced copy of the orders for our relief team, Doc, they're coming from the Amphib Base at Little Creek, Virginia. They will be from what is now SEAL Team Two, designated MTT 4-63. From the way the orders read, they will have two Corpsmen with them. Mr. Shurburn and I will stay on to orient them. I'd like you to stick around too."

"I'll be glad to, Bill. It's going to be quite a transition going back to Pearl and spending eight hours a day watching submarine crews splash around in the escape training tank."

"That's something I've been meaning to talk to you about. Would you consider sticking with SEAL? I already told the people in Coronado about the job you've done here and I talked about it to the team, you're one hundred percent welcome as far as your fellow team members are concerned. Coronado said they would welcome a letter from you requesting a transfer to SEAL."

"I hadn't really thought that much about it. I am honored to be accepted by all of you. I've had my career on track for a few years now aiming at a commission. I'm due to finish my undergraduate degree when I get back, I guess getting that will have a lot to do with what I decide. Thanks, nothing like being made to feel welcome! I've really enjoyed this tour. There's not a finer group of men in the navy than this team."

Bill made another stab at convincing Doc, "the one thing I can tell you is that you are badly needed. There are very few independent duty qualified, Diving Corpsmen in the pipeline, the training is tough and long, as you know, and the volunteers are few."

"I will give it serious consideration." Doc changed the subject, "what about Junk? Does she have to stay here? If she doesn't, I'll take her back to Pearl with me."

"I don't know about that, do you, Dale?"

"Yeah, there is a rule about taking pets out of country, you can't."

"What's going to happen to her? We can't turn her over to just anyone."

"I'm sure there are other people in the team that would like to have her, Doc. Since she can't be taken out of the country by any of us, I'm hoping that the next team will keep her, she's a valuable asset," Bill said, attempting to reassure himself.

As they entered the base area that housed the trainees, they were surprised to see the entire trainee group assembled in three ranks standing at ease. The new uniforms were in sharp contrast to the attire worn during training. As a special touch, each man had a dark blue scarf around his neck tucked neatly into the shirt and crossed at the throat. The top two buttons of the shirt had been un-buttoned, adding an attractive and distinctive flare to their uniforms. As the SEALs approached the group, Lieutenant Lin called the trainees to attention and gave the command for a hand salute.

The SEALs lined up behind Bill, Dale, and the Chief, who stood in a straight line facing the trainee ranks.

Bill looked around expecting to see Commander Vinh. He was nowhere in sight.

The Chief apparently was thinking along the same line. "No Vinh," he commented, "can't say I'll miss him."

Lieutenant Lin marched forward to face Bill and rendered a smart salute. He then told Bill that the trainee squad was ready for graduation inspection. Bill, Dale, and the Chief proceeded to the first of the three ranks. Bill did a facing in front of each trainee, shook his hand and gave him a graduation certificate. They moved down the line conducting the same ritual with each trainee. Dale and the Chief shook each trainee's hand. Several of the trainees stepped forward and embraced the Chief then fell back in line. When the last man had received his certificate, the three men returned to the original position and Lin resumed his troop commander position.

Bill delivered a series of remarks telling the trainees that it had been an honor working with them and wishing them the best of luck in their upcoming assignments. He relinquished command of the group to Lieutenant Lin.

Lin faced the trainees and gave a command in Vietnamese. Turning back toward the SEALs he said, "we will never be able to repay you for the training you have given us and the comradeship you have shown us. We will carry the memories of this training forever. As a small token of our dedication to the cause you have instilled in us we have done the following…"

At that point, he gave a command in English, "open shirts."

The trainees did as ordered. On the upper left chest of every trainee was a tattoo, in large letters that said, ***SAT CONG.*** The meaning of that phrase would be a death sentence for any trainee captured by the VC. Translated, the words Sat Cong mean ***Death to the Viet Cong.***

Although individual team members voiced their appreciation of this gesture, it was evident by the sad looks on the faces of many SEALs that they were dismayed, their trainees were dead if captured. It was overwhelming to realize that this gesture of appreciation could be a death sentence to a trainee.

Chapter Twenty Two

When the trainees broke formation following the graduation ceremony, they began to mingle with the SEALs. They offered individual appreciation for the training and the effort shown by the Americans to help them achieve an effective fighting force.

Doc saw Ramsey and Smith jump into one of the weapons carriers and head out of the base and turn toward town. "Where are they headed, Les?"

"They're going after the graduation present for the group...100 bottles of San Miguel beer. We managed to have it flown in from the Philippines. The air force has a regular logistics flight from there, once a week, out of Clark Air Force base. We thought the trainees should have a chance to taste something other than their local brew."

"Can I help with the cost? I haven't had a bottle of San Miguel since I was in Subic Bay in 1960."

"Sure, Doc. We chipped in ten bucks a piece, that should cover it."

"Great, I'll catch you with it at the house, didn't bring any money with me this morning."

"Doc, I need to talk to you about something else. The rest of the team has been talking to me about you. We would all like to have you stay with SEAL. Any chance you might?"

"I just can't say at this point. The Skipper talked to me about that on the way out here this morning. I'm due to get my degree when I get back to Pearl and I hope that will give me a start towards getting a commission in the Medical Service Corps. If that doesn't happen, I will seriously consider requesting a transfer to SEAL."

"Good enough. We just wanted you to know that all of us would be proud to serve with you again," Les assured Doc.

"Can I interrupt this conversation, men?"

"Sure Lei, what's on your mind?" Doc used Lin's first name, as Lin had asked him to do the first time they met.

"I thought this would be a good time to thank you again for the job you did on my arm, he flexed his injured arm, works just fine. I was lucky I didn't get an infection but thanks to you, I didn't. Where do you go when you leave here, Doc?"

"Back to Subase Pearl, Lieutenant, back to the Submarine Escape Training Tank and some less demanding duty…I hope!"

"I've never been to Hawaii. Is it as beautiful as they say?" Lin asked.

"It's spectacular, the only problem is that too many people are discovering that beauty, most of the time it's tourists from wall to wall. There are a few places yet that aren't overrun but you have to know where to find them. If you ever get there, I'll show you around."

"Thanks, I may take you up on that in the next couple of years."

A little later, Ramsey and Smith returned with the weapons carrier and pulled up to the training field where the graduation had taken place.

Chuck Ramsey called, "come and get it, all hands! The beer truck has arrived."

Everyone headed for the truck and within minutes, they each had a cold bottle of San Miguel. The beer had been placed in large tubs in the back of the weapons carrier and completely covered with ice; it was a real treat for everyone. The trainees drank from the green bottles and licked their lips. Many exclaimed they had never tasted beer like this before.

"Hey, Skipper," Smith hollered, as he walked toward Bill with a piece of paper in his hand. I picked up this message for you when we were at the airport; they had a notice posted on the board that there was a priority message for the CO of MTT 10-62."

Bill extended his hand to take the sealed envelope. "Thanks. I wonder what's up now."

Bill opened the envelope and read, 'Priority/Confidential…Your presence in Saigon required immediately. Top priority air transportation approved and arranged. Rudd'. Bill folded the single sheet of paper and placed it back in the envelope. *What is going on now*? he thought.

"Hey, Chief," Bill quietly addressed the Chief.

"Yes, Sir."

"I gotta make a quick trip to Saigon. I don't have a clue what it's about. Can you handle everything here?"

"Sure Skipper. I have Mr. Shurburn to work with. We'll concentrate on planning the boat thing and have the details worked out by the time you get back."

"Great, I'll take the Jeep back to the house and pick up a few things. I'll leave it at the airport if you want to pick it up later."

"That'll work, Bill, have a safe trip…again."

Everyone at the graduation party seemed to have a good time. It was a new experience for the trainees to mingle on a social level with the SEAL Team members, but both sides accepted it with comradeship and congeniality. Previously, the members of the SEAL Team had purposely isolated themselves from the trainees, socially, to maintain an environment needed to conduct successful training, not unlike what they had each experienced in BUDS. Within two hours, the beer supply was exhausted and the former trainees were anxious to get on with the matter of their coming transfer.

Lieutenant Lin called the newly graduated commandoes to order and began distributing written orders to each man. Some appeared pleased with their assignments, others look depressed. Many of their attitudes were the result of the physical location that their orders placed them. The ones closer to home were grateful, others realized that it would be difficult to stay in touch with their families. Family ties being the fundamental strength of the Vietnamese society.

During the entire graduation, Junk had done her usual thing by first setting close to the SEALs during the formalities, then circulating among the trainees and team members. She seemed to sense something was about to change and went about saying goodbye by greeting each trainee, with whom she had casual contact over the past five months. Several of the trainees dropped to one knee in order to embrace her and give an extra pat on her head.

The team members gradually assembled around the vehicles and prepared to head back to town.

"Anybody seen Doc?" Les looked around as he questioned.

The Chief answered, "yeah, he said he would be over in Sick Bay. When we're ready to head out, I'll swing by there and pick him up."

Doc did not know if he would be back to the base soon. He wanted to clean and re-arrange the medical items in his locker before he left. As he finished up, he looked around the small space remembering the early days and doing initial physicals on all the perspective trainees. He had felt a little overwhelmed then, now it seemed like a simple matter. He realized that in the past five months, he had grown in confidence regarding his medical ability. He had also improved his ability to cope with difficult and dangerous circumstances. He knew he had to think long and hard about requesting that transfer to SEAL.

Bill arrived at the Da Nang airport to find an Air Force EC- 47D sitting on the apron next to the small terminal. He entered the building and was immediately greeted by an Air Force Captain in a flight suit who hollered at him, "are you Lieutenant Evans?"

"Yes, I am, Captain."

"You're my passenger. Headed for Saigon are you?"

"That's right, you must be my ride."

"You can go on out and get aboard, I have to file my flight plan and I'll be right along."

At the center hatch of the aircraft, an Air Force Sergeant, who helped him aboard, greeted Bill, "you must be a V.I.P., Lieutenant?"

"No just a man who needs to get to Saigon in a hurry."

"Have a seat, Sir. We'll be airborne in about five minutes.

Bill moved to one of only six seats in the forward portion of the aircraft and strapped in, the other seats were empty. A minute or two later the man, he had encountered in the terminal, jumped through the hatch and went directly to the cockpit. In another minute, the engines were turning over and shortly after that they were airborne. The Sergeant moved forward and took the seat next to Bill.

"What type of aircraft is this, Sergeant?" Bill inquired.

"It's an EC 47D, in civilian terms a DC 3. We were out on a test flight in this area and got a message that we had an urgent requirement to pick you up on our way back to Saigon. Really important for you to get there, right?"

"That's right, Sergeant." Bill let it drop at that and turned his attention to look at the interior of the aircraft. The entire aft section was empty except for multiple boxes of .30 caliber ammunition. Swung out of the way, inside the large mid-section cargo door, was a weapon Bill had never seen before, it looked like the old Gatling gun of civil war and cavalry days. He wondered what the application of this weapon could be but was hesitant to ask the Sergeant, maybe Commander Rudd would know.

They arrived in Saigon in less than two hours, about the same as the C 119 could make it but Bill knew that the DC 3 was a much older plane. Would you call that progress?

He was offered a seat in Rudd's office and the usual cup of coffee, he accepted both.

"I hate to summons you down here so soon but what we have to discuss is a pressing matter and I need your suggestions. We have lost two additional junks in the last twenty-four hours to those damn North Vietnamese gunboats. I know you haven't had time to finalize your plans yet, but we need to move on this. Another topic is equally pressing. You know of Tom's involvement with this Vietnamese woman you hooked him up with?"

"Yes, Commander, I know about Pearl."

"Did you know she is a North Vietnamese agent? Goddamn it, anyway."

"I obviously hadn't known when we introduced Tom to her. It was just happenstance."

"Well he came in this morning and spilled the beans, so to speak. He says he is in love with her and she with him, a bad scene but out of my control. Would you mind talking to her with me?"

"I will be happy to do anything I can to help Tom and you."

"Good, I appreciate that. I'll have him bring her in; she's next door right now."

Rudd went to the phone, dialed a two-digit number, and said, "bring her in, Tom. Bill's here to talk with us now."

In a moment, there was a quiet knock on the door; Pearl entered the office followed by Tom. They each took a seat next to Bill's and across from Rudd's desk.

"This is a touchy situation, I hope you realize that, Pearl," Commander Rudd got right to the point, "to find out that my primary assistant is involved with an agent of the North Vietnamese government, gives me no end of troubles, not to mention what it might do to Tom's career. Tom has told me that you want to sever you association with the folks up north but you're concerned about the ramifications for your family. Is that correct?"

In perfect English Pearl responded, "that is correct, Commander. I am afraid that if the authorities in Hanoi find out that I have quit my job they will be after me and probably kill my family."

"I keep trying to figure out a way to make this go away, I haven't had any luck yet. Do you have any ideas, Tom?"

"Yes, Commander, I have a couple. First, I have discussed this with Pearl for hours. She feels great regret for what she has done to date. She also expressed her willingness to help us in a way that might make up for some of her acts. Second, she has agreed to marry me in the near future, we're committed to make this situation right."

"Bill, do you have any ideas?"

"Pearl, do you have access to information about the movements of those gunboats?"

"I haven't in the past. I probably could learn about their movements, but I would need a reason."

"Could that reason be that you suspect someone in the Da Nang area of being a double agent who is passing information to the Saigon government?"

"What the hell do you have in mind, Bill?"

"Just this, Commander, who do we know that is most possibly a VC/NVA spy?"

"BINGO. Commander Vinh. But how can this work? I think I see it but please explain."

"Pearl, do you know who we are talking about?" Bill asked with some excitement in his voice.

"Yes, I do. I've had little contact with him, he operates through different people than I. My primary contact has been directly with people in Hanoi."

Commander Rudd leaned across the desk and looked directly at Pearl. "I have to ask this question. Why this change of heart? I mean why are you now willing to help us when for three years you have worked against the legitimate government in Saigon?"

Pearl was glad to have an opportunity to explain. "There is a difference, Commander. I have not worked against you or the Americans. My mission was to gain information about the actions and activities of the Saigon government. They don't represent my people, the people of the north. They are corrupt and the Diem regime is a dictatorship surrounded by murderers. When he cancelled the elections, he broke the back of any support he had in the north. The night I met Tom, all I knew was that he was an American naval officer. I was doing as directed by my contact in Hanoi. I assure you I never learned anything from Tom. On the other hand, gaining information from government officials in Saigon is easy. They have an eye for attractive young women and drink too much."

Pearl sat rigidly with her hands clasped in her lap. She looked at Rudd with cool resignation. "I need to ask this, Commander. If I can help you, is there a way for me to escape the country? They will be looking for me to silence me."

"I can work on that. In fact, we can all work on that part of the problem. Do you think you can get information on those boats?"

"I will try, Commander. What exactly do you want to know?"

"We need to know their schedule and the locations where they can be attacked. Also, can you come up with something to feed the north about Commander Vinh that will raise suspicion?"

"I will try. I have seen what your people are trying to do for the Vietnamese people. That is partly why I am willing to help you. The other reasons are my love for this country and this man," she looked longingly at Tom as she said this.

"Bill, do you have anything to add?"

"No, Sir. I think you've said it all."

"Tom, let's work on this non-stop until we get it resolved. I need to make some phone calls right now, please excuse me." Commander Rudd picked up his phone.

Bill, Tom, and Pearl left the office quickly. Bill was going to ask about the strange weapon he had seen on the airplane coming down but decided another time would be better. He decided to stay over until he had some answers to his many questions; having no idea how fast things might move along.

In Tom's office, the three sat down for further discussion regarding what they had talked about with Rudd.

Bill looked directly at Pearl. "Do you feel your parents might be in danger if you help us?"

"Yes, without a doubt, they will be in danger. My father has a relatively high profile in our community as a physician."

"Your father is a physician, you never told me that," Tom responded with a surprised look on his face.

"I guess I didn't think it was important, our relationship has moved along rapidly…I had no idea it was going to take this turn until recently. Love makes a difference. When your Commander asked about my safety, I was tempted to mention the safety of my parents, as well, but I thought better of it. I didn't want it to look as though I was doing this just to get my family away from the north."

Tom shook his head mumbling, "I still can't believe this whole thing is happening, it's too bizarre."

"You and I are in the same boat, Tom," Bill added. "Where do we go from here?"

"If I'm going to be successful at turning this thing around, I need to ask some questions." Pearl appeared to be dead serious and resigned to making every effort.

"Go ahead, Pearl, we'll do our best to answer them," was Bill's immediate response.

"Your recent raid in the Mekong, was Commander Vinh informed about it?"

"Not directly, but how did you know about it?"

"It was common knowledge among my contacts in Saigon."

Tom responded in a loud voice, "how in the hell was it known, except for the ARVN review, no one else knew about it."

Bill frowned, "you probably answered you own question, Tom."

"Yes, you did, Darling." Pearl looked at Tom lovingly. "ARVN is infiltrated with people from the north who sympathize with the north's cause."

"My big question is, can you find out anything about the movements of those gunboats…anything that would help?" Bill asked.

Pearl looked gravely first at Tom, then at Bill. "I can't promise. I must be very careful. I will try."

Chapter Twenty Three

Two days passed while Bill hung around Saigon waiting for events to unfold. Primarily, what and when would additional information be available on the gunboats, with some understanding of their schedule. Pearl had embarked on a trip to Hanoi early in the week and Tom was anxious for her safe return to Saigon. She had indicated that she crossed the border at some low profile point and had no difficulty getting back and forth.

In early afternoon, Bill paid Commander Rudd a visit to find out whether anything new was known. He found the Commander setting in a straight back chair with a stack of papers on his lap. "Hey, Bill glad to see you're still around. We had a bit of luck yesterday, the skipper of one of the junk units that was sunk by the gunboats managed to make it out alive. He hid under a piece of debris and swam toward shore, after the gunboat left the area... they assumed they had killed everyone. After a couple of hours in the water, a fishing boat from Da Nang came along and rescued him. They got back late yesterday."

"What can he tell us about the boats, Commander?"

"They're working up a formal report over at Junk Force command but I managed to get a preliminary draft of the document, it's on my desk." The Commander pointed toward his grey metal desk.

Bill walked to the desk and picked up two sheets of yellow typing paper. He sat down across the coffee table, where the Commander did much of his work, and began to read.

The Commander began to relate the content of the draft report while Bill read. "Looks like they are sixty feet long, give or take a foot or two. We guessed right about the weapons they carry with one exception and it's an important one. It sounds like they carry a rocket launcher on the bow, probably 30mm."

"Did you say a rocket launcher, Commander?"

"Yes, also two of the 12.7 mm machine guns, one on either side of the bridge. That's a lot of firepower for one small boat. The boats were built in Russia, no surprise. They are powered by twin engines and have a top speed of somewhere around thirty knots."

"That makes them about three times faster than a motorized junk…we may have a problem here. The only way we have a chance at taking one of these suckers out is by surprise."

"That has been the name of the game from the beginning, hasn't it?"

"I've got the whole team thinking on this operation, maybe they'll come up with a bright idea. What about a junk for this exercise? You indicated that you could come up with one."

"Just like so many other things you've done out here, I think you'll have to steal one. Now, before you react, let me tell you that, if we send one up there for your use, there will be a million questions to answer. Our friend, Commander Vinh, is bound to find out about it. If one turns up missing we can claim ignorance…right?"

"Do you have any ideas as to how we should go about this?"

"I have made a few inquiries about junk movement and deployment. There will be a junk coming out of maintenance later this week in Da Nang. When they go into maintenance, the crew is removed and re-assigned. Often the boat will sit idle for a few days, until they assign a new crew. It would seem to me, that would be your best opportunity to snatch one. The one coming out of repair got a new engine and should be in excellent condition. The security on that boat will be next to none. Night 'liberation', so to speak, should be easy."

"Could I shanghai a couple of Lieutenant Lin's crew to help us with the cover?"

"Yes, I'll run that by my contact here but I'm sure that can be arranged. By the way, Lin's force will be assigned to the Da Nang area so that will help; he'll function independently, not under Vinh's control, taking his orders directly from Saigon."

"We'll need a location to set her up, we should be able to come up with that and be ready to go if and when we get some information from Pearl. I would like to stick around for another day and see what she comes up with, if that is alright with you, Commander."

"By all means, I like having you around, it helps to break up the tedium of this job, makes me remember the days when I was an operator."

"Speaking of being an operator, do you have any idea where I could come up with a VC flag?"

"What do you want with that?"

"It's an idea I'm working on for a cover, do you have a source?"

"I have an excellent source, take a look in the bottom left hand drawer of my desk…I think you'll find what you need."

Bill got up and walked across the room to the Commander's large metal desk and opened the drawer. He found a piece of brown paper covering the contents. Moving the paper aside, underneath, was a selection of what he recognized as VC flags. "Anyone of these you had in mind, Commander?"

"The second one down is a VC battle flag and would be the best for your needs, if you intend to use it as I think you might."

Bill moved the top flag aside and took out a red and blue flag with a yellow star in the center. The top panel, covering half of the flag, was red, the lower half was blue with the star imposed in the center of the flag where the two colors met. "Where did you come up with this?"

"Normally, it would be a need to know situation but in this case, I'll let you in on it. That flag was a present from our mutual 'friend', Commander Vinh. He gave it to me shortly after I arrived in country. He said it was one that he captured during one of his 'clandestine' operations up north…what a bunch of bull that was, it's probably one that he had at home for future use."

"Vinh gave it to you? I didn't realize you were such good friends with him," Bill said, as a big grin spread across his face.

"Yeah, well there you have it. Let me tell you what I've done about this Pearl situation. Right after we had our discussion about her wanting to help us, in effect to defect, I sent a classified message to our friends in Okinawa telling them that we had a VC spy who was interested in defecting. Their response was quick, as I expected it would be, they want her to come to Okinawa and talk to them. There was also mention that they might be able to find a job for her in their organization, they didn't say what that would be, however, she has to have some valuable information. I just don't know yet whether she can be trusted completely."

"I think she can, Commander, but you're the better judge of that. I know it would suit Tom to have her out of the country and safe, but what about her parents?"

"I did mention that part of the problem in my message to Combined Studies. They can't address it fully, indicating that something could be worked out."

"Thanks for keeping me in the loop, I really appreciate it. I have a couple of errands to run today but I'll stick around tomorrow in hopes that we hear something from Pearl."

"O.K. See you later, Bill."

The following day, about mid-morning, Bill stopped by Commander

Rudd's office. The door was open so he knocked on the jam and stuck his head in, "what's going on, Commander?"

The Commander looked up from a piece of paper he held in his hand. "Come on in, Bill, and have a seat we've got some really bad news."

"What kind of bad news?"

"The 93rd just lost another one of their birds about fifty klicks north of Pleiku. They were examining potential landing sites and a few VC got lucky with ground fire and knocked the copter down. Everyone on board is dead."

"Do I know any of the crew?"

"Yeah, you sure do. The unit is the one that's been working with you all along, Warrant Officer Jim Deal and Andy Kraft."

"Oh god, why them, a couple of great guys. Who else was aboard, anyone we know?"

"No, the other two, the Crew Chief and Copilot were new. They're dead too!"

"Can you fill me in on the details? I know my team, particularly Doc, is going to want to know. Andy's death is going to hit Doc hard."

"I'll tell you what I've learned so far. They were looking for landing sites, as I said, and evidently didn't see any hostiles near the site. They were probably hovering, judging from the reported angle of the bullet holes in the bird. A group of VC must have come out of cover and opened up on them. They took several rounds in the rotor transmission and some through the cockpit; the scene looked like they went right down. They had been out of contact with Pleiku for some time so another bird was sent out to look for them at their last reported position. When the relief chopper arrived, they found the co-pilot and the crew chief dead in the chopper. Jim Deal and Andy were outside the aircraft but were both dead. They must have put up a good fight because the weapons they carried were empty. Jim had been shot several times in the chest and head Andy Kraft had two bullet wounds, which probably would not have been fatal but he died from other complications."

"What other complications?"

"The relief crew found Andy tied to a tree and eviscerated, they opened him up from crotch to brisket. What a hell of a way to die!"

Bill sat for several minutes reflecting on the horrible nature of Andy's death. He was dreading the role he must play by informing his team.

When the conversation resumed, the Commander said, "you know the really sad part of this whole mess is that the 93rd is less than thirty days from being withdrawn. They have lost sixty percent of their aircraft and forty-five percent of their troops in this non-war shit hole."

"I didn't realize they had lost so much, they never mentioned it in all the time we spent together."

"Their losses are classified. You really didn't need to know, now did you?"

"I could use a drink. How about you, Commander?"

"Go on, Bill, I'll join you shortly."

Chapter Twenty Four

All that night Bill did nothing but think about Andy, CWO Deal, and the loss of the 93rd chopper. His mind kept playing back the events as he imagined them, too horrible to forget and impossible to get out of his mind no matter how hard he tried. He wasn't looking forward to carrying the news back to Da Nang, maybe, if he was lucky, they would have already found out. Bill thought of the lives that had already been lost in this support action in this remote corner of the world. Most people had never heard of Vietnam. *Was the price worth it* ? He hoped that the activities of our forces would contribute to some sort of peace in this country that had been torn by wars for thousands of years. Did most of the South Vietnamese really care about the central government in Saigon or would they be content, to farm their rice and raise their children, no matter what the politicians said or did. From his personal experience, he would surmise that who ran the government made little difference to most of them.

The following afternoon, Bill checked in with Commander Rudd to see what information he had gained in the past twenty-four hours. The Commander was at his usual workstation, seated by the table, when Bill entered his open door. He was surprised to see Tom and Pearl seated around the table. All three looked up as he entered the room and closed the door. Pearl had a tense look about her. Tom waved but said nothing.

The Commander nodded Bill to a chair at the table. "We have the information you wanted about the boats, Bill. Pearl did a great job on her little trip up north. You tell him, Pearl."

Pearl, tense and very serious, looked at Bill, "North Vietnamese operate the boats that have been running down here but occasionally they may also carry an advisor from the Russian navy. One of the boats is currently in dry dock at Hyphong, having something replaced, I wasn't clear on that, it will be out of commission for several weeks. The other one will be running another patrol south in the next week to ten days and will be in the Da Nang area toward the end of that period. I was able to discover that they plan to work the area as close as twenty-five miles from Da Nang and, in particular, the region around Chan May bay and inlet. One of the crewmembers told me that they often overnight at Chan May. It seems the captain of the boat visits a girl friend there."

"That really helps, Pearl. I couldn't ask for much better information. We have an excellent starting point to plan from now. We will have to get our act together rather soon to make this work. I'll proceed with the arrangements you and I discussed, Commander."

"Good, Bill. Tom, can you get him on the first flight to Da Nang?"

"I'll go check, be back in a minute."

Nothing was said as the three sat in silence. Pearl was still tense and the Commander seemed preoccupied. In less than two minutes Tom reentered the office."There are no flights to Da Nang for the rest of the day, Bill. I got you on a flight at 0600. Sorry about the hour but the next one won't go until early afternoon and I knew you wanted to get back ASAP."

"Thanks, I don't mind getting up early. I can beat the traffic that way," Bill responded with a sly smile.

"I almost forgot, personnel got message orders for some of your team a couple hours ago. Sounds like they want them back in Coronado soon," Tom said as he re-took his seat next to Pearl.

"Do you remember who they were? I wonder what the hurry is. I informed Coronado that we had completed our training session a few days ago, but I didn't expect this quick turn around."

"I can go check if you would like to know now."

"No, I'll pick up their orders after we're finished here. Would you like me to stay for anything, Commander?"

"Yes, Bill why don't you. I have some things to tell Tom and Pearl and, since you've been involved with this situation from the start, you'll be interested. Pearl, I told you about the organization in Okinawa. Do you remember?"

"Yes I do. The group is referred to as Combined Studies that may or may not represent the CIA. Correct?"

"Correct. They would like to talk to you. They can arrange for you to defect with total secrecy and have offered to assist your parents as well."

Pearl got to her feet, moved around the table, and threw her arms around Rudd's shoulders. Rudd drew back at first, then let her embrace him, and hesitantly put an arm around her shoulders. She had tears in her eyes when she looked at him. "Thank you, Commander. I can't tell you how much this means to me and my parents. I hate to be thought of as a traitor but, if what I'm doing will save any lives on either side, it will be worth it. There has been too much killing and it must stop. I hope your government realizes what a terrible choice they have made in supporting President Diem. He is a corrupt man and those around him are murderers."

"I can't comment on that point. Maybe you can repeat that in Okinawa… it might help. Do you think your parents will have trouble getting out of Hanoi?"

"I don't think so. My father has many colleagues in the south and several relatives. He and my mother have traveled to Saigon numerous times for visits and conferences. He is trusted by the powers in Hanoi, so there should be no difficulty."

"That's good news, Pearl," Tom said as he took her hand and gave her a one arm embrace.

The Commander continued, "once you're in Okinawa, the people there can arrange for a place for you to settle and keep it secret. Do you think your parents would like Bangkok?"

"I think anywhere away from Hanoi would please my parents. My mother has a cousin who lives in Bangkok. How will we get to Okinawa?"

"We can arrange for you to fly there on a special plane that they will send for you. How soon can your parents come to Saigon?"

"I will have to get them because I know a special way of getting across the border. I could have them here in three or four days."

"How do your parents feel about this defection?" The Commander leaned forward as he spoke, while Bill and Tom listened intently.

"Three years ago they would not have considered leaving the north. The principles that were used by Ho Chi Minh, to found our government, were copied from your very own. In fact, the Declaration of Independence is almost verbatim. Father Ho has traveled and studied extensively throughout Europe and your country, searching for the best principles on which to found a government. However, as in history, outside forces infiltrate the structure of government and bring their own values with them. The activities of our current regime are abhorrent to my father in many ways. He is opposed to killing and, in particular, killing our own compatriots whether they live in the south or north. There is a debate in process now, in the western world, about the threat of communism in Asia. The fact that our people have lived under a communal system for thousands of years seems to be lost on the major world powers. It may not be the best system for the west, but it is thought to be a system under which my people can live and prosper. This war must stop, no one will benefit from it, that is the reason for my decision and that of my parents."

There was a pause around the table as Bill, Rudd, and Tom looked at Pearl and one another. Commander Rudd questioned our part in this conflict.

Were decisions based on knowledge of the situation and the people or scare tactics put forth by forces that stood to gain the most from a major war in Southeast Asia? The question was beyond answering, at this point, but it was a valid consideration.

Commander Rudd continued the conversation by saying, "Pearl, I have to ask you if you were able to soil Commander Vinh's reputation while you were up north?"

"I told some of the party leaders that the information he passed to the forces in the Mekong was totally false. That he misrepresented the size and the purpose of the mission, causing them to expend extra manpower and weapons unnecessarily. I don't know if it was effective, I did see some stern faces and looks of concern at our meeting."

The Commander complimented Pearl, "well done. When can you leave for Hanoi, Pearl?"

"I need a day or two here but certainly by the weekend, Commander."

"Then I should be able to schedule a plane from Okinawa toward the end of next week, right?"

"Yes, I think that will give me adequate time to bring my parents back. They must not try to bring anything with them; it would arouse suspicion. I know they have money in Saigon and Paris banks so they should be alright."

When the meeting broke up, Bill headed to the personnel office to pick up orders for part of his team. Tom, Pearl, and he had agreed to meet for dinner later that evening.

At the personnel office, Bill gathered up transfer orders for Ramsey, Smith, Soule, and Carey. The orders required their immediate transfer back to Coronado on the first available flight. The orders also authorized these men to carry weapons onboard the aircraft, as well as up to 2000 pounds of personal items. Bill had requested this wording on all orders for his team's return to Coronado, since it would provide a means to transport the weapons they had acquired while in Da Nang. They could be used to supplement the supply of weapons available to the team in Coronado.

Bill's flight arrived in Da Nang by mid-morning the next day, as the plane taxied toward the terminal he saw, through one of the small port side windows, the Chief driving the Jeep toward the apron of the taxiway. When the plane pulled onto the apron and shut down the engines, the Chief drove up next to the port hatch of the plane and was waiting only a few feet away when Bill disembarked. Bill often wondered just how the Chief was able to always be waiting for him.

"Welcome home, Skipper. Got some good news for us?"

"Yes, some of both, Chief. I'll tell you later. Don't drive back to the house just yet. Remember that boat yard we saw on the waterfront a few weeks back?"

"Yeah, I do. Why?"

"Let's take a ride by that place and see what they have going."

The Chief took a left out of the airport entrance instead of the usual right turn and headed toward downtown and the boat yards.

"Let's not be obvious. What we're looking for is a junk that looks like it's about to go back in the water, maybe all shiny and refurbished. Let's make it look to anyone watching like we're out for a late morning joy ride."

"That one, two slips down, looks like what you're talking about, she's already in the water and looks real good."

"That's probably the one that will be our ride to take out that gunboat. I'll tell you more back at the house."

As Bill concluded this statement, he felt something being pushed into his back just below his left arm. Not knowing what it was at first, he thought it must be someone or something in the back of the Jeep. He hadn't seen anything when he threw his bag on the back seat. As he turned his head, he saw movement and Junk emerged from the floor with a happy whine and her special grin.

"My god, I didn't see her back there."

"She must have been asleep. Junk has wanted to go with us whenever we leave the house lately. I think she senses something is about to change."

Bill patted her on the head as they changed course and headed for the house.

When they arrived, Bill told the Chief that he would like a team meeting as soon as everyone could be assembled. Since the entire team was at the house, it didn't take long to get them together. In less then fifteen minutes the windows and doors were closed and everyone was around the table. The meeting began as Bill told the four team members about their orders and the need for them to depart as soon as they could get it together, no later than tomorrow. He then brought them up to date on the information Pearl had gained about the movement of the gunboats on her trip north. He added that, with this information, the plans for their actions should be finalized and the team members involved could brief him on their plan after the meeting. Next was the most difficult part of the meeting, the loss of the 93rd chopper.

He paused for a moment before launching into that subject."I have some bad news regarding the 93rd."

"Yeah, what's with those guys, we haven't seen them around for quite a while?"

"The reason for that is they are being withdrawn, Doc. They've lost too many units and personnel. The last unit they lost included our good friends,

Jim Deal and Andy Kraft. I don't know any other way to tell you all except to say it. They went down a ways out of Pleiku while looking for potential landing sites. They were taken down by small arms ground fire."

Doc leaned forward and looked intently at Bill, "Andy's dead…is that what you're saying?"

"Yes, Doc, he died along with the other three crew members on the chopper."

Chapter Twenty Five

October 1962

THE FOUR MEN, BEING TRANSFERRED, left the table to begin a hurried packing for their departure. The rest of the team, including Les, Boats, Doc, and the Chief, stayed with Bill and Shurburn to continue the discussion of other matters.

Bill took up the topic of the gunboats. "The VC have two gunboats, one is in dry dock in Hyphong the other is operational. It will be headed our way in a couple of days and will be near Chan May which is only twenty or so miles up the coast. It sounds like they overnight in that area because the skipper has a girl there he visits."

The Chief excused himself from the table saying, "I'll be right back. I want to grab a chart out of my room."

He returned to the table and spread a chart of the South China Sea out so that all could see it clearly.

He pointed to a place on the map, "Chan May is about twenty-five miles, Skipper. It's right up the coast, with a neat little inlet that might be navigable at high tide. That's way inside South Vietnam waters, if you consider the seventeenth parallel as a real boundary, other than one thought up by a bunch of politicians. Maybe the gunboat runs in there. What do you think?"

Bill studied the map, "I doubt they would chance getting into a confined area. I know I wouldn't if I was running their show. I don't know the draft on those boats but I wouldn't want to get in there with a junk. Speaking of junks, we need one for this operation, as you know, we will have to resort to our usual practice, since we've been out here, and *liberate* one. Commander Rudd assured me that the people who are responsible here in Da Nang would look the other way if we borrowed one for a few days."

"Oh boy, here we go again. Do I have to hot wire a junk, Skipper?"

The conversation was interrupted by an outbreak of laughter and Doc slapped Les on the shoulder.

"No, Les. All we have to do is sneak it away from the boatyard here in Da Nang, the Chief and I saw it earlier today."

"Did you say 'sneak it away', Bill?"

"Yes, Boats. We need to do it at night and have the equipment and everything ready to load on at the same time. I thought we might be able to run it up to the practice bay, so we would be off the beaten path, so to speak. I'd like to hear what you guys have put together for a plan of attack."

The Chief looked around the table and nodded at Boats.

Boats nodded back and began, "well, Skipper, we figured that these boats have been doing anything they damn well please for quite a spell. They haven't ever been opposed by the south, have they?"

"No, not to my knowledge," Bill responded.

"Right, we have the element of surprise on our side and that's a big advantage." He looked around the table with a slight smile. "Our plan is to take the junk out and act like innocent fishermen and somehow get the gunboat within range. Now, since we know how close they are operating to Da Nang, that can't be too hard. At first, we thought it might be best to do it at night, but that would screw up our accuracy and we might not get them on the first shot. Les and I took the recoilless rifle out to the Special Forces firing range the other day and ran off five rounds. We thought that would be the best place to do it without attracting too much attention. There's always something going BOOM out there. That sucker shoots; let me tell you, I'd forgotten how powerful those things are. We blew a hole in the side of a hill big enough for a bus. We were out about 300 yards. Therefore, any range out to 500 or so would be good. They have an effective range of over 4000 but my aim isn't that good, without a lot more practice."

Bill leaned back in his chair and looked around the table. "So far so good. I have a couple of ideas to try and round it out. We can recruit a couple of Lieutenant Lin's men. Did I mention that he and part of our graduates are going to be attached to the Junk Force unit here in Da Nang, They won't be under Commander Vinh. They will work directly for Junk Force headquarters in Saigon. I'm sure some of his men have done time on a junk so that would help us out, maybe we can even entice Lieutenant Lin to go along. Once we grab the junk and get it up to the practice bay, we can load the weapons, food, water, and whatever else we might need, and get underway. We can access the bay with the weapons carriers so that would make loading easier. I managed to come up with a VC battle flag from Commander Rudd. I thought we might run that up after we get the bad guys in site..."

"Great minds work in similar ways," Les interrupted with a smirk, "we had that same idea but didn't know where to come up with a flag. The other idea we had, once we had them looking us over, was to pop a smoke grenade in the engine space and make it look like we were on fire. If they think we are a 'friendly' and think we're in trouble, they might just ease up close enough for Boats to get a couple of rounds off. That will definitely be the end of them."

Boats was nodding in agreement, "I thought I would hit the pilot house first, Bill. The recoilless should take out the two machine guns on the wings of the bridge and their ability to direct and fire the rockets. I thought I'd put the second round deep in her belly and inflict one hell of a big hole, it might even break her in two, if I hit it right."

"Are there any more thoughts on this?" Bill asked.

"Yeah, who goes on this little picnic?" Dale Shurburn wanted to know.

"We can't all go. I think Les, Boats, and me. Do you want to go, Doc?"

"Yes, we've been talking about this ever since I got here. I would like to be in on the final event, Skipper."

Bill addressed the Chief, "Chief, do you mind watching the store with Mr. Shurburn? We really need to have someone here to keep the house in order and watch for the arrival of our relief team. I got some advanced word on their arrival, should be sometime next week when they start getting into Saigon. When they get in, I think Dale should run down and bring them up. O.K. with you, Dale?"

Dale nodded his head in the affirmative.

The Chief then responded, "I can live with that, Bill. Junk and I will do a few things. Maybe I can finish my rock blowing. Although, I do so hate to miss this thing. After all, who got the recoilless?" He extended his arms and smiled as he made the statement.

Bill smiled, shaking his head. He knew the Chief was only half kidding."We're all set then. I'll talk to Lin tomorrow and set it up with him. We should plan on snatching the junk soon, like tomorrow night or the next. Les and Boats can do that while the rest of us haul the gear out to the bay. We should be underway by daylight the next day. Questions?"

"Bill?"

"Yes, Doc."

"Can you tell me about Andy? It's really important for me to know how that whole thing went down."

Bill reluctantly related the details of Andy's death, as he had been told by Commander Rudd, and ended with the fact that Andy and CWO Deal's weapons had been empty when they were found. "They must've put up a hell of a fight and probably took several VC along with them. It really hit Rudd hard. He had tears in his eyes as he told me and that's something for an old sea dog like him. He worked very close with the 93rd and relied on their support capability. We all owe that outfit a lot, I'm truly sorry about Andy's death, Doc. I know how much you two had in common. He was quite a man."

Doc sat stark faced and listened to all of the information then got up from his chair and headed for his alcove. There was nothing to be said and, even if there had been, he didn't feel like saying it.

Later that evening Doc was having trouble going to sleep, he couldn't get Andy out of his mind. *What is this whole thing about when good men are killed, men who have spent most of their adult lives trying to help others who suffer from diseases and injuries.* He'd felt close to Andy because they had so much in common, they were dedicated to the same mission, keeping their men healthy. Maybe there was some part of the big picture, he didn't have, that made sense of this non-war war but he doubted it. Doc would never forget Andy and the terrible and senseless way he met his death. They were just out trying to find safe landing areas so they could help other people. He wandered how Andy's death and the many other deaths happening every day out here were being treated in the Pentagon. Since this was an undeclared war, how would the families of these non-combat deaths be dealt with? Would there be appropriate recognition of their sacrifices and would their loved ones be informed about the nature of their death? No one knew at this point. Maybe it would be handled appropriately.

The four team members, who were headed back to Coronado, had finished packing and were booked on an early evening flight to Saigon. The rest of the team had decided to go to the airport to see them off, even though all, except Doc, would see them within a couple of weeks back in California. The C119 was on the runway apron, ready for the flight. They helped the four get their gear aboard.

The Chief offered a final word of advice to the four. "Keep your dumb asses out of drafts and stay the hell away from Charlie's." Charlie's was a bar in Coronado, well known as a UDT hangout.

"Same to you, Chief, it's been nice knowing you. Doc, Go SEAL…O.K.?" one of the departing men called out.

Doc responded with a smile and a wave of the hand, shouting after them, "don't forget to take your malaria pills; the Primaquine for seven days after you get to California."

They watched as the plane taxied to the runway and turned for its takeoff position. After what seemed like an extra long takeoff run, it was airborne and turning South.

Les noticed a group of strange helicopters setting on a side apron across from the terminal building with US Marine Corps (USMC) markings below the tail rotor.

"Where did those guys come from, Chief?" Les asked with a frown.

"I heard they were working down in the Mekong delta but some must have been rotated up here since the 93rd is pulling out. What makes you ask?"

"I don't know, just curious I guess. Have you guys been to that little beer shack the air force guys built over behind the terminal? Let's stroll over there and have a beer before we go back to the house, sort of a farewell drink to those guys who just got on the plane."

"Thanks, Les," Bill answered, "but Dale and I are heading back to the house. Coming with us, Chief?"

"Yeah, wait up. I'll be right with you. You guys stay out of trouble. You hear?"

Les, Boats, and Doc held up their hands in farewell as the Chief trotted to catch up with Bill and Dale.

In the beer shack, which measured about twenty by thirty feet, were a couple tables and a makeshift bar put together using shipping crates with planks across the top. There wasn't much activity as yet. A few air force enlisted people were sitting around having a beer, while the bartender related a war story from the Korean era. At the bar were three young marines, who had obviously consumed more then enough beer for one day. The SEALs discussed quietly among themselves that they must be members of a helicopter group newly arrived in Da Nang. One of the young marines looked at the three SEALs and then covered his mouth to say something to his buddies. They began to laugh. Les, Boats, and Doc ignored their antics until one of them got up and staggered toward the table where the three were seated.

As the young marine approached them, he looked over his shoulder at his buddies as he made obscene gestures with his hand. "What fucking outfit do you clowns belong to? Did you get those clothes out of the dumpster, must be one of those pussy groups out cleaning up after the army. I heard they hire shit heads to do that stuff around here."

The SEALs ignored this remark, but Doc could feel his anger mounting and surmised that Les and Boats felt the same.

"You know that pussy group, the Army 93rd, got pulled out of here because they did a piss poor job. The brass in Saigon realized that they needed some real men, not those army ass holes. They brought in the best, Marine choppers. Right buddies?" With this remark, he glanced at the other two marines who gave him thumbs up.

Doc stood, "you better watch your mouth when it comes to talking about the 93rd, Private. Those men lost over half of their complement and a very good friend of mine was among them. How long have you been in-country... two weeks?"

Les came to his feet and moved closer to the marine, the other two marines at the bar kept their positions. The air force group stopped talking and intently watched the confrontation.

"So you like those army pussies, right?"

One of the other marines at the bar hollered. "Let it be, Jake. Those people aren't worth getting put on report over. Remember what the skipper said this morning at quarters? No trouble with the locals or any foreign military."

"Yeah, well these bastards are asking for it and I'm going to show them how marines handle shit like this." He turned his attention back to the SEALs. Addressing the three, he said, "who wants to be a hero and stand up for those army pricks?"

Les responded, "Doc asked you to watch your mouth, you fucking jar head."

"And what the hell do they call you, Shrimp?"

The marine was a head taller than Les and outweighed him by at least fifty pounds but a thing like that never stopped Les. The marine began to stagger back toward the bar and his buddies for reinforcement. Boats and Doc were now on their feet.

Then the marine made a big mistake, after a few steps backward, he lunged at Les. Les made a quick sidestep to his left and as the marine passed by grasp his shoulder and leg and hoisted the marine over his head and heaved. The private flew the six or so feet up and over the makeshift bar and into the wall behind it. The wall collapsed. The marine found himself, dazed and bleeding, laying on the ground behind the shack. No one in the place made a move. The other two marines busied themselves looking at the hole in the rear wall.

Les looked at Doc and Boats, "I've had enough fun for one day. You guys ready to hang it up and head for the house. Foreign military no less."

As the SEALs left the beer shack, the old Sergeant behind the bar looked after them and asked, "who the hell are those guys anyway?"

One of the air force men spoke up, "I don't know for sure but I've seen them around here, getting off and on planes to and from Saigon. They might be from that group of Navy Special Forces that was written up in the Stars and Stripes a few months back, I think they're training some Junk Force people to be commandos. I know I wouldn't want to tangle with any of them and particularly that little guy."

The two marines got up and went behind the shack to check on their buddy. He was not seriously hurt, just a few minor cuts and bruises. However, he had a changed attitude.

Chapter Twenty Six

By sundown the next evening, the rain had begun to fall heavily. Gear for the operation had been assembled and loaded into the two weapons carriers, in preparation for the trip to the practice bay and transfer onto the 'liberated' junk.

It had been decided that Doc would drive Boats and Les to the harbor area where, Boats and Les, would 'barrow' the junk and then navigate it to the practice bay. The night grew darker, the rain came down in sheets, and the roads were partially covered with water, as Doc drove the Jeep to the harbor area. The three men appreciated the new canvas top and side curtains, the Chief had acquired for the vehicle. Doc stopped on the edge of the wharf ramp, looking for the poorest lit area to discharge his passengers.

"Where is the junk, Boats?" Doc didn't see a junk anywhere.

"The skipper said it was at the far end, next to the haul out basin. That must be it down there." Boats pointed to the far end of the wharf.

"Looks pretty dark down there. Is it dark enough for you to get out?" Doc was concerned about where to unload his passengers.

"I think all the spectators are hiding from the rain. There doesn't seem to be any security on or around the junk."

"I think you're right, Les, should be an easy heist."

Les directed Doc, "drive down there and we'll get out."

Doc quickly turned off the headlights and eased down the wharf area toward the junk.

As the two men left the Jeep, Boats touched Doc's shoulder and in a whisper said, "see you at the bay… in a while."

The two men virtually disappeared in the rain and darkness as they moved across the wharf to where the junk was moored.

Doc decided to hang around for a few minutes in case Les and Boats ran into trouble. There was a small stand of trees nearby where he could park the

Jeep and wait. He moved into the area, shut off the engine, and listened. He heard nothing for several minutes.

Les and Boats were now onboard the junk and Boats, in a low voice, said, "check out the engine and controls, I'll get the lines."

Under the trees, Doc sat with his side curtain open to listen for the junk engine to start. Without any warning, he felt a hand on his shoulder and turned quickly to see Lieutenant Lin standing beside the Jeep.

In a low voice, Lin asked, "are they on the junk?"

"Yes, the one there." Doc pointed in the general direction where Les and Boats had disappeared into the night.

"I'll go with them in case there is any trouble. I'm not sure they know the harbor well enough to get out in this weather. I can help them with the navigation."

"Be careful when you go aboard, Lieutenant, they're not expecting you."

"I will, don't worry." Lin trotted toward the junk and disappeared into the darkness.

Onboard the junk, Boats had freed up all the lines and was ready to slip them on deck when the junk moved away from the pier. He heard someone coming down the pier and dropped below the railing out of sight. Lin came abreast of the junk and leaped onto the deck, landing about six feet from Boats who was immediately on his feet and ready to attack. He grabbed the intruder by the shoulder and spun him around, his Browning Hi Power at the ready. Then he recognized the man. "My god, Lieutenant, what the hell are you doing here?"

"Bill told me of your plans to use this junk. I thought you could use an extra hand."

"Welcome aboard, we sure as hell can. I'm not sure I can get this tub out of here. Maybe you can help?"

"I know this harbor well, Boats…we'll make it out."

Below decks, Les had checked out the engine, the fuel supply, and the controls. He now went to the pilothouse to see how to start the engine and control the speed. Boats and Lin had retrieved the lines, faked them out on deck and headed for the pilothouse. Les was surprised to see Lin onboard and welcomed him.

"What do we have for locomotion, Les?" Boats was anxious to learn.

"A new Yanmar diesel, probably about 200 horsepower, it should push this thing at a good clip, maybe twelve to fifteen knots. The fuel tank is full and everything looks in good order below. It almost looks as though they were expecting us."

Lieutenant Lin had a sly smile on his face in response to this remark.

Boats suggested, "why don't you see if you can get that hummer running while the Lieutenant and I look around for a chart."

Les located the engine controls on the helm station, flipped on the start switch and pushed the start button. There was a delay while the engine cranked. Les let off on the start switch for a few seconds then pressed it again. There was a low rumble as the big diesel started; Les could feel the vibration through the deck under his feet. Alerted by the engine start, Boats and Lin returned from the chart house, aft of the pilothouse, and Boats took the helm of the fifty-foot craft.

"I would normally say, 'underway-shift colors', but there are no colors up." Boats shrugged his shoulders with a big smile.

He carefully backed the craft out of its berth, came about, and headed for the opening out of the harbor. Lin stood beside him offering suggestions for the best headings to avoid obstacles. It was even darker out in the bay and the rain was now running squall lines across the bow from the port side. The junk moved along nicely under half power, probably six to seven knots. Boats could just make out the bow, which seemed further away than it really was. This junk was no exception to the seaworthiness designed into junks in general. They were sturdy, well built, and perfect for navigating the costal waters in the South China Sea.

As they cleared the harbor entrance, Lin suggested that they should turn on running lights, which they had avoided turning on in the harbor, to lessen the chance of being seen. Now that they were in the open sea, they didn't need a collision with another ship. After entering the open sea, the swells grew larger until they were reaching a height of six to eight feet, a rough ride in a fifty-foot craft.

As they headed south, toward the Junk Force base and the practice bay, Boats began to feel concern about finding it in this low visibility. He hadn't had a chance to fully examine the controls in the pilot house so he asked Lin if he would mind taking the helm for a short time.

About that time, Les came up from the engine spaces and sat on a seat just aft of the wheel. "Everything is ticking along great down there, that's one hell of an engine. How do you guys know where you're going?"

Boats looked slightly worried, "we're running by dead reckoning, I laid out a course before we left the house and made some heading notes. The problem is, I don't know our SOA with this weather, so I really don't know where we are in relation to the beach. We should be able to pickup some landmark lights and the base should be visible once we are offshore of it. There are plenty of lights around the buildings." (SOA - speed of advance)

Lin was working the wheel trying to hold a steady course on a heading of 185 degrees. "I'm concerned about the mouth of the practice bay, Boats.

It's not very wide and if we miss it, well you know the rocks on either side are bad."

"Yeah, I was just thinking about that. I thought this boat might have a searchlight mounted up here or on the forecastle but I didn't see one and I don't see any remote controls for one." Just then, he spotted a switch he had overlooked. "I just found something let's see what we got." He turned the switch and a brilliant bolt of light shot out from the roof of the pilothouse. Next to the switch, he had just flipped on, was a small knob. He turned the knob and the beam of the light began to shift to starboard.

"We got light now, Lieutenant. That sucker must be five million candlepower. We should be able to use that to navigate the mouth of the bay, don't you think?"

"Yes, Boats, that should do it. I think you might want to turn it off until we need it though. It could attract attention."

They continued at a slow pace since their course at 185 was directly into the swells and the wind. Another thirty minutes passed and Les had taken up a position on the starboard side of the pilothouse to watch for shore lights. "There are some lights abeam of us but they don't fit a pattern that looks familiar to me. Do we have any binoculars?" Les questioned.

"There are some in the bag I brought aboard," Lin pointed to a small leather bag lying on the aft seat of the pilothouse.

With the binoculars, Les began scanning the shoreline looking for anything that seemed familiar. After his second sweep off the starboard bow, he shouted, "there we go. I can make out the lights above the trainees barracks. That should put us abeam of the north end of the base in a few minutes. It's what, about two miles to the practice bay from there?"

"You've been below, Les. What would you say our draft is forward?" Boats needed to know.

Lin interceded, "these junks have a rocker keel shaped like the rung of a rocking chair so our draft forward will be considerably less than that amidships. I would put it at something around one foot at the bow and probably four at the center of the keel."

"We should be able to run pretty close to the beach to load the gear. If I remember right, the end where we brought in the LST was about as shallow as we could find."

"Yeah that's the way I remember it, Boats. Say, Lieutenant, what are the Junk Force folks going to say when they come up missing a junk in the morning?"

"Not much, at least not in a fashion that anyone will get alarmed about. I spoke to the yard Commanding Officer earlier today about that very subject. He had a heads up from Saigon HQ recently that told him of the operation and what our goal was. He was very pleased; he doesn't like losing boats at the rate the VC have been taking them out. He told me that he would report the missing craft in a routine letter report at the end of the week. It will take a few days to get into the right hands and by that time...who knows."

"That sounds like a good arrangement. Another question, these junks are primarily a sailing vessel but they have added power to many of them to improve their handling and utilitarian value. Could this one be sailed if needed?"

"Yes, Les. All of her rigging has been replaced, the sails are stowed in the forward locker."

"There's only one problem. I don't know how to sail a boat, do you?"

"You ask a graduate of the French Naval Academy if he knows how to sail a boat, really, Les," Lin responded with mock indignity.

"Sorry, Lieutenant. I didn't intend to question your abilities, I didn't know."

"Just kidding, you would have no way of knowing, but I believe your Naval Academy teaches it's cadets to sail."

"You're right about that, I had a good buddy who was a sailing instructor there a few years back. He was a Chief Boatswainmate. Had a hell of a good time with all those Midshipmen, thought they were a great group."

"Hit that searchlight will you, Les. I think we should be coming up on the bay real soon." Lin was serious now.

The rain was still falling hard but, as the night began to clear, the visibility was getting better. After Les turned on the searchlight, they saw that the mouth of the practice bay was about 500 yards ahead. They had made the navigation work and they were almost there. Now if they could get the junk in close enough to make a transfer of the gear the rest of the team had brought out. They hoped the team had arrived by now.

Doc was to return to the house, after making sure that Les, Boats, and Lin had successfully 'borrowed' the junk. On his way back, Doc thought that using the junk shouldn't be a problem since, after all, Lieutenant Lin was a Junk Force Officer but you never knew in these circumstances.

The weapons carriers were ready to go, the Jeep could be left at the house. Mr. Shurburn and the Chief would drive the carriers back to the house after the junk got underway.

The plan was to swing by the base, on the way, to pick up Lin and his men. Lieutenant Lin and two of his men had enthusiastically volunteered for the mission, Doc knew Lin was already on the junk, but in the hurried atmosphere he didn't bother to mention the fact.

As they sat at the head of the bay, waiting for the junk to show up, they chatted about the plan for attacking the gunboat. Based on earlier conversations they had had, it appeared those involved had a clear understanding of the techniques to be used.

They allowed Junk to come along for the ride. She now stood in the back of a weapons carrier and looked out across the bay, as though she knew someone she was familiar with was out there.

A few minutes later, a flame of light stabbed through the darkness from the mouth of the bay and they heard the low throb of a diesel engine, getting louder, as the junk navigated its way toward their location.

"You guys been waiting long?" was the question Les shouted from the bow of the junk as it approached the beach.

"Hell yes, we've been waiting for hours. But we've enjoyed the beautiful evening rain," the Chief shouted as he jumped from behind the wheel of the weapons carrier and prepared to take the line thrown to him.

"We had some rough seas out there, sure glad I'm not a real sailor," Les joked.

Another figure emerged from the darkness and took up a position next to Les holding a coil of line ready to throw.

"Hell, that's Lin. How the hell did he get out there?" Bill shouted as he jumped from the second weapons carrier. He understood that Lin would join them at the bay, at least, that's what the two other Junk Force graduates had told him when they picked them up on the base.

There was a small rock outcropping at the center of the beach that provided a convenient loading point to transfer the weapons and other gear onto the junk. Boats managed to maneuver the craft in such a way that, by slightly broaching the junk, he could place the outcropping amidships. Fore and aft lines were passed to the Chief and Doc, who made them fast to trees a few yards back from the beach. After loading the junk, it would take some effort to loose her from being slightly aground but this was preferable to wading to transport all the gear.

Lin and Bill shook hands as Bill boarded the junk while the rest of the group stowed the gear and weapons below in the aft cabin.

"I think we would be wise to hold off until we have more light to navigate the bay entry point, Bill," Lin said as he passed the M60 machine gun over the gunwale to Boats.

"Yeah, I don't see any hurry to get out there either."

"I thought we could run out into the open sea on the engine and then we can rig the sails, even a better low profile than running on power." Lin looked at Bill for approval.

"Can you sail this thing, Lieutenant?"

"That question came up while we were running down here, Bill. The answer is yes."

With the weapons stowed below, out of sight, and the other gear organized, the entire group was on deck awaiting their next move.

"It should be light enough to get underway in another thirty minutes. Everyone should relax for a spell and get any organizing done that needs attention."

The group acknowledged Bill's statement and some of them began to chat in low tones while the others busied themselves by going forward to break out the sails and extra lines needed to sail the junk.

When there was enough light to get underway, all hands went over the rail to move the junk off the beached position. After a few minutes, it was obvious that the junk had taken a hard set in the sand and, in spite of their efforts, it would take more push than they could muster.

"I'll get a weapons carrier. I think I can ease the front bumper against the beam and push her out," the Chief hollered over his shoulder as he headed up the bank toward the vehicle.

In four wheel drive, low range, the weapons carrier 'growled' down the slight incline to the beach and, with the front bumper padded with a piece of canvas, eased into the side of the junk. After a little wheel spin, the junk began to move and finally broke free from the sand. All hands scrambled back aboard and the lines were taken in. The Chief and Ensign Shurburn waved at the men on deck, as they heard the diesel engine start and saw that the junk was underway. They then crawled back into their respective vehicles and headed for town. There hadn't been a formal goodbye to the men on the junk. The possibility they might never see their team mates again, never occurred to them. Failure isn't a word in their vocabulary.

After all, they are NAVY SEALs.

Chapter Twenty Seven

The Chief and Shurburn glanced at each other as each headed for a weapons carrier It was evident that they trusted the mission would be a success and their teammates would return unharmed. As they headed out from the bay and back to the house, the Chief took the lead. Once back on the gravel road he could see the sun just coming over the horizon.

As Shurburn passed the entry road to the Junk Force base, he saw what appeared to be a small boy lying by the roadside. The Ensign stopped the vehicle and walked over to the boy, who he would guess to be about five or six years old. He shook the boy gently and the little fellow opened his eyes. He looked the boy over for injuries or a visible medical condition and saw nothing. He tried to get the boy to stand but he seemed unable. Without further delay, Shurburn picked the boy up and carried him to the weapons carrier. To the big man, the boy was as light as a feather. Shurburn placed the boy in the front passenger seat and got back behind the wheel. The boy said something in Vietnamese and pointed to the village that was just outside the Junk Force base. The Ensign nodded his head and started the engine. He drove to the main path entering the village, driving as far as he could before encountering a deep ditch. He went around to the passenger's side of the vehicle, carefully lifted the boy out, trying not to worsen an unseen injury. Carrying the child, he walked toward the group of huts that comprised the village, seeing no one outside, stood for a moment and wondered what to do next.

He shouted, "hello."

In a moment, an old woman stuck her head out of the second hut on the left. She looked at him fearfully, from a distance of about thirty feet, before recognizing the little boy. She ran screaming toward them. As she approached, Shurburn could tell she was very old, possibly the boy's grandmother. She took the boy from the Ensigns arms and headed toward the hut she had come from. After a few steps, she turned and motioned with her head and body for Shurburn to follow her. He wasn't sure about the idea but reasoned, *what can it hurt.*

In the meantime, the Chief had made steady progress toward the house and town, but soon realized that Shurburn was no longer following him. He had watched him, off and on, in the rearview mirror to make sure he was not having any trouble. The weapons carrier the Ensign was driving had been running poorly, for the last few days and the Chief reasoned it might be due for another tune-up. When he determined that the vehicle was definitely not behind him, he decided that might be the reason. He turned his truck around and headed back toward the Junk Force base. As he approached, he saw the other weapons carrier setting at the edge of the village but Shurburn was nowhere in sight.

The Ensign had followed the old woman down the path between the huts, to the door of what was apparently her hut. She stood in the door and again motioned him inside, this time with her hand. He hesitated for several seconds wondering if this was the smart thing to do, not knowing what was inside. The team had often wondered about the connection of this village with the local VC activity. Oh well, he was armed and would walk in with his eyes open.

The inside of the hut was dimly lit with meager furnishings. In the middle of the room was a small, square, low table that you would have to be sitting on the floor to use. In one corner was a set of shelves holding a few cooking pots and some unmatched dishes. Next to that was a small cooking appliance which may have been charcoal fired. On one side of that appliance sat a teapot with steam coming out of the spout. The old woman had placed the boy on a small cot in the opposite corner. He appeared to be sleeping now with an occasional low moan. The old woman motioned the Ensign to sit at the table while she readied a cup and saucer. She then spoke a word that Shurburn recognized from hearing the cook at the house use it, the word was Vietnamese for tea.

All of this, he realized, was a way for her to show her gratitude for bringing her grandson home safely. He accepted it as that and took a seat on the floor with his legs partially under the table. The old woman bowed and made a gesture for him to wait by putting her index finger and thumb together, holding it in front of her and smiling, as she hurried out the door. She was absent only a few minutes, but this gave him time to look more closely around the interior of the place. All the items noted so far were unremarkable.

Along the far wall was a row of woven baskets covered with cloths. These caught his attention. He could reach the nearest one with his foot so he extended his left leg from under the table and moved the cloth slightly aside. What he saw came as a surprise. The basket contained empty cartridge cases, primed and ready to be loaded with bullets and powder. The cartridge cases looked like the ones used in an AK47, 7.62x39. A few others among them appeared to be .30 caliber cases used in an M1 carbine, they were also primed but not loaded. He quickly got to his feet, pushed the cloth back over the basket and thought for a moment. There must be more in this hut and began looking intently into all the dark corners. Under the head of the cot where she had laid the boy was an old hand reloading tang tool, a tool made by Lyman in the U.S. for hand loading rifle and pistol cartridges. He was familiar with the tool since he had used one as a boy to reload cartridges for his deer rifle, when he could not afford to buy ammunition.

He heard footsteps on the path outside. He quietly resumed his seat. The old woman re-entered the hut carrying a small glass jar containing a white granular substance. *Sugar.* She hadn't any sugar for his tea so she had gone to a neighbor to barrow some. *Just like back home.* Now that he knew what went on in this hut and probably a good part of the village, what should he do about it? Sit and drink the tea that the old woman had so thoughtfully made for him.

The old woman refused to sit at the table but knelt beside it while she served him tea with sugar. He smiled at her and she returned the smile with a big toothless grin. Then putting her hand on his arm, she gestured to him her thanks by moving her hand from the level of her heart, palm up, toward him.

He heard someone shout his name from outside and realized that it must be the Chief. Since he hadn't followed the Chief to the house, he must have come back looking for him...*that's a Navy Chief for you!*

He rose from the table and gave the old woman a slight hug. She bowed to him as he went out the door but didn't follow.

"Here I am, Chief. Had to stop to help a little boy and, well, I'll tell you later."

They both got into their vehicles and headed for the house. This time the Chief did not let the Ensign out of his sight in the rearview mirror.

Junk, who was riding with the Chief, jumped from the vehicle as soon as they entered the backyard and stood by the back door waiting to get in. Once inside, the Chief saw her race upstairs and systematically go from room to room checking for the people who were normally there. Satisfied that no one was there, she came into the main room and looked up at the Chief.

"I know girl, they're all gone," the Chief tried to console her with an ear rub.

"What do you think she's doing, Chief?"

"She knows where everyone should be and she's probably puzzled why they aren't where they belong."

They both sat down at the table and began to eat a cold meal left for them by the cook.

The Chief looked at the Ensign. "What was all that about at the village, Dale?"

Mr. Shurburn related the entire story and provided some detail of what he had found in the baskets.

"Hell, we've felt all along that they had some VC connection but never had any real evidence. Now we have something solid…right?"

"Yes, but I don't think we should try to deal with it, it's really a job for ARVN. What could the two of us do anyway?"

"I can think of several things but some innocent people might get hurt. I guess the best thing to do would be to tell Captain Marz at Special Forces and let him take it from there."

"My thought exactly. Do you want to run out there with me?"

"No, you should be the one to tell him about it. Besides, I have a few things that need to be done here. I need to get the rest of the weapons packed up to send back to Coronado."

In early afternoon, Ensign Shurburn made the trip to the Special Forces compound and, after looking for several minutes, found Captain Marz on the firing range with several members of his group.

"Target practice, Captain?" Dale Shurburn asked.

"Yeah, we need to keep a hand in it even though we haven't had much action lately. Nevertheless, that will change soon, I'm sure. What can I do for you, Dale?"

"I need to tell you about something I found at the little village outside the gate to the Junk Force base."

"Let's walk over to my 'office tent' and talk over a cup of coffee. I haven't had my usual eight cups today."

The rain had finally subsided and the sun looked as though it might soon break through the clouds. At the office, they each grabbed a cup and filled it with coffee from an urn in the outer section of the tent.

"You know we are running a mission against those VC gunboats, right?"

"Yes, Bill told me a little about it the last time we spoke. How's it going anyway?"

"The crew left after daylight this morning. We think we have a good plan. Time will tell. What I need to tell you about is…"

Ensign Shurburn then related the story of the little boy and the old woman who had invited him into her hut for tea.

"I would guess there are several thousand rounds ready to reload in those baskets and we, or you, will see them coming back at us in a few days. My real concern is that those people seldom have any choice in the process, do it or we will kill you. That would be typical of VC strong arm tactics imposed on local villagers, wouldn't it?"

"Yeah, that's the way they operate. I wouldn't be surprised to find a few resident VC in that village though. There has been more activity out there and in the hills above the village for several weeks now. We had a brief run-in, with a small band, a couple of weeks ago but they turned tail and got out of range real quick, when we opened up on them. I should probably take a crew out there tonight and see what we can find. I definitely want to get rid of that ammunition. You said it looked like .30 caliber carbine and 7.62 x 39?"

"I can't be certain but at a glance that's what it looked like to me. The one thing I would ask is take it easy on that little old woman. I don't know what the story is with the little boy but she did show gratitude and even went to a neighbor to barrow sugar for my tea. I pity those people when they have no choice in what they have to do."

"I'm concerned also. Which hut does she live in?"

"The second one on the left from the road, the lane runs up to a ditch and you really need to stop a vehicle there."

"We'll come in on foot from the road and not make much noise…we do these things pretty well you know." He laughed as he made this statement and looked Dale in the eye with a smile.

"I've been curious, have you seen Vinh around? They told Bill in Saigon that he was on special assignment. That sounds like trouble to me."

Captain Marz got up from the table and replenished his coffee. Before answering he returned, setting across from Shurburn. "He is on special assignment alright. His ass is in deep shit with the folks in Saigon. I shouldn't probably tell you any of this, but you will be pulling out of country soon and Bill would probably fill you in anyway. Evidently, one of the undercover VC agents in Saigon did some reporting up north about the false information he passed to Hanoi, concerning your recon in the Mekong. It didn't make them happy and they decided to see how far they could run him up the flag pole with the powers in Saigon. Hanoi didn't want to have a direct hand in his demise so they leaked a bit of communication to him which spelled out his role in assisting them. It was intercepted and went right to the top dogs in Saigon. They landed on him, like stink on you know what. He has been stripped of his commission and will be court-martialed, as a traitor, sometime next week. He stands to get the death penalty, at a minimum."

"That's quite a piece of good news, Captain. Wow, wait until Bill hears this, he'll jump up and down and that's something for him. How did all this information come to you, or shouldn't I ask?" Ensign Shurburn inquired.

"There is a Combined Studies agent here in Da Nang. I talk to her on a regular basis, just to keep the communication lines open. She has been trying to nail Vinh for a long time because she knew he was VC, but couldn't come up with anything to jar him loose from his connections in Saigon. This will do it and the very people that will rid the earth of that SOB, are the people he has been working against, only they didn't know it. A real stroke of genius on the part of the VC, except they are killing off one of their own because they don't have the facts. Whoever planted that information in Hanoi did a first rate job."

"I know something of that arrangement but its ancient history now. I never imagined that Combined Studies would have an agent here in Da Nang."

"I don't think you ever met her, but Bill has."

"It wouldn't be Madam Chang by any chance?'

"Bingo. Can you see the connection now? The house you rent, the frequent visits by Bill, him being recruited by Combined Studies. Where do you think that recommendation came from?"

"I got it. I don't need to know any more. It won't go any further."

"Good. We'll watch out for your little old grandma out at the village, you can bet on that."

Chapter Twenty Eight

The junk cleared the practice bay just after daylight and headed north east on a course of 065. This would take it out to sea from the Da Nang shipping lanes. The sun had emerged from behind a cloud front and the seas were moderately calm with three to five foot swells. All on board had donned the traditional black pajama type wear and added a dark green hooded slicker. As they moved away from the shore, they had shut down the diesel engine. Lieutenant Lin, with the help of his two Junk Force men, had rigged the sails and the junk was now running with a ten-knot wind astern. The members of the SEAL Team mostly stayed below, to avoid being seen by passing boats, occasionally coming above deck to catch a breath of fresh air and take a quick look around. As an added precaution, they had agreed to have the hoods of their slickers pulled up to minimized their Caucasian appearance.

"What kind of speed do you think we're making, Lieutenant?"

"With this wind, I would guess about five to six knots, Bill. At this speed, we should make the Chan May area by early afternoon. I guess we'll just hang out and watch for the VC boat at that point. Is that the plan?"

"I think that's the general idea. How do we look like a fishing boat, we don't have the rigging for it?"

"Well, I'm no fisherman, but I think if we move about slowly in some sort of pattern it should pass with the casual observer. I doubt if the crew on that gunboat are fishermen either. I guess the secret is to look busy," Lin spoke as if totally relaxed.

"If you or your men get hungry there's plenty of food below, help yourself and tell your men to do the same. I'm going to check the charts and talk to Boats about the profile he needs for a shot with the recoilless. Do you need any help with the sails?" Bill asked.

"No, everything is going smoothly. The two men I brought along are experienced sailors, they both served on junks before coming into our training program."

In the chart house, Bill found Boats drinking coffee. There was a small diesel fuel powered hotplate below decks to heat food and make coffee. He had a chart spread out on the chart table and was laying out a preliminary course to points north.

"What if that boat doesn't run down here, Skipper? I think we should head north and try to have them find us off shore. There are so damn many fishing skiffs in these waters it's going to be tough to get a clear shot and still be low profile. I would like to approach the gunboat from the stern, for the best shot, and avoid the rockets and machine guns. As I understand the design of that boat, the rockets are mounted directly in front of the pilothouse. The machine guns are mounted on the wings of the pilothouse. If we can achieve an approach on her port quarter, the machine gun mounted on the starboard side won't have a clear field of fire at us and the rockets will be useless. The rocket launcher rotates but that won't do them any good with us approaching from the stern."

"You have several good points there. I guess I would like to see that sucker before he sees us anyway. How far do you figure we should go?"

"I thought it might work to just keep sailing along, maybe we'll get lucky and run into them if they are running this way. Once we have a fix on the gunboat, we can follow and choose our moment."

"Sounds like a good idea. I'll let Lin know what we think we should do and get his take on it. The information that Pearl gave us wasn't cast in stone, but it's the best we have."

By this time, everyone on the SEAL Team knew of the intelligence information Pearl had provided Commander Rudd, about the suspected schedule of the gunboats, although it was far from firm data.

Bill went back up on deck and found Lin getting ready to come about and make a course change, which would put them more on an easterly heading and away from the cluster of fishing boats that surrounded them.

"If we did run into that gunboat, there's no way we could get a clear shot, with all these little boats around," Lin said as he finished tightening a sheet coming off the mainsail boom block.

"I was just talking about that with Boats. He thinks we should steer a course north and try to run into the gunboat. That way we might see them before they see us. At the worst, we can follow it back down here and find out where they are going to end up."

Lin agreed, "I can adjust our course and head in that direction. I think that might be the best tactic. We can set up a starboard tack and come back in a more northerly heading."

"Sounds good, Lin, let's do it."

Bill headed aft and down to the berthing spaces of the small vessel. There he found Doc and Les just rolling out of their bunks.

"About time you guys hit the deck. How long have you been asleep anyway?"

"Not long enough to suit my body, Skipper. That was a long night we just put in and I need my beauty sleep, you know."

"Sleep isn't going to help you that much, Les, and Doc is beyond help."

"I didn't see the results, Bill. Just exactly which beauty contest did you win?"

"That's a trade secret, Doc. In case you guys wondered, we are sailing north to try and head off that gunboat. We figured it would be better to get an eye on them before they see us."

"Do we have any idea when the boat is due in these waters?"

"You know what Pearl told Rudd. Should be anytime in the next two or three days, Les. In the meantime we just go about our business of looking innocent and local."

The balance of the day passed, without event, and the evening brought on stronger winds and an increase in sea height. The junk was pitching now and it made moving about hard. Most of the 'crew' stayed in the pilothouse or on deck tending the sails. After dark, it was decided to rig in the sails and revert to diesel power to maintain a better course heading and an easier ride. The night passed with each of the men taking a two-hour turn at the wheel and acting as lookouts. By daylight, the weather had calmed again and the surface of the South China Sea became almost flat, except for a continuous series of long interval five to six foot waves. With little or no wind, they continued to run on diesel power so the batteries could be charged and radio communication remain on line. The radio was a cheap little marine version, but Lin was able to raise other vessels and occasionally a shore station would answer up.

As the sun rose higher, the temperatures began to climb and by noon, it was becoming too hot to stay below decks.

Boats was at the wheel and had just marked their estimated position on the chart. "Looks like we've come almost 100 miles, Skipper. If that gunboat is heading this way we should run across it before too long."

"I hope so. I don't like the idea of slopping around out here for a week. I'm glad I never had any sea duty if this is any indication."

"Sea duty is great, Bill. I had a few years of it before I joined the teams; it's not quite like this though, there's always something to do even if it is work. You had some sea duty didn't you, Doc?"

Doc stood in the back of the pilothouse scanning the horizon with the binoculars. "Yeah. I had an ASR, great duty. We were a SUBPAC command

and there's no shortage of funds in SUBPAC. We had everything we wanted, the best, if you know what I mean."

"I heard about you guys. The best food, the best gear, and the easiest diving there is. If you don't mind hanging out at 300 plus feet down I mean."

"Hey, Skipper, take a look to the north east at about 050 degrees. It looks like a grey boat on the horizon, could be our friend," Doc said, handing the binoculars to Bill.

Bill took the binoculars and brought them up to look at what Doc was referring to. "Hot shit, I think that's our baby going like a bat out of hell. It must be doing thirty knots and then some."

"At that speed we won't be more than a blur on the horizon. What do you think, Doc?"

"I think you got it right, Boats."

They continued to watch the object, which now came into clear view, although it was still miles to the east of them on a southerly course and moving so fast it would soon fade out of sight.

"Looks to me like their heading for Chan May, sure as hell, Skipper," Boats declared.

"They're on the right course it seems, Boats. I think we should slowly come about and follow them at a long distance. I just hope we can keep them in sight."

"Unless they slow down a lot, that isn't going to work. I think they'll have to let off some to get through all those little fishing boats we left behind a while ago," Doc observed as he brought the binoculars back up to his eyes to follow the progress of the gunboat.

Then Boats added, "those Russian boats are fast. They're not pretty but they're built like a brick shit house. I saw some like that one in Cuba, you know when." Without further comment, Boats spun the wheel to starboard to set up a heading for a gradual arching turn back to the south and increased the throttle setting to 'all ahead full'. This course change would gradually bring them to a heading of 190 degrees.

"Hey, Boats. Watching this thing, I get the feeling of picking a fight with a destroyer in an aluminum canoe with a Beebe gun."

"Not to worry, Doc. We've got plenty of firepower, with the right range and a good angle. Those boats are made of steel, unlike our WW II torpedo boats that were made of plywood. That one looks like its running gasoline engines, not enough smoke for diesels at that speed."

Back on deck, Bill stood next to Lin as they both watched the gunboat speed south.

"Was that a junk that passed abeam of us a while back?" Bill asked Lin.

"Yeah, it was one of ours on a southerly heading. They run supplies along the coast to our forces on garrison duty. That's one of the reasons for the gunboats you know. They take out as many as they can, up until now, they have been unopposed."

"How do they tell the good guys from the bad? They have junks running the coast as well," Bill asked with a concerned look.

"I can give you several answers to that, for one thing, all of our junks carry a hull I.D. number on a plate, on the bow. It has been suggested that those be removed because they're a dead giveaway, but nothing has been done yet. If you noticed, this junk doesn't have any of those numbers. I took the liberty of removing them yesterday before Boats and Les 'lifted' this junk. *Lifted* is the right word isn't it? I'm never quite sure when it comes to your slang."

"Yes, that's right. English is a hard language to learn."

The speed of the junk was now well up and the seas had shifted to off the port quarter, this added even more to the engines top end. The junk was approaching fourteen knots as best Boats could estimate. All eyes were still on the gunboat that had now slowed, as it worked its way through the myriad of small fishing boats off shore from Chan May. Boats estimated the range to be about six miles.

Then suddenly there was a bright flash of light just ahead of the gunboat and an orange fireball spewed skyward from an object that had obviously exploded.

"They got that junk we were talking about a minute ago, Bill."

"Sure as hell did, son of a bitch. It looked like a rocket judging from the bright light it gave off, that rotten bastard."

"Should we go in to see if there are any survivors?" Lin asked.

"No, probably not without tipping our hand, they would spot us in a minute. If there are any survivors, there are plenty of fishing boats around to help. In the past there have been damn few survivors."

Bill went immediately to the pilothouse to advise Boats. "Better back off on the speed, we don't want to get any closer to that bastard for now."

By this time, everyone onboard the junk was out on deck watching the action of the gunboat. Although there was considerable time delay of the sound, they could hear the bark of the big .50 caliber machine guns as they worked over what little was left of the junk they had just blown up.

"We gotta give that bastard some of his own medicine, Doc. Jesus Christ, that damn junk never had a prayer." Bill hit the bulkhead with his fist as he spoke.

"It seems the South Vietnamese are powerless to do anything about it. When are they going to wise up and get some protection for their junks?" Doc asked knowing it was a rhetorical question.

"They had better do it soon. We can help a little now but there will be more and, until they learn how to defend themselves, it will be wholesale slaughter, as it has been for the past several months," Bill responded.

They took turns watching through the binoculars, as the gunboat circled the area where the junk had gone down. The VC were obviously looking for survivors, who they could machine gun, but the guns were silent. It was a total and complete kill.

Later that afternoon, Lin re-rigged the sails and set a course for Mui Chan May Dong (Chan May), in order to be in the area when the gunboat returned. The course it had taken from the site where it sank the junk, was in the opposite direction of Chan May and it looked as though they were headed for Lang Co, down the coast another ten or so miles.

Bill was in the pilothouse with Lin as they both looked over the chart to determine the best position to spend the night. "I can't understand why they are headed that direction, it will bring them even closer to Da Nang," Bill said as he refolded the chart.

Lin looked at him carefully. "They may be looking for another target before they head in for the night. Going closer to Da Nang would increase their chances."

"I hope you're wrong. I can't wait to get at that son of a bitch."

Right before dark, they had seen the gunboat running north and put in at the first pier on the south side of Chan May harbor. The plan was to hit the gunboat in the morning as soon as it cleared the harbor, when the crew was still getting organized. Everything was ready for the action that would come in the morning.

During the night, each man took his turn at the wheel and tending the sails. There was little wind now, so the sails were not much of a chore. In fact, there was little movement of the junk as it drifted slowly with the tide, still a few miles off Chan May.

Daylight was just breaking and the crew of the junk assembled what they could find for their first meal of the day. The day looked as though it would be sunny with light wind and no apparent rain as yet. They had rigged in the sails and started the engine. The junk was lying about three miles off Chan May with the engine mostly at idle. As the visibility improved, Bill and Lin were in the pilothouse watching the pier where the gunboat had moored overnight. Les and Boats had broken out the recoilless rifle and M60 machine gun, placing them in a handy position just inside the pilothouse door. The two Junk Force sailors busied themselves on deck, primarily to keep up appearances.

Bill was looking through the binoculars. He turned and handed them to Lin and said, "I see movement on the boat and it looks like they lit off the engines, I think that is exhaust I see coming out the stern."

Lin took the glasses and looked long at the boat. "Yes, I think I see someone in the pilothouse and they are singling up the lines."

"Let's come about and head north. They may think we are trying to get away." Lin headed for the wheel as he added, "what do you think, Bill?"

"It's worth a try. Les, do you have that smoke grenade planted in the engine space?"

'Yeah, Skipper. I did that last night just in case we got an early start."

The gunboat had taken in all its lines and was backing away from the pier. When about two boat lengths back, it came about and headed on a southeasterly course and away from the junk.

"Those bastards haven't seen us or they're not interested. I don't get it, Bill."

"Give them a little time, Lin, they'll have to see us soon. What's our heading, Boats?"

"Our course is due north our speed is all ahead full."

The gunboat had cleared the harbor and slowed to about one-third speed. Then it altered course and began to head north, directly astern of the junk.

"They're coming, guys, and picking up speed. Doc, why don't you take the wheel when Boats and Les man the recoilless rifle. You can handle a boat, right?"

"Yes, Bill. I am a sailor you know," Doc said with a little jest in his voice.

"If they come up on our starboard side, try to steer under them and come up from behind. Got it?"

Doc looked directly at Bill and nodded his head.

The gunboat was coming on fast, closing the distance between them in short order. One of the Junk Force sailors, at Lin's command, ran up the VC battle flag on the main mast. Les scrambled below and in a minute, there was black smoke billowing out of the engine space. The gunboat slowed and headed to come alongside of the junk. As they passed at about 100 yards, Doc spun the wheel to come astern of them, which would take the junk to a position off the gunboat's port quarter.

"They haven't manned the machine guns yet but be ready, guys. Slow your speed, Doc," Bill hollered as he moved into the pilothouse.

The junk settled into the water, as the speed dropped from all ahead to about half throttle. The gunboat also reduced speed but kept on a straight course heading. A man on the gunboat appeared next to the pilothouse with binoculars and began scanning the junk from stem to stern. The junk was in almost perfect position for the shot. Boats, with the recoilless rifle and Les with three rounds at the ready, stepped out from behind the wing of the pilothouse as the recoilless came to Boat's shoulder.

From inside the pilothouse, the firing sounded like a puff-ca-boom. The men on the gunboat were now racing for their stations and four headed for the machine guns on the wings of the pilothouse.

Everyone on the junk watched as the white tail of the round from the recoilless rifle passed fifteen feet over the pilothouse and landed in the sea about 2000 yards on the far side. The .50 calibers on the gunboat were now manned and were about to open fire. Bill grabbed the M60 and took it to the front corner of the pilothouse, where he would have some protection if the gunboat returned fire.

"I can't believe I missed that fucker. We took a roll from those damn ground swells just as I squeezed the trigger. I need to get another shot at her before all hell breaks loose with those .50 calibers." Boats let his words reduce the tension as Les prepared another round.

The men on the gunboat were now positioning their guns to fire on the junk, but they had a difficult situation. The gunboat was heading away from the junk, which was now on it's stern, the starboard gun could not get a clear field of fire with the pilothouse in front of it. The port side machine gun had to swing a rearward arc that would place the muzzle blast adjacent to the open pilothouse door. Before the port side machine gun could open fire, there was another puff-ca-boom. The range was now no more then seventy-five yards. In an instant, the entire bridge of the gunboat disappeared in a flash of yellow fire and a resounding boom. The shot had done as hoped and took out the entire pilothouse and the machine guns on either side of it. How many men went with the structure would never be known. Boats fired the third shot. This round hit the boat dead center just above the waterline. On impact, what remained of the Russian built gunboat rose into the air, broke in the middle, and the pieces fell back into the sea. On close observation, it was obvious that none of the crew had survived the attack.

Boats looked at Les. "I got the goddamn fuel tank on the third shot. I was guessing at its location, I figured it would be close to the engine spaces. The Russians build them strong, but they're not too fussy on sophistication. They wouldn't run more fuel line than necessary."

"That's one down and one to go, Lin. The other one may not be out of the repair yard in Haiphong in time for us to take a crack at it. I think we can leave that for another day," Bill said as he leaned against the side of the pilothouse and looked out to sea.

As was the case following the earlier ambush of the VC outside the village, there was little talk of the success of the attack. From the expression on their faces, the SEALs did not enjoy the idea of taking human life and had little inclination to discuss it. The junk came about and headed for Da Nang.

Chapter Twenty Nine

After the encounter with the gunboat, Bill decided to hang loose and take their time returning to Da Nang. It was now mid-morning and he thought an after dark return would avoid going to the practice bay to offload their gear. With the diesel engine thumping along at half speed, the crew relaxed and pretended it was a one day cruise. The sea was calm and the sun was bright, a great day to be on the water. As they got nearer to Da Nang, Lin turned on the small ship to shore radio and began attempting to raise the officer in charge of the junk repair facility in Da Nang. After several attempts, a voice came up on the radio and Lin recognized it as the man he had spoken with before they took the junk. Bill was concerned about making any statements over an open circuit radio that might be listened to by people they didn't want to know their identity. When Lin was certain to whom he was speaking, the language changed from Vietnamese to a language Bill didn't immediately recognize. Doc perked up and began to smile.

"Do you recognize that 'lingo', Doc?"

"Sure do. It's Japanese; I didn't know Lin was fluent in that language."

"I didn't either but he sure is making it sound convincing."

When Lin finished the conversation he replaced the microphone on its hook and turned to Bill, "I didn't want to compromise our conversation and I learned that the officer in charge spoke Japanese so I though that would be a good language to use…worked out fine."

"I wasn't aware that you were fluent in Japanese. What did you tell him?"

"I'm not fluent; I know just enough to get along when it stays simple. My father had a man on our plantation who had been a prisoner of the Japanese during WW II and that's where he learned it, he taught it to me but that was several years ago, I haven't used it much since. To answer your question, I said we would be in after dark, for security reasons and that his junk was unharmed with no damage. I also indicated that our little trip was a success and asked him if he could get word to Ensign Shurburn or the Chief to let them know of our ETA."

Bill was grateful. "Thanks, Lin. I was wondering how we were going to let the men know we were back. I'll bet he was pleased that he has one less gunboat to worry about."

"Yes, he said there will be something waiting for us when we get in."

They arrived well after dark and placed the junk in the exact same slip. As they approached the pier, the Chief and Mr. Shurburn were there to take the lines and help secure the junk. All hands quickly removed the weapons and other gear, loading it in the weapons carriers the two men had arrived in.

As they loaded the gear, Les noticed a case of Vietnamese beer setting inside the tailgate. "Where did this come from, Chief?"

"The officer in charge of the repair shop brought it out and threw it in just as we arrived. He said it was a present for a job well done!"

Ensign Shurburn sat next to Bill, in the front seat, while the Chief drove. "I swung by the communications center at the airport this afternoon, Bill, and picked up the message traffic. There are some things in there you'll be interested in." He handed Bill a folder containing several sheets of paper and a small penlight.

Bill opened the folder and began to read as the Chief drove the weapons carrier with all aboard toward the house. In the folder, Bill found a message from the Chief of Naval Personnel informing him that his Chief had been selected for Senior Chief (E8). He looked at Shurburn when he had read this message and Shurburn shook his head 'No', indicating he had not told the Chief of his selection. The next sheet held a message from Commander Rudd asking for a full report on their 'hunting trip', when they returned. The message also included the fact that Pearl had been successfully extracted from the country along with her parents. Also, in the folder was a small envelope, hand addressed, and labeled 'Lieutenant Evans - Eyes-Only'. There was no return address on the envelope and no postage had been affixed. Bill opened the envelope and read the one line note. 'It is very important that you contact me upon your return', signed Madam Chang. *How the hell did she know I was away*, Bill thought as he refolded the note and placed it in the envelope.

"Anything hot in that note, Bill?"

"I don't know until I go see her, Dale."

"Ah, Madam Chang, no doubt."

When they arrived at the house, Doc took the Jeep and drove Lieutenant Lin and the two sailors to the Junk Force base. He shook their hands and thanked them for helping with the mission. All three embraced him before heading into the barracks. Doc realized that he might never see these men again but knew that they had the training and stamina to give the VC hell.

Back at the house, Les and Boats busied themselves by cleaning and stowing the weapons. When this was done, they headed for their rooms and the shower. The cook had stayed late that night and prepared an excellent dinner for the team. It consisted of pork chops, scalloped potatoes, and of course, egg plant. They never discovered the source of the pork chops but they tasted like real pork.

After a shower and change of clothes, Bill headed for Madam Chang's house. He was away about thirty minutes. When he entered the back door he was met on the stairs by Ensign Shurburn.

"What's the big secret?"

"Let's get the guys together, I have some interesting news."

When they were all seated around the table, Bill took the message from the Chief of Naval Personnel and laid it in front of the Chief. "Congratulation, Senior Chief Volkert!"

The Chief looked at him, puzzled, picked up the message and read it. A big smile came across his face as he said, "well I'll be damned, I passed that test after all. I never thought I would see this day. Promotions tend to be a little slow in my rating and I suspect even more so when you're with the teams. This is quite a day. I get promoted to E8 and finished splitting that rock, out at the base, in the same twenty-four hours."

Everyone around the table got up and passed by the Chief shaking his hand.

"What should we call you now, Chief?" Les asked with a firm pat on the Chief's back.

"I still go by my same title. Chief will do just fine, men."

Junk must have been confused by the unusual behavior, as she suddenly stood up, raised her head in the air, and let out a howl. She sounded almost like a wolf. Doc reassured her, giving her caring pats on the head.

The Chief smiled at Doc and shook his head. He knew Doc wasn't the only one having difficulty with the fact that Junk would be left behind.

After the congratulations, when everyone had settled back at the table, Bill continued with his briefing. "I need to send a report to Commander Rudd. Do any of you have anything in particular you want in that report?"

"Yeah, Skipper. I think we should advise Rudd that he should strongly encourage the Junk Force Command to buy some weapons to outfit their junks. We saw how vulnerable they are, sitting ducks." Boats pushed his chair back from the table with a look of disgust on his face as he spoke.

Les joined the discussion, "I agree, Boss. They won't have a team like ours to fight their battles for them. They need to defend themselves. I have a thing about wiping out a whole command without ever seeing the men we killed. I don't mind killing, when our people or our country are in jeopardy, but killing in this non-war war for someone else just strikes me as wrong. I'm not going soft, you asked and that's how I feel. Maybe as this thing develops and we get deeper involved it will change. Why are we here anyway? We are supposed to be advisors not mercenaries."

"I think you both made good points." Bill gave his head a slight shake before continuing, "I don't have the answers and Rudd probably doesn't either. I do wonder why we are involved as deeply as we are. I can see training these people to defend themselves and we have done a good job of that. I took on this mission because Rudd had no other resource, he knows our capability to do the tough things. I would guess that future SEALs will be involved in things like this and even more so as time goes along. However, I agree, it needs to be action involving protecting our country and our way of life… maybe we just don't have the big picture. Things being as they are, enough of that for now.

Bill looked around the table to make sure he had everyone's attention. "I have some interesting news about our next-door neighbors. Vinh has been charged as a traitor and will soon stand trial by courts martial in Saigon. During his interrogation, he spilled the beans on his VC contacts in this area, Madam Chang told me this evening. People in Combined Studies advised her that he identified the folks next door as one of his primary conduits, for getting information back to the VC. Seems they have been at it since they came in country over three years ago. Our suspicions have been confirmed, those 'prayer meetings' were heavily attended by VC representatives from all over the area. Several of them had direct communication with Hanoi."

"Well I'll be damned," the Chief said as he looked around the table, "that would explain a lot about the gathering of 'Gooks' across the street."

"That's why Madam Chang wanted to give me a heads up ASAP. There will be a unit of the Saigon security police hitting town early tomorrow and she wanted to let me know what to expect before it happens."

Doc instantly questioned, "how does Madam Chang get information from Combined Studies unless she is… you don't need to answer that, Boss."

"That's O.K., Doc. I thought some of you might have figured it out with all my meetings. I did learn a lot about Mandarin Chinese dialect but that wasn't all the lessons were about. Show and tell time isn't it?" Bill said with a smile.

Bill continued, "our replacements, SEAL Team 2 MTT 4-63, will start arriving in Saigon in two days. I'll go down and meet them since I need to brief Rudd about our little foray with the VC. and I would rather brief him in person. I had asked Mr. Shurburn to go if we were still out chasing VC gunboats, since that's been taken care of, I'll go. I understand the SEALs will arrive in two increments, the second increment will accompany a pallet of equipment and weapons. Seems they're coming loaded for bear. Too bad, we didn't have some of that gear when we came. Oh well, next time? While I'm in Saigon, the rest of you can help the Chief get the remainder of our gear packed up and get the vehicles squared away for our replacements. They'll need vehicles. We should pass along the ones we have. Doc, the Corpsmen will be in the first increment. I would like you to brief them about the process you followed. This will all be new to them."

"I sure as hell hope they can handle the workload. I wonder where they came up with those guys?" Doc said in a joking manner. "What about Junk? Will we also pass her along?" too?" Doc had become very attached to Junk.

"I guess so, since none of us can take her home with us. Junk will be as valuable to them as she was to us." Bill attempted to reassure Doc.

Junk had been lying near the end of the table, upon hearing her name, she looked at Bill and made her usual rounds around the table greeting each man as she passed him.

"I have another question. What will happen to our neighbors?" Doc asked.

"As I understand it, Doc, they will have their visas pulled, if they haven't been already, and they will be expelled from the country. The State Department has a few questions for them about aiding and abetting an enemy of an ally. Not treason exactly, but very unpopular as foreign relations go, they could get some jail time out of it. I doubt if they'll be offered a church in the states. Maybe one in Hanoi?"

The entire group laughed at this remark and then headed for their rooms. It had been a long three days.

Bill caught the first flight to Saigon the following morning and ran into Lieutenant Beck as he was entering his office in the intelligence complex.

"Hey, Bill. Welcome back from your trip. Come on in and we can chat a minute. The Commander is tied up now, he told me to keep an eye out for you. We didn't know when you would make it down, thought it would be soon after your return."

The two men entered Beck's office and poured themselves a cup of coffee from the server on the side table.

Bill took a seat across from the desk and leaned back with a sigh."Well we did it. I don't think the skipper of that gunboat ever did figure us out, if he did, it was already too late. Petty Officer Vail, Boats as we call him, missed on his first shot with the recoilless. By that time, it was beginning to dawn on the crew of the gunboat that something wasn't exactly right. They were ready to open up with their .50s just as Vail hit them with the second shot.

That did it. He took off the pilothouse and both .50s with that shot. The next and final shot went into her guts and she blew sky high, probably got the fuel tanks. She was fueled with gasoline as opposed to diesel, not a good choice in that situation. The best part is that they never laid a hand on us. No damage to the junk or any of us. I don't imagine it will be that clean the next time someone tries to take out one of those things." Bill finally wound down and took a deep breath.

"That's really great news, I'm sure the Commander will be flying high when he hears it. When is the remainder of your crew heading back to the states?"

"We're just waiting for our replacements to arrive, we'll brief them and then we're gone. I'm going to hold Doc for an extra day or so to give him time to work through all the things the incoming Corpsmen will need to know to function."

Tom Beck nodded in understanding, then proceeded to tell Bill how much he had enjoyed the time they had spent together . He added that the time he spent with the team had been great and gave them credit for finding Pearl for him.

Bill asked with interest, "how's Pearl? I understand she's getting settled in Okinawa."

"I flew over there last weekend and spent two days with her. The place they gave her isn't real fancy but it's better than anyplace she could go in this country. Combined Studies has a regular flight that goes to Okinawa on Friday afternoon and comes back on Monday morning, works just great. I should be able to get over a couple weekends a month."

"So, do you have any long range plans?"

"We haven't quite gotten to that point yet. I do want to spend the rest of my life with that woman, she's so special to me. How about your future, is there a place for Combined Studies in it?"

"I haven't made that turn in the road quite yet. There are many things to consider and I've been too busy to spend much time on it. It's an attractive offer but, the navy has done so much for me, I don't know if I want to desert the ship."

The phone rang and Lieutenant Beck picked it up.

"The Commander is ready to see you now. I'll go in with you."

Commander Rudd greeted Bill with his hand held out."Hey, Bill, tell me a story. We've been on hold until you got back from your little trip up north. Sounds like it went well from the minimal reports I've received."

Bill related a detailed description of the mission and concluded with the ideas and suggestions made by members of his team.

Commander Rudd pursed his lips while nodding his head."Your guys have their heads screwed on in the right direction, Bill. The problem is that we are only the instruments of political policy. As long as the powers in Washington support this government in Saigon, the deeper we'll get into this thing. Right now, it's looking more like a political ping pong match than preparation for a war we want to win. I really don't think our President favors some of the suggestions being passed his way. The people who lobby congress are the source of many of those suggestions, not the senior military advisors. On that note, I want to tell you that the next SEAL Team that comes out here, not your replacements, the one following them, will be designated as a combat unit, not advisors. It would keep this situation more in line with the thinking of hitting the VC with their own tactics. Large-scale military operations will be a bitch in this terrain. Can you see heavy tanks operating in the Mekong delta? As long as we can keep this thing at a low profile level, I don't see the north responding with massed forces or heavy artillery and we shouldn't think in that direction either. But who am I? I don't set military policy. I just try to keep an intelligent lid on this thing."

As Bill and Tom left Rudd's office, Rudd thanked Bill and his team for an excellent action against the VC and wished them well in the future.

Back in Lieutenant Beck's office, Tom reminded Bill, "your replacement team, at least the first group, is due in tomorrow about noon. You're going to hang around and usher them back up north, right?"

"Yeah, that's one of the reasons I came down. I am free for dinner but I thought you would never ask," Bill said while trying to look serious.

"You got it buddy. Is the Golden Pheasant O.K.?"

"They have the best steaks in town. Are you kidding?"

The next morning Bill caught a MACV bus to Tan Son Nhat airport in Saigon to wait for the first increment of SEAL Team Two to arrive. A while later, he heard an announcement over the terminal public address system informing the waiting passengers of the arrival of a flight. A Pan American Airways flight number fifty-six from San Francisco and Agana Guam was on final approach. *That must be the one their on*, he thought as he walked toward the immigration area in the terminal. *Why the hell couldn't I catch a Pan Am flight when I came out here*? The beautiful blue and white Boeing 707 made a smooth landing and taxied to the unloading area next to the terminal. About half way through the disembarking process, he saw six men in UDT greens coming down the stairway from the front hatch of the aircraft. *There they are, sure is good to see some replacements*, Bill thought with relief.

The group cleared immigration quickly and soon entered the main terminal building. Bill approached the man in the lead noticing he wore the collar devices of a full Lieutenant. 'Oh shit, outranked again', Bill moaned to himself as he walked toward the man and extended his hand in greeting.

"You must be Bill Evans; I'm Tom Dolph, CO of this bunch of miss fits. Hot here isn't it."

"This is the cool part of the year, Tom, and Saigon is cooler than where we're going."

"Yeah, they told me we would be working out of Da Nang. How far is that from here?"

"It's about 300 air miles, about one and a half hours flying time if we get a good plane." Bill pointed to a C 119 setting near the terminal and shrugged his shoulders, "that's probably our ride north setting over there."

"Good god. You mean they still fly those things out here. I thought that aircraft had been abandoned by the air force years ago."

"They get the job done, just maybe not as quick or efficient as some newer models but that's our primary transport aircraft for now anyway. If you want to get your team together, we can sit down and handle the introductions. We'll take the evening flight to Da Nang. I need to take you and your men to MACV headquarters, there's some in-processing to do before we head out. I also want to introduce you to the Naval Intelligence crew; we've been working very closely for the past six months. I think you'll like them."

As their entire group boarded the bus for the MACV compound, Bill sat next to Lieutenant Dolph and thought *this indoctrination may be a bigger job than I thought.*

Chapter Thirty

The in-processing at MACV had taken longer than Bill thought and by the time they spent a few minutes with Commander Rudd and Tom Beck they had to hurry to make the afternoon flight to Da Nang. After boarding the Fairchild C 119, the pilot gave the routine speech regarding the loss of power on takeoff and crashing. This time he added the fact that there was a severe weather front moving in off the ocean, which they would attempt to avoid by flying inland, a greater distance than normal. Even with that effort, they still might encounter the perimeter of the front and experience some turbulence. To Bills surprise, the engines started on the first try and they taxied to their take off position at the end of the runway. As the pilot ran-up the engines prior to takeoff, the port engine began to sputter and died.

"Is this routine, Bill?" Lieutenant Dolph asked as he displayed a look of concern.

"Pretty much, Tom, they can usually keep them running long enough to get to Da Nang though."

"How often do you have to come down here on one of these things?"

"During the last six months I've averaged three to five trips a month, a couple times a little more."

"My god, do you think I'll need to come that often? I'm not sure my nerves can take it."

"You get use to it after a while. I've only been involved in one crash landing since I've been here. I think that's pretty good for these old birds." Bill was enjoying watching Lieutenant Dolph squirm.

As the plane sat behind the takeoff line at the end of the runway, a group of air force ground support men rushed out with their fire truck and a tool truck. They pulled the cowling off the failed engine. In a few minutes, Bill saw the chief of the ground crew give the cockpit crew a thumbs-up. The engine began turning and, after the second try, started…not without a cloud of black smoke. The run-up went smoothly and the plane was airborne slightly before it reached the end of the runway. As they flew north, the atmosphere seemed calm. For the first part of the flight, everything went smoothly. Bill got up from his seat and moved forward to the cockpit. The co-pilot was checking a chart while the pilot wrestled with the controls.

The pilot saw Bill standing behind him and diverted his attention from piloting long enough to say, "see those big black clouds on the coast. We need to get north of here before those suckers roll in. We're at full power; I just hope the old girl holds together."

Bill responded with, "I hope so too," and went back to his seat next to Lieutenant Dolph.

"How's it looking Bill?" Lieutenant Dolph asked with obvious concern.

"Not real good. We're going in the right direction, away from the storm front, but there's some question if we can go fast enough."

During the next fifteen minutes, the turbulence continued to build and soon the Fairchild was bouncing around like a gull on a rough sea.

Bill leaned close to Dolph to be heard, "on one of my first flights from Saigon to Da Nang there were two crates of explosives for cargo. We didn't make it off the ground with that plane and ended up switching to another. The replacement plane blew a tire on touchdown in Da Nang and caught on fire. We were all glad the explosives had been left behind in Saigon."

"We do draw hazardous duty pay for this tour of duty, don't we, Bill?"

"You're kidding, right, your normal pay and allowances plus a quarters and subsistence allowance, not even sea duty pay."

Lieutenant Dolph looked at Bill with raised eyebrows and a shrug of his shoulders and said, "it's not fair."

The ride was now severe and the plane buffeted with first one wing low then the other. As suddenly as it had begun, the air smoothed out and the ride was stable and consistent.

Mr. Shurburn and the Chief were waiting at the airport in Da Nang when the C 119 taxied to its designated spot on the runway apron. A couple of the new SEALs appeared to be delighted to be on the ground and said so with gusto. During the flight north they had expressed among themselves their objection to having all forms of identification taken away in Saigon. They followed those remarks voicing acceptance that their mission was still of a covert nature and it might be in the best interest of the team.

The men loaded themselves and their gear into the two weapon carriers and were soon on their way, heading toward the house. In Saigon, Bill had explained the housing arrangements his team had made when they arrived last April and Lieutenant Dolph seemed more than happy to continue that arrangement. The price was reasonable and the indoor plumbing was a real plus, even though there was only one shower. As they drove, Bill explained how he thought they should handle the situation at the Junk Force base, the training regimen, the risks connected in selecting a group of men to be trained, and the transfer of command to the new team. He also included an explanation of their relationship with the Army 93rd helicopter squadron and how valuable they had been in the training exercises. He wasn't sure how the new marine chopper squadron would work out but that was something Lieutenant Dolph would need to explore and develop.

When the group arrived at the house, Doc, Les, and Boats met them in the backyard and welcomed them to Da Nang. Junk was part of the welcoming committee, though reluctant at first, she soon accepted the new men as part of her 'family'.

After showing the men through the house and explaining the duties of the cook, laundress, and housekeeper, Bill settled at the big table where everyone joined him for the first of several briefings. Once the basics had been covered, a period of about two hours, it was time for a break. Doc motioned the two new Corpsmen off to the side and had them join him in his alcove. He began by explaining the physicals he had conducted on the prospective trainees and the number he had eliminated during that process. When he finished he asked if the two had any questions so far.

"Yeah, Chris, it is Chris isn't it?" After a nod from Chris, he continued, "where is your physician backup?"

"There isn't any in the vicinity. I hear there may be a Navy M.D. that will come to the Da Nang marine helicopter unit but there will be no permanent presence. I think the marines will have a field medicine trained Corpsman with them eventually, but he hasn't reported in yet."

"Well, how far is it to the nearest military physician?"

"There is an army doc at Na Trang, that's about an hour by chopper."

"One more question. They told us in Saigon that we would normally get a briefing on the conditions 'in country'. Did you have that briefing when you got here?"

"Yes, I did. It amounted to who points a weapon at you is probably VC. That's the best means of identifying VC. Nevertheless, the real secret out here is, *if you want a friend, get a dog,* to paraphrase something Harry Truman once said. We are leaving you the best damn dog in this country and she will be your friend."

Doc could tell the new Corpsmen were not comfortable with the arrangements and there was nothing he could do about it. That was the situation he had faced for the past five months, *tough it out guys and be Navy Hospital Corpsmen,* he thought as he went on to the next topic on his mental briefing list.

The briefing process went on for the next two days and at the end of that period, there were no unanswered questions and the new team began to settle in. The remainder of Team Two was due the following day. Doc thought he had done all that was possible to prepare the new Corpsmen for the task ahead.

In the time they had been in Da Nang, the new team had established a relationship with Junk. That pleased the Team One members. She had taken to them and them to her. The departing SEALs felt good about leaving her with their east coast 'cousins'.

That evening, after dinner, Doc took Bill aside and told him that he felt his briefing of the two SEAL Team Two Corpsmen was complete. Unless Bill had additional duties for him, he was ready to head out for Pearl.

Bill thought for a moment and responded, "Doc, I wasn't so sure about it when I found out you were coming as our team Corpsman. I can see now that you were the right person for the job. I have written to the SEAL Team One commanding officer about you and he knows what you are capable of. I hope to see you again, maybe our career paths will cross someday. As far as I'm concerned, you can head out on the first plane for Saigon, good luck, Doc."

Doc thanked Bill before going from room to room to tell Boats, Les, Mr. Shurburn, and the Chief that Bill had released him so he would head out on the first plane. He received a hardy embrace and handshake from each of them. Les gave him a scrap of paper with his address in San Diego and included his home address in Los Angeles, just in case. Before he left Les's room, he asked if Les knew what weapons the new team had brought with them. Les said he had been discussing that subject with a fellow Engineman from Team Two and the man had indicated that they had each been issued a new fully automatic Colt AR15. Les proceeded to explain the weapon to Doc. Les said he had been briefed on the AR 15 in weapons school and that it was likely to be selected as the replacement weapon for the M 14. He voiced some concern about the stopping power of the round as compared with the M 14, however, the AR 15 was a much lighter weapon with substantially less recoil. Doc was always eager to increase his knowledge of guns and thanked Les for the information.

Doc's orders did not include transporting weapons aboard aircraft, he wanted to keep the Walther P38 that Boats had given him. He asked Dale Shurburn, whose orders permitted him to carry weapons on aircraft, if it would be possible for him to drop the P38 off in Pearl when he came through a few weeks later. Dale agreed that it would be no problem and Doc gave him his phone number in Pearl. Doc would give him the weapon before he departed tomorrow. He headed for his alcove to begin the packing process... time to head for home.

The next morning, Les and Boats drove Doc to the airport in time to catch the first flight to Saigon. There was another round of good byes. They left him saying that they hoped to follow in the next few days and each encouraging him to think hard about joining SEAL and becoming a permanent part of the *Teams*.

The plane left almost on time and had a routine flight to Saigon. Arriving in Saigon, Doc caught a bus to MACV headquarters and checked in with the navy personnel office. The Chief there recognized him and reminded him to turn in the weapon he had been issued. He also advised Doc that the transportation options heading for Hickam Air Force Base in Hawaii were limited. The wait would probably be several days if not a week.

Great news, Doc thought as he headed for the armory. The Sergeant there was not in a good mood. That was obvious, from the look Doc got when he walked in and laid the .38 special on the counter.

"Where are the cartridges, Sailor?" While Doc was dressed in civilian clothes, he had laid his newly returned I.D. card on the counter with the weapon.

"They're right here in my pocket, Sergeant," Doc dropped them, one at a time, on the counter and with each impact the Sergeant's face grew more crimson.

"You didn't really need the weapon, in a safe zone, no doubt." The Sergeant smirked as he picked up the cartridges.

"You should have been with me, Sergeant. Have you been involved in any ambushes while in Saigon?"

The Sergeant looked at Doc, began to say something then thought better of it.

"There are six cartridges there, the same number I was issued. I can help you if you can't count that high." Doc turned after that remark and headed for the door. The Sergeant had no parting remarks.

The next stop was the transportation desk in the center of the MACV compound. It was a small office, currently empty but probably big enough to handle the minimal transportation demands at the time. He entered the office and found a small empty counter with an office behind it. He saw someone sitting behind a desk in the office so he called out.

A voice answered his call with, "just a minute." A few seconds later, a husky six-foot ruddy faced man, wearing the navy white uniform with First Class Boatswain Mate stripes, came through the office door. "My god, if it ain't Doc David. Christ man, where have you been?"

Doc looked closely at the man for a minute then threw out his hand.

"Boats Cruz, I haven't seen you since diving school. I just came in from up north."

"What can I do for you, Doc?"

"I need a ride to Hickam, the sooner the better. I've been in this country for over five months and I need to get back to Pearl and resume a more normal life, if you know what I mean."

"Boy that's gonna be tough. We don't have much going that way but let me check my flight lists and see what I can come up with."

He came back to the counter with a long list of scheduled flights and went through them one by one. "Let me check my 'fly through' list real quick." He went back into the office and in a moment, he came back out smiling. "I got ya one, it's a KC 135 inbound from New Delhi, bound for Edwards with stops at Clark in Manila and Hickam Field. Comes in tonight at 1900 and leaves at 2100. There are no passenger spaces per se, on these planes, but I think I can get you a ride on it. They'll be picking up a diplomatic pouch here and delivering it to Manila."

"Do you need a copy of my orders? I can get them in a minute."

"Naw, this is strictly a courtesy placement. I do it all the time with these KC crews. You need to be out there at about 1830 to connect. Just grab the pilot and give him this," he handed Doc a small pre-printed form. Boats Cruz had entered Doc's last name and signed the form at the bottom. "There you go, buddy. Hope you have a good flight."

Doc had noticed during their conversation that, even though Cruz had graduated from First Class Diving School, he no longer wore the distinctive patch that identified him as a First Class Diver. "What happened to your diving qualification, Boats?" Doc questioned after thanking Cruz for the flight arrangements.

"I went to the escape training tank at Subbase New London, when I came out of diving school, and really liked it. Unfortunately, I got what they call a pneumothorax that ended my diving career."

"Did you experience that while you were in the tank?"

"We were doing free ascents from the bottom. It hit me at about the fifty-foot level. I was exhaling as always. I had made several ascents from that depth and never had a problem."

"Sounds to me like an air embolism rather then a pneuomothorax, it's hard to tell without having been there. Did they treat you in a recompression chamber?"

"They did a short run with me, a table two, I think."

"You feel all right now?"

"Yeah, feel great. I do miss that diving pay though, but I guess I will never dive again...oh well."

"Tough luck, buddy, I hope the rest of your tour here is ship-shape. Thanks again for the plane ride. If you ever get through Pearl, look me up at the escape training tank at Subbase." Doc waved goodbye as he went through the door. Now he needed a ride to the airport. It was already late afternoon and he sure didn't want to miss that flight.

At Tan Son Nhat airport, he found a small lunch counter and ordered an egg sandwich with coffee. He realized later that he hadn't eaten since dinner the night before...getting home was distracting. When he finished his sandwich, he took a seat where he could see the incoming aircraft traffic, keeping an eye peeled for a KC 135, thinking, *they look just like a Boeing 707 with no windows.* At 1903 hours, he saw a silver aircraft on final approach for the main runway and watched it touch down as smoothly as any plane he had ever seen. The aircraft taxied to an apron to the side of the terminal and, in a few minutes, he saw two officers and an enlisted man exit the plane. As the men entered the terminal, Doc walked up to the man who appeared to be the pilot, a Lieutenant Colonel, and introduced himself, holding out the slip of paper Cruz had given him. The pilot took the paper and smiled.

"Welcome, Mr. David, we will be underway in about a half an hour, we'll overnight at Clark, then head on to Hickam first thing in the morning. You can board the aircraft anytime. Bring what luggage you have with you."

"Thank you, Colonel. I'll be there."

Doc grabbed his Valpak and headed toward the terminal exit leading to the boarding area and the apron where the KC was parked. The enlisted man he had seen was the Crew Chief. He greeted Doc at the top of the moveable stairway leading to the forward hatch.

"Welcome aboard, Mr. David. Our flight to Clark will take about forty-five minutes once we get airborne. You can probably get accommodations in the transient facility there, not fancy but they do have decent beds."

"Thanks, Sergeant, I'll check that out."

Doc took a typical canvas metal frame seat, there were only six directly behind the cockpit, and tried to get comfortable. In a few minutes, the pilot and the other officer came aboard and the hatch was closed. The engines were started without incident and the plane taxied to the takeoff end of the runway. With what seemed a severe degree of acceleration, the big plane was airborne and climbed at a steep angle into the night sky. Doc took particular note of the smoothness and the rate of climb since this was his first experience in a jet aircraft. *Wow, what a plane*, he thought. A few minutes later the Crew Chief stuck his head through the cockpit door to tell Doc they were at cruising altitude and would be letting down for Clark in about fifteen minutes.

Clark was hot and uncomfortable. When Doc asked, at the air force courtesy desk about transient quarters, the young Airman directed him to a bus stop outside the terminal complex. The bus dropped him in front of an old Quonset hut building at the edge of the base. Inside, there were two rows of double deck steel bunks with a pillow stacked on top of a set of sheets and a blanket on each bed. The floor was dirt. The only concrete in the building was in the shower stall that had one faucet marked, 'cold'. The windows were cutouts in the sides of the building with screen stretched over them. After making up a lower bunk, Doc tried to get some sleep but the best he could do was doze for a few minutes at a time. During the night, he got up to make a head call forgetting the floor was dirt. When he returned to his bunk, he used a pillowcase from another bunk to clean his feet. At daylight, he was ready to get back on his way, since there was no way to sleep in that hovel.

The KC 135 departed Clark at 0600 hours bound for Hickam and home to Pearl. After takeoff, the Crew Chief came back to where Doc was seated indicating that he needed to take a nap and Doc was welcome to take his seat in the cockpit if he liked. Doc went forward and found a seat on the left side directly behind the pilot. The pilot was trying to read a newspaper; the co-pilot was sleeping. The plane must be on autopilot, Doc guessed. There was a third officer in the cockpit whom Doc had not seen before. This officer sat in front of a huge panel of gauges and switches with a small radar screen directly in front of him. Doc assumed this must be the navigator because he was regularly passing heading and altitude changes to the pilot who interrupted his reading to dial them into, what Doc assumed was, the autopilot control. Every aspect of this experience fascinated him.

The cockpit crew later introduced themselves, once the plane reached its cruising altitude at 43,000 feet. The flight time to Hickam was estimated at nine hours and twenty-five minutes, which would place the ETA in early evening. Just nine more hours and this tour of duty would end in the paradise of the Pacific, Hawaii, and home...for the next couple of years anyway.

Chapter Thirty One

As they flew across the Pacific, Doc chatted with the cockpit crew about the plane and the flight path. He was amazed when the co-pilot said that they would not take on fuel again until they reached Hickam, the first time since they left New Delhi. Doc questioned the range capability of this particular aircraft. The pilot told him they were in what was known as the "ferry configuration", which gave this KC 135 a range of just over 11,000 miles, flying half way around the world without refueling, this struck Doc as astounding. As the flight progressed, Doc dozed and reclined the seat slightly to catch a nap. The next thing he knew, he heard the landing gear coming down. He sat up quickly and saw the runway lights of Hickam Air Force base in the distance with the lights of downtown Honolulu off to the right and the lights of Pearl Harbor to his left. The pink color of the Royal Hawaiian hotel was illuminated with special lights making the historic edifice visible for miles. Those same lights also cast direct beams on the white sand of Waikiki with its interlacing palm trees. The lights of many businesses along Ala Moana Boulevard and the huge shopping center led, like a magic path, towards the fun places at Waikiki beach. A gigantic hotel complex, on which construction was just starting, when Doc left for Vietnam, now stretched its structural steel arms skyward for what looked like thirty stories. The massive construction lights made the steel look like a huge woven basket. Doc had heard it was to be called the Ilikai.

The landing was again feather smooth and the plane taxied to a space a short distance from the MATS passenger terminal. After thanking the flight crew, Doc was the first down the moveable stairway that had been rolled to the front hatch of the plane. In the terminal, Doc looked for a phone. Finding one at the air force passenger service desk, he called a close friend asking for a ride home. The friend lived in an apartment adjoining Doc's. While Doc waited, in front of the terminal for his ride, he sat on a bench and took in the marvelous night breeze that is so often present in Hawaii. Just the smell of the place made him feel at home again. His friend arrived in a short while and gave Doc a hearty embrace and a lingering kiss. *Wow, this is better than I expected*, Doc thought as he put his Valpak in the trunk. She was full of questions about the activities Doc had been involved in for the past five months, of course, there was little Doc could tell her...he was dealing with information that was classified. He was able to tell her, as they drove toward their apartment complex, that he had been in the central portion of Vietnam helping to train Vietnamese sailors in special techniques. Kit, his neighbor's name, started to ask more questions about those 'special techniques' but let it drop when she realized Doc was limited in what he could tell her.

Back in his apartment, Doc just walked around handling his personal treasures, pictures of his folks, his weapons collection, and his guitar. His housekeeper had done an excellent job of maintaining the place during his absence. All the dishes and linens were clean and for a short time, would be in perfect order...until he started to use them. He would give her an extra twenty dollars the next time she came. It was a Friday evening so he decided to just relax and take the weekend off. He thought he had earned some quality time with Kit.

On Monday, it was time to go back to work so he dressed in a tropical white long uniform and headed for Subase and the escape training tank. He left home early enough to catch the morning run that the tank crew did regularly. It had been a week since he had run any distance. At the tank, he changed into his running gear, consisting of khaki shorts, white tee shirt, and sneakers. When he joined the group in front of the tank, everyone greeted him and ask about the TAD assignment.

He answered them by saying, "it was just, routine, but the climate in Vietnam was too hot and humid."

After finishing the three miles around the Subase, he took a shower and dressed in his tank togs, form fitting red swimming shorts, a white Terry Cloth robe, and shower shoes. He checked the training schedule, posted on a white plastic note board next to the elevator. There was a submarine crew due at 1000 hours for buoyant ascent training. It would be a full day. On his way to the elevator, that would take him to the top of the tank where his training station was located, he passed the office of the Master Chief of the tank, who was also the Master Diver.

As he passed the door of the office, he heard the Master Chief call out to him, "hey, Doc. Come in here."

Doc entered the office and stood in front of the Master Chief's desk.

"Welcome back, Doc, really glad to see you in one piece. I have a question for you. What the HELL are you doing here?"

"This is where I work, Master Chief," Doc responded with a sly smile.

"Don't give me that shit, Doc. When did you get in?"

"On Friday evening, a non-stop flight from Clark to Hickam in a little over nine hours."

"Well, welcome back, again, now get the hell out of here. I don't want to see your ugly face around here until next Monday, at the earliest. I wrote up some leave papers for you, they're in my top basket and that's where they'll stay, seven days of 'basket leave'. I don't want any arguments. Now get the HELL out of here!"

"What about the training you have scheduled today?"

"I've got that covered. One of the Submarine Medical Officers from the dispensary has been covering for you along with another Diving Corpsman who reported in while you were on TAD. That's my last word, out, out, out!"

"Thanks, Chief," Doc said as he headed for the locker room to change back into uniform and head for home. On the way, he thought he should swing by Tripler Army Hospital and see if he could get in to see an Ear, Nose, and Throat physician to find out how much damage had been done to his ear in that explosion months earlier. At Tripler, he was welcomed in the ENT clinic, which was typical of the all the clinic staffs. As an independent duty Navy Corpsmen, he had built a close professional working relationship with the staff in most of the clinics, since Tripler was the source for definitive care for sailors. He met with Dr. Masters, an Army Major and an ENT specialist, who did a complete evaluation of Doc's ears and hearing loss. After the audiogram, Major Masters took Doc into his office to read him the results of his evaluation.

"You said that was a block of TNT that went off?"

"Yes, Doctor, a few feet away from my right ear. It knocked me out for a short time and I had a hell of a headache for several days afterwards. There was no one around to evaluate it for me, so here I am."

"Well, Chris, you have severe damage to your right auditory nerve that will not get better. You will never regain any of the hearing loss you now have in that ear and it will probably deteriorate over the next few years. You need to avoid exposure to loud noise or it will go even faster."

"It's going to be tough working as a diving Corpsman, Doctor."

"I don't think you should make a decision right now, David. Why don't we schedule you for another visit in a month and check it again. That will be even more meaningful once you've had a chance to get some rest, get back to work, and see how the diving affects any increased hearing loss."

"Sounds good to me, Major, I'll see you in a month."

Doc swung by the tank on his way back to his apartment to pick up some clothing items that he wanted to have cleaned.

When he got to the tank, the Master Chief saw him and again called Doc into his office. "I know I gave you a week off, Doc, but I just got this phone message a while ago. You probably should respond. I was going to put a call in to your apartment but since you're here." He slid a pink colored phone message across the desk to Doc.

Doc picked up the slip of paper and read, "HM1 David, Contact the Fleet Medical Officer's Office immediately upon your return from TAD to set a time and date for a de-briefing conference." *Well I wonder what the hell this is about*, Doc thought as he folded the note and put it in his pocket.

Doc looked at the Master Chief inquisitively.

The Master Chief answered his unspoken question."I don't have a clew, Doc. Can you tell me anything about the unit you were with? That might have something to do with that phone message."

"Not much, Master Chief. Everything we did was classified, including the name of the parent unit. The crew was all former UDT sailors."

The Master Chief took a small phone message pad from his desk drawer and wrote something on it in large letters. He then pushed it across the desk to Doc. He had written the word 'SEAL' in large capitol letters. Doc picked up the piece of paper, read it, then rolled it up into a ball and stuck it in his pocket. He gave the Master Chief a subtle smile and a nod.

Master Chief Petty Officers in the Navy have information sources that the rest of the Navy will never understand, Doc told himself.

"Before you run off, what do you plan to do with all your time off?"

"I haven't made any plans, Master Chief. Why?"

"Just a suggestion, have you ever been to the island of Kauai?"

"We did a diving job off the coast there once but we didn't get ashore. I was aboard an ASR then."

"I mention it because I have a friend, a retired E9, who manages a hotel over there. I was telling him about your TAD and he said for you to give him a call and he would cut you a special deal for a few days stay."

"Thanks, Master Chief; I'll give it some serious thought. That might be fun."

That night, Doc thought he was due for a little entertainment. He knew it was Kit's night off so he called her and asked her if she would like to take in Waikiki sites. She enthusiastically accepted his invitation; she was ready to go in ten minutes. They drove to Waikiki and parked on a street near the

Royal Hawaiian hotel. As they walked down the street which separated the Waikiki Beach from the International Market Place, Doc heard some really exceptional guitar music coming from a bar a few doors down. With Kit on his arm, he stuck his head in the door and they were immediately greeted by a cocktail waitress who showed them to a table directly across from a small stage. On the stage was a dark haired, stocky man, dressed in white, playing a double neck guitar. The music he was making with the instrument was nothing short of fantastic. They decided to spring for a couple beers so they could stay and listen. There was normally a cover charge but if you purchased a drink, the charge was waived.

They each managed to nurse two beers through three performances. This man was the best guitarist Doc had ever heard; Doc had been playing the guitar for over fifteen years so he was especially appreciative. During a break, Doc invited the performer to their little table and offered to buy him a drink, the man selected ice water. They learned that the performer's name was Adamono and he was from California. He would be in Honolulu for the next few days, then head back to California for a recording session. After that, he was off on tour of Europe to perform in most of the major cities. The price of two beers each had been well spent that evening.

On the drive home, Doc asked Kit if she could take some time off from her job at Tripler Army hospital, where she worked in Civil Service as an R.N. She thought for a minute. She did have quite a bit of vacation time built up. What did he have in mind? He told her about the offer from the hotel manager in Kauai and asked if she would like to fly over there for a couple of days. She said she would check with her supervisor and let him know.

Doc had called the Fleet Medical Officer, to arrange for the 'command performance' de-briefing. The secretary wavered for several minutes while she checked schedules and finally selected Wednesday at 0900. The meeting was to be held in the Commander in Chief Pacific (CINCPAC) Flag Conference Room. That date and time bisected Doc's week off but he could look forward to a weekend with Kit if she could arrange to get the time off.

Doc hadn't asked about the required uniform for the de-briefing session but he assumed that service dress white would be acceptable. So, on Wednesday morning, he dressed and headed for the CINCPAC headquarters building. When he arrived, the Marine sentry scrutinized him. After showing his I.D. card, he was admitted to the building. At a reception desk in the lobby, he was directed to the conference room, on the second floor of the building. He found the room and knocked on the door. There was no answer so he opened the door just enough to peek inside, what he saw was a little overwhelming.

Seated around the table he saw more gold than one would see in a top rated jewelry store. *Holy Shit*, he thought. An officer at the head of the table got to his feet and motioned Doc into the room.

"Petty Officer David?" The man looked directly at Doc as he spoke.

"Yes, Sir," Doc answered.

"Come in, David. We'll be with you in a moment."

The men around the table continued a discussion of some topic, which meant nothing to Doc, so he spent the time doing a visual survey of the officers present. There were three Captains, four Commanders, a Rear Admiral, and two Lieutenants...wow what a collection of rank. Doc did not feel intimidated since he had worked with senior officers throughout his career. When they had completed their discussion, the Captain at the head of the table, a Medical Service Corps officer, looked at Doc and introduced himself as the Administrative Officer for the Fleet Medical Officer, he asked if Doc knew any of the officers at the table.

Doc responded that he had never met any of them but he looked forward to discussing whatever they had on the agenda.

The Captain at the head of the table smiled at this remark then addressed Doc, "we have asked you here, David, to brief us on your recent TAD to Vietnam. Our involvement with Vietnam is something new to many of us and we feel that any information you can provide will help to expand our knowledge base. My primary concern is with the medical support available to our force levels, which may expand in the future. Others around this table have questions regarding other subjects that you may or may not be able to address. Feel free to tell them if you have no knowledge of the subject areas they mention. The gentlemen around this table represent the major commands under CINCPAC. First, what can you tell me about the medical support conditions in Vietnam?"

Doc thought for a moment wondering how he could explain a non-existing resource. "Well, Captain, the only major area I was exposed to was Saigon. As I'm sure you're aware, there is a navy dispensary there that seems to be well staffed. They provided some support to me in the form of medical supplies. My unit was operating in the Da Nang area where no U.S. medical support exists; the nearest U.S. military physicians are in Na Trang which is over 100 miles away."

The Admiral interrupted Doc at this point in his presentation. "Just exactly what unit were you assigned to, Petty Officer?"

Doc looked to the head of the table for some guidance. He received a pained look from the Medical Service Corps Captain, Doc then addressed the Admiral. "The unit I was assigned to is classified as SECRET, Admiral.

Can I assume that everyone at this table has sufficient security clearance for me to reveal that information?"

The Admiral looked to the head of the table for the Captain to respond.

The Captain addressed Doc, "everyone in this room has sufficient security clearance to hear whatever you may say, David."

"Yes, Sir," Doc responded. I was assigned to a unit designated as MTT 10-62. That unit is the first increment of a specially trained group of former UDT members. They are being referred to as SEALs. The team was to consist of ten enlisted men and two officers. When I arrived in Vietnam last May, two of the enlisted members of the team were gone. One I believe was injured and returned to the states. The whereabouts of the other missing man was never revealed to me. I suspect that there may have been some family problems or other serious problems that caused him to return to the states early in their deployment."

One of the Commanders addressed Doc, "what was the function of this team you were assigned to?"

"Our primary mission, Sir, was to train a group of Vietnamese Junk Force personnel in counterinsurgency, marine warfare, and jungle warfare. We began the training with 120 candidates and finished with thirty. The first sixty or so I eliminated because of their physical condition, because of possible disease or physical abnormalities. Others were dropped or withdrew from the training regimen because they were unable to cope with the physical demands of the training."

Now a Captain entered the questioning. "Were you supposed to be covert, David?"

"Yes, Sir. As we were processed through the Navy Unit at MACV headquarters in Saigon, all of our personal identification was taken away. We were told that if anything happened they would claim we never existed."

"That sounds a little far fetched to me, Petty Officer," the Admiral remarked with a smirk on his face.

The Medical Service Corps Captain jumped into the conversation, "no Admiral, that's the way certain select units, headed in-country, in Vietnam are being handled, at least at this point in time."

The Admiral looked at the Captain and responded with, "hmm," and continued, "was this covert nature effective, did it shelter you from hostile actions against your unit?"

"Yes, Sir, it did for quite a while until a reporter from the Stars and Stripes came to Da Nang, an unauthorized visit I might add, and blew our cover with a front page story. That story was entitled 'Secret Navy Group Training Junk Force Commandoes in Da Nang'. That blew our cover permanently."

"Did your CO attempt to do anything about the story?" a Commander asked as he leaned closer to the table.

"Yes, Sir. He raised hell about it in Saigon but nothing ever came from his complaints and they never retracted the story. I doubt it would have done any good if they had."

Another Captain leaned closer to the huge table and looked at Doc, "I'm curious about the facilities and material support you had to perform this training mission. What about billeting, food, vehicles, and the like. What resources were in place when you arrived at, was it Da Nang?"

"Yes, Sir, it was Da Nang. When the team arrived, a month before I did, there was nothing in place. Our CO rented a house in Da Nang for our quarters, we made our own meals. Later, we were able to hire a cook. We stole all of our vehicles from the Vietnamese motor pool, with the exception of one, which we were able to check out from the air force facility at the Da Nang airport. My uniforms for this assignment were specified in my orders as whites, not a suitable uniform for working in a hostile environment in the jungle. The men in the team outfitted me with UDT greens. Our weapons and explosives were supplied through an army Special Forces Unit stationed outside Da Nang."

"These weapons and explosives, what was their source? In other words, where did the Special Forces unit come up with them? They certainly didn't bring that many extras with them." The Admiral demanded an answer to his question, as he glanced at the Captain at the head of the table.

The Captain looked to Doc for an answer. "The weapons and explosives and many of the camouflage uniforms we wore were supplied by Special Forces." Doc tried to evade giving a direct answer.

"You didn't answer my question, Petty Officer. Where did they get them?"

"Sorry, Admiral, I was about to tell you that. The Special Forces team was supplied with many of their needs from an organization in Okinawa called Combined Studies."

This statement brought an immediate silence around the table and several questioning looks from the Admiral and others.

The MSC Captain again entered the questioning. "Do you know the identity of this organization you just mentioned?"

"No, Sir, only scuttlebutt."

"And what was that scuttlebutt, David?"

"That the organization was a part of the CIA, I was never told that directly by anyone in authority." Doc lied, just a little, since the relationship between Combined Studies and the CIA had been revealed to him more then once by Bill and the Chief, he couldn't involve anyone who might get in trouble for giving him that information. If he indicated that he had confirmation of this relationship, the next question would be, *who told you that.*

One of the Commanders looked at Doc, "I'm curious, David. Did any training you gave these Vietnamese involve actual combat situations and if so, against who?"

"Yes, Sir, it's difficult to train a group of men about counterinsurgency and marine warfare without some exposure to a combat environment. We conducted an operation, an ambush, in conjunction with the Special Forces team. It was their mission but we thought it would be good training for a select group of our trainees. The insurgents in that case were a group of Viet Cong who had been harassing one particular village for several months. They had stolen food, raped women, and even killed one old couple. The operation was a success, although one of our Junk Force trainees was shot and one of the Special Forces trainees was killed in a grenade accident. To further answer your question about the enemy, they are Viet Cong. Mostly from the northern part of the country, although, there are many who live in the south and pass themselves off as loyal to the south but fight on the side of the Viet Cong after dark. That's what makes this action so difficult, gentlemen. Enemy identification is a real problem."

The same Commander had more questions. "What can you tell us about other actions your team took, I'm speaking of actions of a combat nature. Did your unit carry out any missions exclusively?"

"Yes, Sir. There were two other operations that were conducted by our team members. One operation included three of our trainees after they had completed our training program."

"What were those actions?" The Admiral asked with a frown on his face.

"One involved the recon of a Viet Cong base on the Mekong river delta. The other was sinking a North Vietnamese gunboat."

"Come, come, David, I think you can be more specific than that."

At this point, the Medical Service Corps Captain intervened, "Admiral, a full report of those actions is available in transmissions made from David's unit commanding officer to Coronado. I can make them available to you if you like."

The Admiral directed his trade-mark frown at the Captain but said nothing.

I doubt that, Doc thought as he leaned back in his chair for the first time. *I don't think Bill ever reduced much of this to writing, maybe to Combined Studies.*

"Does anyone have more questions for Petty Officer David?"

"Yes", one of the Lieutenants raised his hand. The Captain at the head of the table nodded permission.

"Petty Officer David, how long have you been back from Vietnam?"

"About four days, Sir. It's great to be back in the world!"

The same Lieutenant continued his questioning. "Where are you assigned in Pearl Harbor, what is your duty station?"

"I am an instructor at the Submarine Escape Training Tank on Subase, Sir."

"Are there anymore questions for David?" No one indicated that they had any. The Medical Service Corps Captain, looking directly at Doc, said, "I have one final question for you, Hospitalman First Class David, could you give us your personal assessment of the situation in Vietnam. In other words, do you think what we are trying to do there will be successful?" The Medical Service Corps Captain leaned back in his chair as he spoke.

Doc hesitated for several seconds then thought to himself, *what the hell.* "Captain and gentlemen, the situation in Vietnam is very confusing. As I have already mentioned, it's difficult to tell the enemy from the 'friendlies'. Corruption is rampant in the government. We are being ripped off big time. Material that is sent in the form of aid to the people is being sold on the open market at exorbitant prices. As an example, I saw Johnson outboard motors, in a department store window in Saigon, priced at twice what they cost here. Those motors still had our handclasp emblem on them which states, 'Gift of the United States of America'. Much of the materiel that enters the country for the Vietnamese Army ends up in the hands of Chinese merchants and is sold on the black market. I'm no expert on military strategy, aside from training I had as an NROTC Midshipman, nor have I attended a war college, but in my opinion we need to keep a lid on this situation. Fighting the Viet Cong is one thing but if we expand the war, other countries will come to the material aid of the North Vietnam, such as China and the Soviet Union. They are already supplying weapons and other material to the Viet Cong. The gunboat we disposed of was built in Russia and operated by a North Vietnamese crew, who we believe were trained by Russians. The terrain would be very difficult to conduct any kind of a conventional war, and in my opinion, it would be very costly in men and resources. I hope what I have told you today will be of some value to you and you will be able to reflect on it when future decisions are made concerning this conflict. The sad part is, men are dying over there everyday and many of those men are Americans. The people, the Vietnamese people, out in the countryside, really couldn't care less about the government in Saigon. All the common people want is to be left alone, raise their families, their rice, and live in peace. I thank you for having me here today and I appreciate the opportunity to share this experience with you."

Doc rose from the table. All the officers around the table got to their feet. The Captain at the head of the table came down the isle, shook Doc's hand, saying, "Thank you, David, we appreciate your candor."

It was early afternoon, the de-briefing had lasted over three hours. Doc emerged from the building and stopped a minute at the top of the stairs leading down from the CINCPAC headquarters. He thought, 'I hope that session will have some effect on our future involvement out there. If we fight in a gorilla warfare format, we have a chance, just a chance, to keep a lid on the level of the conflict. If we pursue conventional warfare methods it could end up a mess'! He had noted, in particular, that none of the officers around the table had taken any notes. *So what was it all worth, all the information he had given them…probably nothing.*

When he arrived at his apartment, Kit was sitting on the front steps waiting for him. "Hey, Sweets, how was your morning?"

Kit was a very attractive young woman at age twenty-three, with light blonde hair, five feet three, and figure that would not stop. She was highly intelligent with a marvelous sense of humor.

Doc smiled at her as he ambled up the walk. "My morning was spent talking to a bunch of navy brass about my TAD assignment. I think I made some good points but they didn't seem to notice. All I can do is say, I told you so. What about our trip, can you get away?"

"We're on; can we leave Friday and come back Sunday? I have the three-to-eleven shift on Monday and I will need to get home a little early to get ready for duty."

"That's really strange; those are the exact days I made the reservation for in Kauai. We'll be staying at a place called the Kauai Surf. It's right on the beach on a bay and I have a car rented so we can take a little tour of the island…sound O.K.?"

"Sounds great, Hon, when do we leave?"

"We'll fly out Friday morning at 9 AM; it only takes about 30 minutes or so. The hotel will pick us up at the airport."

"How did you know what days to make the reservations?"

"Just guessed, I got lucky."

They boarded the Aloha Airlines turboprop at Honolulu International airport and the departure was on time. As the plane climbed out through a thin cloud layer, Doc took a backward glance, as the Naval Air station at Barbers Point drifted under the right wing. *Well here I go again, off into the wild blue yonder,* he thought, t*his landing will be a lot different and the climate should be an improvement over Vietnam.*

Doc leaned his seat back as the plane leveled off at cruising altitude and held Kit's hand.

He thought about the past several months and his tour of duty with the SEAL Team. *Should he put in for a transfer to SEAL, so many things to consider. If he received his degree on schedule, he could apply for a commission shortly after and it would change his options completely.* He did know, it was good to be home and great to be alive. He thought, *the men in SEAL were exceptional in so many ways; the best group he had ever served with.*

In his opinion an appropriate motto for SEAL could be, ***The difficult we do immediately, the impossible takes a little longer.***

LaVergne, TN USA
05 December 2010
207402LV00003B/1/P

9 781450 271455